CONTENTS

EVEREST 2000

Mount Everest continues to make negative headlines: as a 'rubbish tip', a 'fatal magnet for adrenaline-freaks', or as 'an amusement park for tourists who have been everywhere else'. Ever since word got out that you could purchase 'the climb of your dreams', an ascent of the highest mountain of the world—revered as holy by those living to the south or north of 'Sagarmatha' or 'Qomolungma' (its local names), it became transformed into a consumer product. In Kathmandu and Lhasa, government departments and service-providers benefit from an Everest boom built upon the mythology which, over almost eighty years, has grown around a couple of dozen expeditionary mountaineers from Mallory to Ang Rita.

Mount Everest tends to shrink in our imagination when we read it has been 'conquered' by a couple of hundred mediocre alpinists, who probably would not trust themselves to climb Mont Blanc without help; but then it grows again, if a half dozen of these trophy-hunters get themselves killed in the process, as happened in 1996 in the course of two commercial climbing trips organised by Rob Hall and Scott Fischer. Jon Krakauer has written a profound book upon the subject, *Into Thin Air: A Personal Account of the Mount Everest Disaster*. Despite this, the hordes came again the following year, and once more there were tragedies.

We seem to have lost sight of the fact that humans cannot survive at heights approaching 9,000 metres. While more and more of us climb where we don't belong, the accidents will go on increasing and, with them, be-cause of them in fact, so will the desire to make such an attempt. Treading the footsteps of those before them, waiting in line at the Hillary Step below the summit, growing numbers of people clamber to heights that offer no retreat for the inexperienced when storm, mist or avalanche play havoc with fuddled brains. What makes Mount Everest so dangerous is not the steepness of its flanks, nor the vast masses of rock and ice that can break

It is a long way to the summit of Mount Everest and even with the route prepared and more or less well trodden, it remains dangerous despite tour organisers treating the world's highest mountain as a consumer article.

away without warning. The most dangerous part of climbing Mount Everest is the reduced partial pressure of oxygen in the summit region, which dulls judgment, appreciation, and indeed one's ability to feel anything at all.

With modern, lightweight oxygen apparatus the mountain can be out-witted, but what happens when the bottles are empty, when descent through a storm becomes impossible, when you can't go a step further? An Everest climb cannot be planned like a journey from Zurich to Berlin, and it doesn't end on the summit. In any sports shop you can buy, for a price, the lightest equipment there is, but you cannot purchase survival strategy. The client surrenders responsibility for him- or herself to the guide—and the higher the mountain, the more personal responsibility is yielded up, even though this is the basic prerequisite for any mountain experience. And what hap-pens when the leader gets into difficulty? Clients are left hanging in the ropes on a mountain they neither know nor understand.

This Everest is no longer the Everest of the pioneers. Increasingly the apex of vanity, it has also become a substitute for something the summit-traveler wants to flaunt on his lapel, like a badge, without taking any of the responsibility in the field.

The more Mount Everest is turned into a consumer article, the more importance attaches to the key moments of its climbing history—with or without supplemental oxygen. As the highest mountain in the world—for trekkers, climbers, environmentalists, and aid workers (to say nothing of undertakers)—it is guaranteed more publicity than other mountain. Its mythos is continually being misinterpreted, so that it becomes a mountain of fortune and fantasy even for those with no need to go there themselves. For them, I tell this story of climbing 'by fair means'.

EVEREST AS CONSUMABLE

Since the beginning of the 1990s more than a thousand people a year converge on the flanks of the world's highest mountain: hundreds on the north side (Tibet), a few on the east side (Tibet), with the bulk continuing to approach from the south (Nepal). Although permits have become more expensive and parties are threatened with all sorts of restrictions, Mount Everest has degenerated into a 'fashionable' mountain. Dozens make it to the summit each year. The increase in numbers attempting the climb produces a correspondingly higher number of successes and, on top of that, with so many expeditions on the mountain simultaneously, the actual climbing has become far easier: the ice fall is protected with fixed ropes and ladders, the trail broken and marked, high camps established, so that the line of the route is obvious for most of the way to the summit. Today's Everest climber is scarcely ever exposed or completely alone; he or she climbs in a crocodile formation. And any exceptions to this scenario are increasingly rare.

For the first time, in the Spring of 1979, a Yugoslav expedition successfully climbed the very difficult West Ridge: over the Lho La, the West Shoulder, and directly up the rocky ridge to the summit.

In February 1980, two days after the winter climbing season ended 'officially', Polish mountaineers became the first to climb to the top of the world at the coldest time of year.

Russian mountaineers claimed the South Pillar in pre-monsoon 1982. Technically, this prominent rock buttress to the left of the South-west Face may well be the most difficult route on the mountain.

In 1983 a team of distinguished American mountaineers at last succeeded in finding a route up Everest's East Face, known as the Kangshung Face.

The Great Couloir on the North Flank, between the North Ridge and a blunt pillar in the central section of the massive face, was climbed by an Australian team in 1984. Variations to the line were done later.

In 1988, ten years after the first ascent of the mountain without oxygen masks, Stephen Venables made it to the top of Everest after an incomparable achievement. Forming a small, unsupported expedition with Robert Anderson and Ed Webster, Venables struggled up a new line to the left of the American Route on the Kangshung Face. All three reached the South Col without supplemental oxygen, climbed higher and survived the panic of losing themselves at those forsaken heights. Venables reached the summit alone and, days later, despite frostbite and complete exhaustion, the crazy trio returned safely to base camp.

There are still possibilities of a pioneering nature waiting to be done on Mount Everest. Even today—should anyone be looking for them. But who cares to take on the challenge of exposure and loneliness away from the beaten track when the summit can be 'bagged' so much more easily?

In 1980 when I made my solo ascent during the monsoon period, there was not another soul anywhere above base camp. For five whole days I climbed in complete isolation, dependent solely on my own resources— and putting myself further from the inhabited earth with every upward step. My body was a wreck at the end of it; I survived despite myself, but as a worn-out shell.

By contrast, many of today's Everest 'conquerors' are far better at managing their bodies than their minds. The preoccupation for this 'no-limits' generation is a quick thrill, rather than choosing the toilsome solitary path with its lengthy periods of sorrow and anguish. They race up prepared trails, ill acclimatised as often as not, from one established camp to the next, all the way to the airy encampment on the South Col. Sherpa Ang Rita, almost 50 years old, who has been to the top of Everest more times than anyone else, shows them the way from there. Some launch themselves back down again from the summit ridge with their parachutes, hang gliders, or skis.

As in the Alps, where it has become modish to rappel into wildwater ravines, bungee-jump, or to go for the short buzz of swarming up an overhang, wealthy, cosseted clients in the Himalaya hope that a dose of Everest will boost their endorphin levels. Without giving much thought to what they do, they follow a trend, an ideology which glorifies the physical and promises recognition as reward for overcoming fear. These people get recognition from others, but less of that feeling of self-worth which comes after putting weeks and months into something where you are dependent only upon yourself, and prey to hopes and doubts.

The kind of excitement offered by travel bureaus is gained for the least possible outlay (in all but monetary terms). The guide and the Sherpa

Since the first ascent of Mount Everest in 1953 (left, Tenzing and Hillary), it is less the equipment that has changed than the attitude of the climber.

assistants take responsibility not only for the camps, the route, and everyone's safety, but also for the client's enjoyment. The promoters of this 'rapture-of-the-heights' know well to let their clients believe that nothing can happen to them, even though they are climbing the same mountain as Hillary and Tenzing climbed in 1953.

More than a hundred people have been killed attempting Everest, including 60 Sherpas and other Nepalis, whose deaths are to be deplored as 'industrial accidents'. A thousand people have reached the summit, ten percent of whom have climbed without oxygen masks, albeit frequently in the steps of trail-breakers who were using oxygen. To date, less than five per cent of the summiteers have been women, but this could be set to change, since women turn out to be stronger than men at high altitude.

The oldest person to get to the top was 60 years old, the youngest 17. All that's lacking is for a couple to get married up there. Generations have

3

moved on: Peter Hillary, the son of the first ascensionist, stood on the summit forty years after his father; the grandson of George Leigh Mallory went up in 1995, and Tenzing's son made it in 1996.

Still, it is not the spirit of the times, nor mass tourism which keeps Everest at the forefront of fashion year by year. It is the hundreds of individuals who foster ambitions for their own personal summit experience.

The thirteen routes which have been established on the mountain so far provide room enough for many; and Mount Everest is only one among millions of high mountains—albeit a very special one. But all the while strings of climbers flock up one single route, the experience brought home from the roof of the world will diminish as each season passes.

SUMMIT REPORT ON TAPE

For a better understanding of this book, it is important to know that during each of his climbs of Mount Everest, Reinhold Messner held in his hand a mini tape-recorder with which he recorded his feelings and impressions—all the way to the summit. He recorded conversations there as they took place. The 24-hour tapes were later typed up and then condensed by the author, but not essentially changed in regards to contents, speech, and testimony. This form of "on the spot" reporting gives the book its character; through its absolute authenticity it produces essentials out of the discussion of incidentals. The immediacy and uncertainty of the climb come through in the conversations. In this way, Messner has preserved his experiences through the descent of Mount Everest and into the reading room. Conversations, as banal as they often may sound, were conducted at 8000 and 8500 m. above sea level exactly as they are written here. It would have been wrong to adorn them later with artistic words. Messner did not do that. Through this oral journal form, he has created a unique document that perhaps does not read smoothly, but in speech and detail could not have been recreated after the fact: a sincere and candid eyewitness account.

THE NATURE OF THE ACCOUNT

An account of an expedition is not a novel. Therefore an authentic account can never be given, let alone written down, by someone who was not present. Any account of an expedition can be checked only by the people who took part in it, and is subject, first and foremost to their criticism. An account of an expedition must, above all, give a true rendering of the facts, and make it possible for all those who took part in it to identify with the tale that is told. That does not mean that there is only one true account of an expedition—there are as many versions of the truth as there are participants.

In the case of a novel any author has the right to project his personal experiences, perceptions and truths into a fictional tale.

An account of an expedition contains no fictional tales, nor any of the heroes of the novel.

The great art of writing the book of an expedition consists in recounting faithfully an actual and inextinguishable experience and in revealing one's own feelings in the first person. If a man is not prepared to reveal anything, he has nothing to say.

— *Reinhold Messner*

5

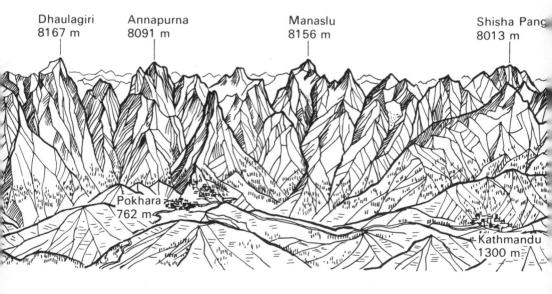

Dhaulagiri
8167 m

Annapurna
8091 m

Manaslu
8156 m

Shisha Pang
8013 m

Pokhara
762 m

Kathmandu
1300 m

THE IDEA

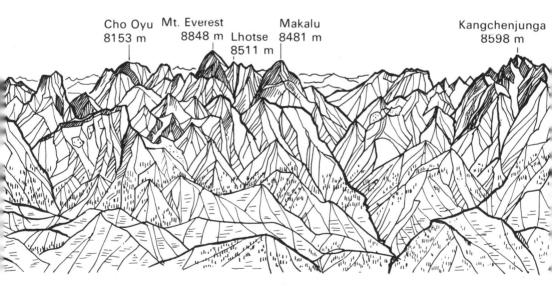

Cho Oyu
8153 m
Mt. Everest
8848 m
Lhotse
8511 m
Makalu
8481 m
Kangchenjunga
8598 m

FROM AN IDEA
INTO AN IDEAL

To begin with, it was just a beautiful illusion, a fantasy, to imagine climbing the highest mountain in the world *without* technical assistance. But out of this illusion a concept grew and finally, a philosophy: Can Man, solely by his own efforts, reach the summit of Everest? Is the world so constructed that Man can climb to its highest point without mechanical aids?

I don't climb mountains simply to vanquish their summits. What would be the point of that? I place myself voluntarily into dangerous situations to learn to face my own fears and doubts, my innermost feelings.

The 'Adventure' is immediately diminished as soon as Man, to further his own ambition, uses technology as a hoist. Even the highest mountains begin to shrink if they are besieged by hundreds of porters, attacked with pegs and oxygen apparatus. In reaching for an oxygen cylinder, a climber degrades Everest to the level of a six-thousand metre peak.

The Himalayan pioneers ventured cautiously up into the great heights, groping their way, sometimes in small groups, sometimes alone. The fascinating tales they brought back of the loneliest regions of the world inspired other adventurers to follow their example. But they all lived in harmony with the *mystery* of the mountains. It was only with the nationalistic expeditions of the inter and post war years and their great emphasis on 'Conquest', that the delicate balance between the Adventurer and the 'Unknown' was destroyed.

Some of the mystery ebbs with every expedition. A mountain region is soon exhausted when no rein is placed on technical assistance, when a summit triumph is more important to a mountaineer than self-discovery. The climber who doesn't rely on his own strength and skills, but on apparatus and drugs, deceives himself.

The face mask is like a barrier between Man and Nature; it is a filter that hinders his visionary perceptions. An Everest ascent without using artificial oxygen is the only alternative to previous ascents, all of which were made with its help.

'Everest by fair means' — that is the human dimension, and that is what interests me.

Mountains are so elemental that man does not have the right nor the need to subdue them with technology. Only the man who chooses his tools with humility can experience natural harmony.

Suddenly, I begin to nurture this idea. I want to climb until I either reach the top of the mountain, or I can go no further. I feel so passionately about this that I am prepared to endure anything, to risk much. I am willing to go further than ever I have before. I am resolved, for this idea, to stake everything I have.

WITH OR WITHOUT FACE MASKS

The idea of attempting Mount Everest without oxygen apparatus is as old as the climbing history of this, the highest of all mountains. Even in 1922 on the second British expedition, the 'with' or 'without' question was hotly debated:

Everyone was agreed about the ultimate goal; the summit of the world! What they were divided about was what technical assistance they could employ to achieve it. The big obstacle, they knew, apart from the wind, was the thin air, the lack of oxygen, which would seriously limit a man's capabilities. At that time, it wasn't yet understood just how the human body could adapt. What more logical than to take to the mountain the oxygen that was lacking up there? That's what airmen already did! Dr Kellas — who died on the march-in to Everest in 1921 — had made the first experiments with oxygen, but was unable to come to any conclusive opinion about it, as the big steel flasks that he took with him were too heavy and unwieldy. Besides this, there was strong prejudice in mountain climbing circles against the employment of oxygen; it was considered an unfair advantage in the struggle of man against mountain — a view that was shared by the Mount Everest Committee, which was comprised of representatives of the Royal Geographical Society and the Alpine Club. But

Norton and Mallory approaching their highest point (8220 m.) on their 1922 attempt.

Captain Finch and Howard Somervell* argued so persuasively for it, that the Committee allowed itself to be swayed. Finch set about producing an apparatus that could be used by climbers and to some extent, he succeeded. He constructed a frame for the climber to carry on his back and which contained four cylinders of oxygen. Each cylinder was charged to a pressure of 120 atmospheres and each would last for about two hours. Copper tubes led the oxygen from the flasks to the climber's chest, upon which a pressure gauge and flow meter were situated. Rubber tubes then conveyed the costly gas to the mask, which practically covered the whole face. Sadly, it later turned out that these masks were quite unsuitable in use, and Finch modified them, producing something significantly simpler and which stood up well. But although everything had been done to

* *Translator's note:* It is true that Dr Somervell was a member of the Oxygen Committee in 1922. However, as a physiologist, and in any case being himself possessed of remarkable powers of endurance, he favoured an attempt without oxygen. Using it, he felt, would prevent the degree of acclimatization an individual could expect to acquire.

make the apparatus as light as possible, each climber still had to carry a load of something over 16 kilos (32 lbs.).*

Two years later, in 1924, Lieutenant-Colonel E. F. Norton climbed without oxygen to a height of almost 8,600 metres above sea level, a record that lasted until 1978. Chinese climbers, who in 1975 followed the North Ridge Route, reconnoitred by the British expeditions, and reached the summit of their Chomolungma (Qomolangma) — as Everest is known in Tibet — claimed not to have used oxygen during their climb but only partook of 'oxygen inhalings', that is to say, they breathed extra oxygen during their rest pauses from cylinders carried with them:

Without having a break and inhaling oxygen, they clambered for one and a half hours at 8000 metres above sea level on Qomolangma Feng, although the air contained only one third of the normal amount of oxgen at sea level. At about 9.30, after a ten minute rest on top of the 'Second Step', or the second major obstacle on the way up, they inhaled oxygen for two or three minutes at a flow of two to five litres per minute. The summiters continued their clamber.†

It was apparent from the film they made at the time, that the Chinese all took doses of oxygen frequently.

THE ATTEMPTS OF NORTON
AND MALLORY

A few days before my departure for Nepal, I receive a letter from Richard Norton, son of the Everest pioneer who has strongly influenced my thinking.

Dear Mr Messner,

I was most interested to read a recent account in 'The Times' of your and Mr Habeler's forthcoming attempt to climb

---

* Rudolf Skuhra: *Sturm auf die Throne der Götter*, Buchergilde Gutenberg, Frankfurt 1950.
† *Nine who climbed Qomolangma Feng* — official Chinese report published in MOUNTAIN No. 46, 1975.

Mount Everest without oxygen. I should explain that I am the son of Colonel (as he then was) E. F. Norton, whose Everest attempt in 1924, when he reached a height of over 28,100 feet without oxygen, you have been quoting.

My father certainly believed that, given the right conditions Everest could be climbed without oxygen.

My mother and my two brothers join me in wishing Mr Habeler and you the best of luck. We shall be following the reports of your expedition with the greatest interest.

Yours sincerely,
Lieutenant-Colonel Richard P. Norton

It is true that E. F. Norton in his day believed that success without oxygen apparatus was possible and had written that he could see no reason why a well-trained, fully-acclimatized man should not climb Everest without oxygen assistance.

Packing for our expedition, I become oblivious of much that goes on around me, I stop reading the newspapers and frequently ignore the telephone, but whenever I find the time I re-read Norton's account of his and Somervell's attempt in 1924:*

Somervell and I started off from Camp III on June 1 to follow in Mallory and Bruce's steps. . . . The porters told off to accompany Somervell and me, and to establish our camp at 25,500 feet (7,800m.), were six in number, and of these three were to come on to 27,000 (8,200m.) . . .

At 3 p.m. (we) reached Camp IV, where Odell and Irvine took charge of us, allotted us tents and cooked and served us our meals, for they were now installed in their new role as 'supporters'. . . .

The morning of June 2 broke fine, and by 6.30 Somervell and I were off with our little party of six porters. The reader will understand that Mallory and Bruce were to have established Camp V overnight; this morning they should have been heading up the North Ridge for Camp VI, carrying with them the tent and sleeping-bags in which they had slept the night before. Our loads, therefore, must comprise one 10-lb. tent, two sleeping-bags, food and 'meta' (solid spirit) for ourselves for a possible three nights and for the porters for one; above the North Col porters' loads were always cut down to a maximum of

* Lieutenant-Colonel E. F. Norton and other members of the Expedition: *The Fight for Everest, 1924* (Edward Arnold, London 1925).

20 lb. a man, preferably a little under that weight. I cannot remember the exact details of the loads our men carried, but I know they were laden so near the limit that Somervell and I had to carry (as we had done the day before) a light rucksack apiece, with compass, electric torch, a few spare woollen garments, a change of socks, etc., for our own personal use.

Our route crossed the actual Col just below the western lip and, as we emerged from the snow hummocks to traverse it, we suddenly found ourselves in shadow and exposed to the full force of the west wind — from which we were completely sheltered both at Camp IV and in the intervening section; that was a bad moment, its memory is still fresh. The wind, even at this early hour, took our breath away like a plunge into the icy waters of a mountain lake, and in a minute or two our well-protected hands lost all sensation as they grasped the frozen rocks to steady us.

Some little way above the Col we emerged into sunlight again, and though we got the full benefit of the wind all the way up the ridge we never again experienced anything quite so blighting as those few minutes in the shady funnel of the Col. Nevertheless the wind was all day a serious matter. Though it seemed to cut clean through our windproof clothes, it yet had so solid a push to it that the laden porters often staggered in their steps. . . .

We followed our old route of 1922 — the blunt ridge known as the North Arête. For the first 1,500 feet or more the edge of a big snow-bed forms the crest of the ridge, representing the very top of that great mass of hanging ice which clothes the whole of the eastern slopes and cliffs of the North Col. Ascending, we stuck to the rocks just clear of this snow-bed; descending it is possible to glissade the whole length of it down to the Col. The rocks are quite easy, but steep enough to be very hard work at those heights. About half-way up this day's climb was the spot where two years before I had, while taking a short rest, placed between my feet my rucksack, containing a few woollen comforts for the night, and something starting it off, it slipped from my grasp and in a second was leaping and bounding like a great football with the evident intention of stopping nowhere short of the main Rongbuk Glacier below. This gives a fair picture of the general angle of the climb.

Somewhere about this same spot we heard something above and, looking up, were not a little disconcerted to see one Dorjay Pasang, descending to meet us. He was Mallory's and Bruce's leading porter, their first pick and one of the men on whom our highest hopes centred. We had hardly heard his tale of woe and read a note he brought from Mallory when we saw above Mallory, Bruce and three more porters descending in his tracks.

The wind was too cold for a long conversation, and their story was distressingly simple. On the preceding day they had met a very bitter wind all the way up the Arête on which we now stood — so bitter that it had quite taken the heart

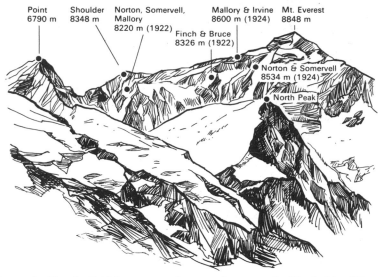

Heights reached by the British attempts of 1922 and 1924 on the North side of Everest.

out of their porters. They had pitched two tents at Camp V at a little over 25,000 feet and spent the night, but next morning nothing — not even Bruce's command of the language and well-known influence over these men — would induce any of the porters to go higher, and the end of it was that they had to return. Incidentally, Bruce had had to help the last two or three porters into camp the night before, carrying their loads for them for a short distance, and it was quite evident to us that these excessive exertions had affected him in some way — a surmise which was later confirmed by the discovery that he had strained his heart. So he himself was in no fit state to go on, though none who knew him will doubt that he would have done so could the porters have been induced to accompany him. Now there is a moral attached to this story. My diary (written at Camp IV) for the day when this fatal wind was encountered mentions the fact that the weather was 'quite perfect'; the porters who failed were the pick of the 'Tigers', presumably among the best men we had. Yet these picked men, under the one Sahib of all our party who knew best how to lead the Sherpa porter and on a day which at Camp IV appeared 'quite perfect', were clean knocked out by wind and couldn't be induced to advance beyond 25,200 feet.

As Camp V had been left all standing with tents and bedding destined to go higher that morning, Somervell and I were able to detach two of the porters who had accompanied us so far, to return with the descending party, and we now continued with four men, the three whose names I have already given and one Lobsang Tashi, a simple, good-natured giant from the eastern borders of Tibet. We reached Camp V without incident about 1 p.m. We had no difficulty in finding the camp from Mallory's description and from certain strips of

15

coloured cloth which each party carried to serve as sign-posts and which had been put up at the point where we were to leave the ridge. The two tents were pitched one above the other on crumbling platforms built on the steep slope just over the edge, and on the east or sheltered side of the North Arête.

The afternoon was spent as every afternoon must always be spent under these conditions. On arrival one crawls into the tent, so completely exhausted that for perhaps three-quarters of an hour one just lies in a sleeping-bag and rests. Then duty begins to call, one member of the party with groans and pantings and frequent rests crawls out of his bag, out of the tent and a few yards to a neighbouring patch of snow, where he fills two big aluminium pots with snow, by what time his companion with more panting and groans sits up in bed, lights the meta burner and opens some tins and bags of food — say a stick of pemmican, some tea, sugar and condensed milk, a tin of sardines or bully beef and a box of biscuits.

Presently both are again ensconced in their sleeping-bags side by side, with the meta cooker doing its indifferent best to produce half a pot of warm water from each piled pot of powdery snow. It doesn't sound a very formidable proceeding, and it might appear that I have rather overdrawn the panting and groans; but I have carried out this routine on three or four occasions, and I can honestly say that I know nothing — not even the exertion of steep climbing at these heights — which is so utterly exhausting or which calls for more determination than this hateful duty of high-altitude cooking. The process has to be repeated two or three times as, in addition to the preparation of the evening meal, a thermos flask or two must be filled with water for to-morrow's breakfast and the cooking pots must be washed up. Perhaps the most hateful part of the process is that some of the resultant mess must be eaten, and this itself is only achieved by will power: there is but little desire to eat — sometimes indeed a sense of nausea at the bare idea — though of drink one cannot have enough. . . .

With one last look at the panorama of glacier and mountain spread out below — a world composed of three elements only, rock, snow and ice, the mountain-tops now gilded by the declining sun and Camp III just discernible in the cold shadow of the North Peak under our feet — we turned in for the night, with gloomy forebodings for the morrow; for there was nothing whatever in the attitude of our porters to-night to encourage us to hope that we should next day succeed any better than Mallory and Bruce. . . .

On the morning of June 3 we were up at 5 a.m., and while Somervell busied himself with preparations for breakfast I climbed down to the porters' tent with some misgivings as to what their condition would prove to be. My fears were justified, and for some time groans were the only answer to my questions. But having at last, as I thought, inspired the men sufficiently to induce them to cook and eat a meal, I returned and had breakfast.

I then again tackled them, for they seemed incapable of making any sort of a move without much stimulating. . . . I talked for a long time to these men, pointing out the honour and glory that they would achieve if they would but carry their loads another 2,000 feet — thus passing by 1,500 feet the highest point to which loads had ever been carried.

I remember saying, 'If you put us up a camp at 27,000 feet and we reach the top, your names shall appear in letters of gold in the book that will be written to describe the achievement.' To make a very long story short I succeeded in inducing the three — Narbu Yishe, Llakpa Chede and Sempchumbi — lame as he was — to come on, and we actually started from camp at 9 a.m. — four hours after we had got up. Truly it is not easy to make an early start on Mount Everest!

Of our ascent of the ridge there is little to tell; it was a repetition of the climb of the day before and was over ground familiar to Somervell and myself, as we had traversed exactly the same route when making for our highest point two years before. . . .

Some time after midday we recognized and passed the highest point that Mallory, Somervell and I had reached in 1922. As I have said before, one's sensations are dulled at these altitudes, but I remember a momentary uplift at the thought that we were actually going to camp higher than the highest point ever reached without oxygen. With a clear day ahead of us, and given favourable conditions, what might we not achieve! . . .

About 2.30 we sent the three porters down. They had nearly 4,000 feet to descend, for we have since estimated the height of Camp VI at about 26,000 feet, and one of them was lame: so there was not too much time for them to reach Camp IV by daylight. I gave the men a note to be shown to the Sahib in charge of each camp to say that they had done splendidly, and were to be fed on the fat of the land and passed comfortably to the Base Camp and a well-earned rest.

We afterwards learnt that on this day, Odell and Hazard, the latter of whom had reached Camp IV the day before, climbed to Camp V, returning to Camp IV the same night. Odell was after fossils, and actually found the first ever collected on Mount Everest,* and Hazard accompanied him for air and exercise. This little stroll is a curious commentary on the fact that two years before the scientists were debating whether human beings could exist without oxygen at 25,000 feet.

Somervell and I spent the afternoon as on the day before, with the exception that we had now no porters to stimulate, and this was fortunate, for as you near 27,000 feet you have no great surplus of determination. My diary for the day finishes with the surprising entry: 'Spent the best night since I left Camp I'; yet

---

* Professor Odell's 'fossils' were, it was discovered later, not fossils at all, but a rare geological form, known as cone-in-cone structure. His full rock collection is now with the British Museum (Natural History) in South Kensington.

it was true in my case, and Somervell was at least fairly comfortable if he didn't sleep quite so well as I did. As one of our doubts had always been whether it would be possible to sleep, or even rest well, at 27,000 feet, this is an interesting point. Besides my boots I took to bed with me in my eiderdown sleeping-bag two thermos flasks filled with warm tea; towards morning I found that one of these had got rid of its cork, and its contents — no longer warm — had emptied into my bed.

Once more our hopes of an early start were shattered; snow had to be fetched and melted to provide the essential drink for breakfast. . . . Yet somehow the job was done and we were off at 6.40.

Perhaps an hour beyond camp we encountered the bottom edge of the great 1,000-foot-deep band of yellow sandstone that crosses the whole north face of Everest from shoulder to shoulder, and is so conspicuous a feature of the mountain as seen from the north. This afforded easy going as we traversed it diagonally, for it was made up of a series of broad ledges running parallel to its general direction and sufficiently broken up to afford easy access, one to the next.

The day was fine and nearly windless — a perfect day for our task — yet it was bitterly cold, and I remember shivering so violently as I sat in the sun during one of our numerous halts, dressed in all the clothes I have described, that I suspected the approach of malaria and took my pulse. I was surprised to find it only about sixty-four, which is some twenty above my normally very slow pulse. I was not wearing snow goggles except when actually on snow — a very small proportion of the day's climb — as I had found that the rims of my goggles somewhat interfered with a clear view of my steps. At a height of about 27,500 feet I began to experience some trouble with my eyes; I was seeing double, and in a difficult step was sometimes in doubt where to put my feet. I thought that this might be a premonitory symptom of snow-blindness, but Somervell assured me that this could not be the case, and he was undoubtedly right, for I have since been told that it was a symptom of lack of control and due to the insufficiency of oxygen in the air I was breathing.

Our pace was wretched. My ambition was to do twenty consecutive paces uphill without a pause to rest and pant, elbow on bent knee; yet I never remember achieving it — thirteen was nearer the mark. The process of breathing in the intensely cold dry air, which caught the back of the larynx, had a disastrous effect on poor Somervell's already very bad sore throat and he had constantly to stop and cough. Every five or ten minutes we had to sit down for a minute or two, and we must have looked a sorry couple.

The view from this great height was disappointing. From 25,000 feet the wild tangle of snowy peaks and winding glaciers, each with its parallel lines of moraine like cart tracks on a snowy road, was imposing to a degree. But we were now high above the highest summit in sight, and everything below us was so flattened out that much of the beauty of outline was lost. To the north, over the great plateau of Tibet, the eye travelled over range upon range of minor hills until all sense of distance was lost, only to be sharply regained on picking up a row of snow-peaks just appearing over the horizon like tiny teeth. The day was a remarkably clear one in a country of the clearest atmosphere in the world, and the imagination was fired by the sight of these infinitely distant peaks tucked away over the curve of the horizon.

Towards noon we found ourselves just below the top edge of the band of sandstone and nearing the big couloir or gully which runs vertically down the mountain and cuts off the base of the final pyramid from the great northern shoulder. The line we had followed was one roughly parallel to and perhaps 500 to 600 feet below the crest of the North-east Arête; this was the line Somervell and I had always favoured in preference to the actual crest, which Mallory advocated.

At midday Somervell succumbed to his throat trouble. He declared that he was only delaying me, and urged me to go on alone and reach the top. I left him sitting under a rock just below the topmost edge of the sandstone band and went on. I followed the actual top edge of the band, which led at a very slightly uphill angle into and across the big couloir; but to reach the latter I had to turn the ends of the two pronounced buttresses which ran down the face of the mountain, one of which we called the second step, and which looked so formidable an obstacle where it crossed the ridge that we had chosen the lower route rather than try and surmount it at its highest point. From about the place where I met with these buttresses the going became a great deal worse; the slope was very steep below me, the foothold ledges narrowed to a few inches in width, and as I approached the shelter of the big couloir there was a lot of powdery snow which concealed the precarious footholds. The whole face of the mountain was composed of slabs like the tiles on a roof, and all sloped at much the same angle as tiles. I had twice to retrace my steps and follow a different band of strata; the couloir itself was filled with powdery snow into which I sank to the knee or even to the waist, and which was yet not of a consistency to support me in the event of a slip. Beyond the couloir the going got steadily worse; I found myself stepping from tile to tile, as it were, each tile sloping smoothly and steeply downwards; I began to feel that I was too much dependent on the mere friction of a boot nail on the slabs. It was not exactly difficult going, but it was a dangerous place for a single unroped climber, as one slip would have sent me in all probability to the bottom of the mountain. The strain of climbing so carefully was beginning to tell and I was getting exhausted. In addition my eye trouble was getting worse and was by now a severe handicap. I had perhaps 200 feet more of this nasty going to surmount before I emerged on to the north face of the final pyramid and, I believe, safety and an easy route to the summit. It was now 1 p.m., and a brief calculation showed that I had no chance of climbing the remaining 800 or 900 feet if I was to return in safety.

At a point subsequently fixed by theodolite as 28,126 feet I turned back and retraced my steps to rejoin Somervell. In an hour I had gained but little — probably 100 feet in height, and in distance perhaps 300 yards — on the position where we had separated. Surveying is an exact science, and I must not quarrel with Hazard for fixing our highest point 24 feet below the height of Kanchenjunga, the third highest mountain in the world.

I feel that I ought to record the bitter feeling of disappointment which I should have experienced on having to acknowledge defeat with the summit so close; yet I cannot conscientiously say that I felt it much at the time. Twice now I have had thus to turn back on a favourable day when success had appeared possible, yet on neither occasion did I feel the sensations appropriate to the moment. This I think is a psychological effect of great altitudes; the better qualities of ambition and will to conquer seem dulled to nothing, and one turns downhill with but little feelings other than relief that the strain and effort of climbing are finished.

I was near the end of my powers, and had for some time been going too slowly to hope to reach the summit. Whether the height I had reached was nearing the limit of human endurance without the artificial aid of oxygen, or whether my earlier exertions and hardships in the month of May accounted for my exhaustion, I cannot, of course, say, but I incline to the latter opinion; and I still believe that there is nothing in the atmospheric conditions even between 28,000 and 29,000 feet to prevent a fresh and fit party from reaching the top of Mount Everest without oxygen.

One small incident will serve to show that I must have been very much below my proper form at this time, and that my nerve had been shaken by the last two hours of climbing alone on steep and slippery going. As I approached Somervell I had to cross a patch of snow lying thinly over some sloping rocks. It was neither steep nor difficult, and not to be compared to the ground I had just left, yet suddenly I felt that I could not face it without help, and I shouted to Somervell to come and throw me the end of the rope. Here again I remember the difficulty I had in making my voice carry perhaps 100 yards. Somervell gave me the required aid, and I could see the surprise he felt at my needing it in such a place.

Then came the descent. Soon after we started down, at about 2 p.m., Somervell's axe slipped from his numb fingers and went cart-wheeling down the slopes below. This must have been somewhere about the point where an hour or two before he had taken his highest photograph; and it is a proof of the deceptive picture of the true angle of the mountain conveyed by these photographs that it does not give the impression that a dropped axe would go any distance without coming to rest, yet his never looked like stopping, and disappeared from our view still going strong.

We retraced our steps of the morning; we made very poor going, descending at a very much slower pace than we had made two years before when we turned back from our highest point some 1,000 feet lower.

We looked in at our tent at Camp VI, finding it without difficulty, collected one or two of our belongings and a section of tent pole as a substitute for Somervell's axe, collapsed and weighted the tent with stones, and started down the interminable North Arête. Sunset found us level with Camp V, which we left below us on the right without departing from the blunt crest of the Arête. We were unroped, for here the going was both safe and easy. Arrived on the big snow-bed I glissaded for some little distance before I realized that Somervell had stopped behind, and I had to wait quite half an hour for him to catch up. I concluded that he had stopped to sketch or photograph the effect of the sunset glow on the great panorama of peaks surrounding us — a proof that I had by no means realized his condition: actually he had been stopped by a more than usually severe fit of coughing which had ended by very nearly choking him, and he was probably only saved by coughing up the obstructing matter along with a lot of blood. When he rejoined me, coming very slowly down the rocks, as he could not trust himself to glissade on the snow, it was already dark and I lit up my electric torch.

As we neared the Col I began to shout to Camp IV, for it was one of our rules that any party of porters or climbers descending from the mountain must be met at the Col and escorted and roped over the intricate route into camp by one or more of the supporters, who knew the way by heart. At last I made myself heard, and an answering shout informed us that our escort was coming and was bringing an oxygen apparatus and cylinder. But there was something we wanted far more than oxygen, for we were parched and famished with thirst. I remember shouting again and again, 'We don't want the d——d oxygen; we want drink.' My own throat and voice were in none too good a case, and my feeble wail seemed to be swallowed up in the dim white expanse below glimmering in the starlight.

A hundred feet or more above the Col, Mallory and Odell met us, and told us that Irvine was in camp hard at work preparing our dinner. Somervell had a go at the oxygen, but seemed to get little benefit from it, and I tried it with the same result. But we were perfectly fit to get along without it, and perhaps another three-quarters of an hour saw us arrive in camp. Mallory and Odell were kindness itself, and they kept congratulating us on having reached what we estimated as a height of 28,000 feet, though we ourselves felt nothing but disappointment at our failure. We reached Camp IV at 9.30 p.m., and what a different welcome it gave us to that we received at the same place two years before on our arrival at eleven at night in an empty and deserted camp! Young Irvine had both tea and soup ready for us, and we had something to eat; but our appetites were meagre, and herein lies one of the difficulties of high climbing: one eats from a sense of duty, and it is impossible to force oneself to take enough food even to begin to make good the day's wastage of tissue.

As Mallory and I lay in our tent, he explained that he had decided that if we two failed to reach the summit, he was determined to make one more attempt, this time with oxygen, and how he had been down to Camp III with Bruce and collected sufficient porters to enable the attempt to be staged. I entirely agreed with his decision, and was full of admiration for the indomitable spirit of the man, determined, in spite of his already excessive exertions, not to admit defeat while any chance remained, and I must admit that—such was his will power and nervous energy—he still seemed entirely adequate to the task. I differed with him in his decision to take Irvine as his companion — for two reasons: firstly, that Irvine was now suffering from the prevalent throat trouble, though certainly not as badly as Somervell had been before the start of our climb; secondly, that he was not the experienced climber that Odell was, while Odell was obviously fit and strong, and, acclimatizing very slowly as he had done, was now beginning to show unmistakably that we had in him a climber of unequalled endurance and toughness. Mallory's reasons for his choice were that though Odell and Irvine were both thoroughly *au fait* with every detail of the oxygen apparatus, yet the latter had a peculiar genius for mechanical expedients, and had taken the lead in devising means to obviate its numerous shortcomings; and he insisted that those who were to use the apparatus must have faith in its efficacy. Odell, having used it with Bruce on the day of their abortive attempt to reach Camp IV without apparently benefiting from it, certainly had not this confidence.

But it was obviously no time for me to interfere with the composition of the party, and when I found that Mallory had completed his plans I made no attempt to do so.

Some time after eleven o'clock that night, as I was dozing off to sleep, I was suddenly wakened by sharp pain in my eyes, and found that I had been smitten with a severe attack of snow blindness. In the morning I found myself completely blind, and I remained in this condition for the next sixty hours, suffering a good deal of pain.

June 5 was spent in the usual preparations for Mallory and Irvine's climb, on which they were to start next day. I was only able to help by periodically coming to the door of my tent and talking to the porters, for, poor though was my knowledge of Nepalese, there was no one else at Camp IV who could do so even as effectively as I; Mallory had learnt a sufficient smattering of Hindustani to communicate with these men to a certain extent, but it was evident that his party might have considerable trouble in getting their porters on from Camp V to Camp VI (though we hoped that their reluctance would be reduced to some extent by the fact that the carry had now been once successfully accomplished), and I had to do my best to stimulate the porters in advance for this crucial moment. That afternoon Somervell descended to Camp III and thence next day went on down to the Base Camp, and Hazard arrived from Camp III to take Irvine's place, with Odell as supporter at Camp IV.

On June 6 at 7.30 a.m. we said good-bye to Mallory and Irvine, little guessing that we should see them no more.

Of this attempt by Mallory and Irvine, N. E. Odell has written:*

On the evening of June 4 Mallory and Irvine with a few coolies came up from III, the two former using oxygen. They were able to cover the distance in the fast time of two and a half hours, and seemed well pleased with a performance which had no doubt been prompted by the wish to demonstrate the real efficacy of oxygen. But in my opinion the demonstration was hardly justified, and Irvine's throat at any rate, that had already given him considerable discomfort from the cold dry air, that at these altitudes can reduce this delicate passage to the consistency of cardboard, was palpably aggravated by the effect of the oxygen. Mallory's throat was less affected, though it was undoubtedly causing him some little irritation; and, besides, his usual equanimity was perhaps a little disturbed by the feeling of responsibility consequent upon this being probably the turning-point in the success or failure of the campaign. Who with the fighting spirit of Mallory, or with the long-tried obsession of attainment of the greatest goal of his ideals, could be otherwise than impatient to be off on the culminating challenge of a lifetime, nay even of a whole generation of active mountaineers! And Irvine, though through youth without the same intensity of mountain spell that was upon Mallory, yet was every bit, if not more, obsessed to go 'all out' on what was certainly to him the greatest course for 'pairs' he would be ever destined to 'row'! I had frequently shared a tent with Sandy Irvine in one or other of our glacier camps, but it was the previous year on our sledging journey across Spizbergen that I had first got to know him intimately. The effects of high altitude somewhat enhanced his natural reserve, but he told me on more than one occasion how much he hoped he would have a real chance of 'a shot at the summit.' And careful and devoted though his work was on making the oxygen apparatus efficient for use, he did not hesitate to tell me that he would rather reach the foot of the final pyramid without the use of oxygen than the summit by means of its aid! He thought that if it were worth while doing at all, it was worth while doing without artificial means. Nevertheless when the call came from Mallory for this one last effort with every means at our disposal, he saw the necessity of foregoing any personal preference in the matter, and welcomed almost with boyish enthusiasm a chance that he had little thought would come his way.

* N. E. Odell: 'Mallory and Irvine's Attempt' in *The Fight for Everest*, 1924 (Edward Arnold, London 1925).

It was late the same evening of Mallory and Irvine's arrival at Camp IV that the former and myself went up to meet Norton and Somervell returning from their record climb, the events of which have already been described. June 5 was spent quietly at the North Col, one and all of us feeling a sense of impotence at our inability to diminish the suffering that poor Norton was undergoing from his painful attack of snow-blindness, and Somervell on account of his severely relaxed throat. The latter, however, with his customary fortitude and resolution, announced that he was fit enough to go down to Camp III, and down to Camp III in the evening, of course, he went. Hazard was signalled for from Camp III by means of our usual code of blankets placed against the snow, and Irvine and I busied ourselves with re-testing and putting further final touches to the oxygen apparatus . . .

Hazard and I were up early the morning of the 6th, and soon had frizzling and crackling over the Primus stove a choice fry of sardines, to be served up in Mallory and Irvine's tent with biscuits and ample hot tea, or chocolate. On the announcement of this breakfast they seemed pleased enough, but I must admit that either owing to excitement or restlessness to be off they hardly did justice to the repast, or flattered the cooks! At 8.40 they were ready to start, and I hurriedly 'snapped' them as they were loading up with oxygen apparatus. Their personal loads consisted of the modified apparatus with two cylinders only and a few other small items such as wraps and a food ration for the day, amounting to not more than perhaps 25 lb. This may sound to many a very heavy load to carry at such altitudes, and in actual fact it is, but it is an easy load compared with the total of 40 lb. or more that the original breathing apparatus as well as the items of extra clothing, etc., that must be carried, amounted to. The eight porters, who accompanied them from Camp IV, carried provisions, bedding, and additional oxygen cylinders, but of course no breathing apparatus for their own use. It always amazed us how little on the whole our Sherpas were affected by moderate loads, though as a matter of fact at these altitudes we contrived to give them no more than 20 to 25 lb. to carry. The party moved off in silence as we bid them adieu, and they were soon lost to view amidst the broken ice-masses that concealed from view the actual saddle of the North Col and the lower part of the North Ridge of the mountain.

Though a brilliant morning, my diary records it as very cloudy in the afternoon and even snowing a little in the evening. It was 9.45 that morning that Hingston arrived and conducted Norton in his sightless condition down to Camp III, Hazard going down as far as the rope ladder and then returning to me on the North Col. I occupied myself meanwhile with various camp duties and observations. That evening, soon after 5 o'clock, four of Mallory's porters returned from Camp V, where his party was spending the night, and brought me a note saying, 'There is no wind here, and things look hopeful.'

THE IDEA

On the 7th Mallory's party was to go on up to Camp VI, and I that same day with Nema, who was the only porter of the two available at the North Col, followed up in support to Camp V. This method of support, a stage as it were behind, was rendered necessary by the limited accommodation at these two high camps, consequent upon the inadequate number of porters available to carry up sufficient tentage, etc. I had expected on my way up to Camp V to find a spare oxygen-breathing set that had been left there earlier, but discovered that Irvine the previous day had taken the mouthpiece from it for a spare, and so rendered it useless to me. However, I carried it on up to Camp V in case another mouthpiece were available there; but this was not so, though it did not bother me, since I found I was able to get along as well without its aid, and better without the bulky inconvenience of the whole apparatus. Not long after my arrival Mallory and Irvine's four remaining porters returned from Camp VI, their advent having been heralded by stones falling unpleasantly near the tent, that had been unwittingly displaced by them during their descent of the steep slopes above. The exposure of Camp V in this respect had been borne in on me during my first visit with Hazard, when Norton and Somervell's returning porters had likewise unknowingly bombarded our frail tents with stones and struck a porter of ours, though fortunately with no severe results. Mallory's porters brought me the following message:

> Dear Odell,
>
> We're awfully sorry to have left things in such a mess — our Unna Cooker rolled down the slope at the last moment. Be sure of getting back to IV to-morrow in time to evacuate before dark, as I hope to. In the tent I must have left a compass — for the Lord's sake rescue it: we are without. To here on 90 atmospheres* for the two days — so we'll probably go on two cylinders — but it's a —— load for climbing. Perfect weather for the job!
>
> Yours ever,
> G. Mallory

That evening as I looked out from the little rock ledge on which my tent was situated, the weather seemed most promising, and I knew with what hopeful feelings and exultant cheer Mallory and Irvine would take their last look around before closing themselves in their tiny tent at VI that night. My outlook, situated though I was 2,000 feet lower down the mountain-side than they, was nevertheless commanding and impressive in the extreme, and the fact that I was quite

* This refers to the pressure, and consequent amount, of oxygen they had been using. For full supply, the pressure stood at 120 atmospheres. . . .

alone certainly enhanced the impressiveness of the scene. To the westward was a savagely wild jumble of peaks . . . bathed in pinks and yellows of the most exquisite tints. Right opposite were the gaunt cliffs of Everest's North Peak, their banded structure pregnant with the more special and esoteric interest of their primeval history, . . . This massive pyramid of rock, the one near thing on God's earth, seemed only to lend greater distance to the wide horizon which it interecepted, and its dark bulk the more exaggerate the brilliant opalescence of the far northern horizon of Central Tibet, above which the sharp-cut crests of distant peaks thrust their purple fangs, . . . To the eastward, floating in thin air, 100 miles away, the snowy top of Kanchenjunga appeared, and nearer, the beautifully varied outline of the Gyankar Range, that guards the tortuous passages of the Arun in its headlong plunge towards the lowlands of Nepal. It has been my good fortune to climb many peaks alone and witness sunset from not a few, but this was the crowning experience of them all, an ineffable transcendent experience that can never fade from memory.

. . . I kept reasonably warm and consequently had a fair amount of sleep. I was up at 6, but the great efforts necessitated and energy absorbed at these altitudes, by the various little obligations of breakfast and putting on one's boots, etc., prevented my starting off before eight o'clock. Carrying a rucksack with provisions in case of shortage at Camp VI, I made my solitary way up the steep slope of snow and rock behind Camp V and so reached the crest of the main North Ridge. The earlier morning had been clear and not unduly cold, but now rolling banks of mist commenced to form and sweep from the westward across the great face of the mountain. But it was fortunate that the wind did not increase. There were indications though that this mist might be chiefly confined to the lower half of the mountain, as on looking up one could see a certain luminosity that might mean comparatively clear conditions about its upper half. This appearance so impressed me that I had no qualms for Mallory and Irvine's progress upward from Camp VI, and I hoped by this time that they would be well on their way up the final pyramid of the summit. The wind being light, they should have made good progress and unhampered by their intended route along the crest of the north-east shoulder. . . .

At about 26,000 feet I climbed a little crag which could possibly have been circumvented, but which I decided to tackle direct, more perhaps as a test of my condition than for any other reason. There was scarcely 100 feet of it, and as I reached the top there was a sudden clearing of the atmosphere above me and I saw the whole summit ridge and final peak of Everest unveiled. I noticed far away on a snow slope leading up to what seemed to me to be the last step but one from the base of the final pyramid, a tiny object moving and approaching the rock step. A second object followed, and then the first climbed to the top of the step. As I stood intently watching this dramatic appearance, the scene became enveloped in cloud once more, and I could not actually be certain that I saw the second figure join the first. It was of course none other than Mallory and Irvine, and I was surprised above all to see them so late as this, namely 12.50, at a point which, if the 'second rock step,' they should have reached according to Mallory's schedule by 8 a.m. at latest, and if the 'first rock step' proportionately earlier. The 'second rock step' is seen prominently in photographs of the North Face from the Base Camp, where it appears a short distance from the base of the final pyramid down the snowy first part of the crest of the North-east Arête. The lower 'first rock step' is about an equivalent distance against to the left. Owing to the small portion of the summit ridge uncovered I could not be precisely certain at which of these two 'steps' they were, as in profile and from below they are very similar, but at the time I took it for the upper 'second step.' However, I am a little doubtful now whether the latter would not be hidden by the projecting nearer ground from my position below on the face. I could see that they were moving expeditiously as if endeavouring to make up for lost time. True, they were moving one at a time over what was apparently but moderately difficult ground, but one cannot definitely conclude from this that they were roped together — a not unimportant consideration in any estimate of what may have eventually befallen them. I had seen that there was a considerable quantity of new snow covering some of the upper rocks near the summit ridge, and this may well have caused delay in the ascent. Burdened as they undoubtedly would be with the oxygen apparatus, these snow-covered débris-sprinkled slabs may have given much trouble. The oxygen apparatus itself may have needed repair or readjustment either before or after they left Camp VI, and so have delayed them. Though rather unlikely, it is just conceivable that the zone of mist and clouds I had experienced below may have extended up to their level and so have somewhat impeded their progress. Any or all of these factors may have hindered them and prevented their getting higher in the time.

I continued my way up to Camp VI, and on arrival there about two o'clock snow commenced to fall and the wind increased. I placed my load of fresh provisions, etc., inside the tiny tent and decided to take shelter for a while. Within were a rather mixed assortment of spare clothes, scraps of food, their two sleeping-bags, oxygen cylinders, and parts of apparatus; outside were more parts of the latter and of the duralumin carriers. It might be supposed that these were undoubted signs of reconstructional work and probable difficulties with the oxygen outfit. But, knowing Irvine's propensities, I had at the time not the slightest qualms on that score. Nothing would have amused him more—as it ever had, though with such good results—than to have spent the previous evening on a job of work of some kind or other in connection with the oxygen apparatus, or to have invented some problem to be solved even if it never really had turned up!... I found they had left no note, which left me ignorant as to the time they had actually started out, or what might have intervened to cause delay. The snow continued, and after a while I began to wonder whether the weather and conditions higher up would have necessitated the party commencing their return. Camp VI was in rather a concealed position on a ledge and backed by a small crag, and in the prevailing conditions it seemed likely they would experience considerable difficulty in finding it. So I went out along the mountain-side in the direction of the summit and having scrambled up about 200 feet, and whistled and jodelled meanwhile in case they should happen to be within hearing, I then took shelter for a while behind a rock from the driving sleet. One could not see more than a few yards ahead so thick was the atmosphere, and in an endeavour to forget the cold I examined the rocks around me in case some new point of geological significance could be found. But in the flurry of snow and the biting wind even my accustomed ardour for this pursuit began to wane, and within an hour I decided to turn back, realizing that even if Mallory and Irvine were returning they could hardly yet be within call, and less so under the existing conditions. As I reached Camp VI the squall, which had lasted not more than two hours, blew over, and before long the whole north face became bathed in sunshine, and the freshly fallen snow speedily evaporated, there being no intermediate melting phase as takes place at lower altitudes. The upper crags became visible, but I could see no signs of the party. I waited for a time, and then I remembered that Mallory had particularly requested me in his last note to return to the North Col as he specially wished to reach there, and presumably if possible evacuate it and reach Camp III that same night, in case the monsoon should suddenly break. But besides this the single small tent at Camp VI was only just large enough for two, and if I remained and they returned, one of us would have had to sleep outside in the open — a hazardous expedient in such an exposed position. I placed Mallory's retrieved compass that I had brought up from Camp V in a conspicuous place in the corner of the tent by the door, and after partaking of a little food and leaving ample provisions against their return, I closed up the tent. Leaving Camp VI therefore about 4.30, I made my way down by the extreme crest of the North Ridge, halting now and again to glance up and scan the upper rocks for some signs of the party, who should by now, it seemed to me, be well on their downward tracks. But I looked in vain: I could, at that great distance and against such a broken background, little hope to pick them out, except by some good chance they should be crossing one of the infrequent patches of snow, as had happened that morning, or be silhouetted on the crest of the North-east Arête, if they should be making their way back by that of their ascent, as seemed most likely. I was abreast of Camp V at 6.15, but there being no reason to turn aside to visit it, situated as it was a hundred yards or so off the main ridge eastward along the face, I hurried downwards. It was interesting to find, as I had earlier, that descending at high altitudes is little more fatiguing than at any other moderate altitudes, and of course in complete contrast to the extraordinarily exhausting reverse of it, and it seemed that a party that has not completely shot its bolt and run itself to a standstill, so to speak, on the ascent, and in any attempt on the summit, should find itself unexpectedly able to make fast time downward and escape being benighted. And as I shall mention later, the unnecessity of oxygen for the properly acclimatized climber seems never more evident than in this capability of quick descent. I was able to speed up my headlong descent upon the North Col by taking to the crest of the snow cornice to the leeward of the North Ridge, and finding the snow between 24,800 and 23,500 feet hard and conveniently steep, it was possible to indulge in a fast standing glissade that brought me to Camp IV by 6.45 p.m. It was rather surprising and withal useful to know that this distance between Camps IV and V, which upwards necessitated at any time three to four hours of arduous toil, could be covered in barely thirty-five minutes descending by means of a glissade, . . .

They would be late, for were they not behind their scheduled time when last seen! And hence they would succeed in reaching Camp VI only, or Camp V possibly, before darkness. The evening was a clear one, and we watched till late that night for some signs of their return, or even an indication by flare of distress. The feeble glow that after sunset pervaded the great dark mountain face above us was later lost in filtered moonlight reflected from high summits of the West Rongbuk. We hoped that this would aid them if perchance some incident had precluded their return as yet to Camp V or VI.

Next morning we scrutinized through field-glasses the tiny tents of those camps far up above us, thinking they must be at one or other, and would not as yet have started down. But no movement at all could be seen, and at noon I decided to go up in search. Before leaving, Hazard and I drew up a code of signals so that we could communicate to some extent in case of necessity: this was by a fixed arrangement of sleeping-bags placed against the snow for day signals, and as far as I was concerned Hazard was to look out for them at stated times at either of the upper camps. Answering signals from him were also arranged. For use after dark we arranged a code of simple flash signals, which included, of course, in case of need, the International Alpine Distress Signal. We had by this time three porters at the North Col Camp, and two of these I managed after some difficulty to persuade to come with me. We started off at 12.15, and on our way up the North Ridge we encountered that bitter crosswind from the west that almost always prevails, and which had really been the means of rendering abortive Mallory and Bruce's earlier attempt. I found my two Sherpas repeatedly faltering, and it was with difficulty that one in particular could be persuaded to proceed. We reached Camp V, however, where the night was to be spent, in the fairly good time of three and a quarter hours. I hardly expected, I must admit, to find that Mallory and Irvine had returned here, for if they had, some movement must have been seen from below. And now one's sole hopes rested on Camp VI, though in the absence of any signal from here earlier in the day, the prospects could not but be black. And time would not allow, even if I could have induced my men to continue in the conditions, of our proceeding on to Camp VI that evening. We made ourselves as comfortable at V as the boisterous wind would permit, but gusts sweeping over the North Ridge would now and again threaten to uproot our small tents bodily from the slender security of the ledges on which they rested, and carry them and us down the mountain-side. Fleeting glimpses of stormy sunset could at intervals be seen through the flying scud, and as the night closed in on us the wind and the cold increased. The porters in their tent below mine were disinclined for much food, and were soon curled up in their sleeping-bags, and I went down and added a stone or two to the guys for the security of their tent. I did likewise to mine and then repaired inside, and fitted up for use next day the oxygen apparatus that had lain idle here since I brought it from the ridge two days previously: having with me another mouthpiece, it was now ready for use.... The cold was intense that night and aggravated by the high wind, and one remained chilled and unable to sleep — even inside two sleeping-bags and with all one's clothes on.

By morning the wind was as strong and bitter as ever, and on looking in at the porters' tent I found them both heavy and disinclined to stir. I tried to rouse them, but both seemed to be suffering from extreme lassitude or nausea. After partaking of a little food myself I indicated that we must make a start, but they only made signs of being sick and wishing to descend. The cold and stormy night and lack of sleep had hardly been conducive to their well-being, and to proceed under these conditions was more than they could face. I told them, therefore, to return without delay to Camp IV, and seeing them well on their way downwards I then set off for Camp VI. This time with an artificial oxygen supply available I hoped to make good time on my upward climb. But the boisterous and bitter wind, blowing as ever from the west athwart the ridge, was trying in the extreme, and I could only make slow progress. Now and then I had to take shelter behind rocks, or crouch low in some recess to restore warmth. Within an hour or so of Camp VI, I came to the conclusion that I was deriving but little benefit from the oxygen, which I had been taking only in moderate quantities from the single cylinder that I carried. I gave myself larger quantities and long inspirations of it, but the effect seemed almost negligible: perhaps it just allayed a trifle the tire in one's legs. I wondered at the claims of others regarding its advantages, and could only conclude that I was fortunate in having acclimatized myself more thoroughly to the air of these altitudes and to its small percentage of available oxygen. I switched the oxygen off and experienced none of those feelings of collapse and panting that one had been led to believe ought to result. I decided to proceed with the apparatus on my back, but without the objectionable rubber mouthpiece between my lips, and depend on direct breathing from the atmosphere. I seemed to get on quite as well, though I must admit the hard breathing at these altitudes would surprise even a long-distance runner.

On reaching the tent at Camp VI, I found everything as I had left it: the tent had obviously not been touched since I was there two days previously: one pole had, however, given way in the wind, though the anchorages had prevented a complete collapse. I dumped the oxygen apparatus and immediately went off along the probable route Mallory and Irvine had taken, to make what search I could in the limited time available. This upper part of Everest must be indeed the remotest and least hospitable spot on earth, but at no time more emphatically and impressively so than when a darkened atmosphere hides its features and a gale races over its cruel face. And how and when more cruel could it ever seem than when balking one's every step to find one's friends? After struggling on for nearly a couple of hours looking in vain for some indication or clue, I realized that the chances of finding the missing ones were indeed small on such a vast expanse of crags and broken slabs, and that for any more expensive search towards the final pyramid a further party would have to be organized. At the same time I considered, and still do consider, that wherever misfortune befell them some traces of them would be discovered on or near the ridge of the North-east Arête: I saw them on that ridge on the morning of their ascent, and presumably they would descend by it. But in the time available under the prevailing conditions, I found it impossible to extend my search. Only too reluctantly I made my way back to Camp VI, and took shelter for a while from the wind, which showed signs of relenting its force. Seizing the opportunity of this lull, with great effort I dragged the two sleeping bags from the tent and up the precipitous rocks behind to a steep snow-patch plastered on a bluff of rocks above. It was the only one in the vicinity to utilize for the purpose of signalling down to Hazard at the North Col Camp the results of my search. It needed all my efforts to cut steps out over the steep snow slope and then fix the sleeping-bags in position, so boisterous was the wind. Placed in the form of a T, my signal with the sleeping-bags conveyed the news that no trace of the missing party could be found. Fortunately the signal was seen 4,000 feet below at the North Col, though Hazard's answering signal, owing to the bad light, I could not make out. I returned to the tent, and took from within Mallory's compass that I had brought up at his request two days previously. That and the oxygen set of Irvine's design alone seemed worth while to retrieve. Then, closing up the tent and leaving its other contents as my friends had left them, I glanced up at the mighty summit above me, which ever and anon deigned to reveal its cloud-wreathed features. It seemed to look down with cold indifference on me, mere puny man, and howl derision in wind-gusts at my petition to yield up its secret — this mystery of my friends. What right had we to venture thus far into the holy presence of the Supreme Goddess, or, much more, sling at her our blasphemous challenges to 'sting her very nose-tip'? If it were indeed the sacred ground of Chomo-lungma — Goddess Mother of the Mountain Snows, had we violated it — was I now violating it? Had we approached her with due reverence and singleness of heart and purpose? And yet as I gazed again another mood appeared to creep over her haunting features. There seemed to be something alluring in that towering presence. I was almost fascinated. . . .

I have already mentioned the possible reasons why Mallory and Irvine were so late in reaching the point at which they were last seen, which if the 'second rock step,' as referred to earlier, would be an altitude of about 28,230 feet, as determined by theodolite from the Base Camp by Hazard; if the 'first rock step,' then not more than 28,000 feet. And in the latter event we must assuredly and deservedly attribute the *known* altitude record, the greatest mountain height definitely attained by man, to Norton, who reached not less than 28,100 feet. I propose, therefore, very briefly just to speculate on the probable causes of their failure to return. From the 'second step' they had about 800 feet of altitude to surmount, and say 1,600 feet of ground to cover, to reach the top, and if no particularly difficult obstacle presented itself on the final pyramid they should have got to the top at about 3 to 3.30. Before, however, he left Camp VI Mallory had sent a note to Noel at Camp III saying he hoped to reach the foot of the final pyramid (about 28,300 feet odd) by 8 a.m. So on this schedule they would be perhaps five or six hours late in reaching the top, and hence they would find it almost impossible to get down to Camp VI before nightfall, allowing five or six hours for the return. But at the same time it must be remembered there was a moon, though it rose rather late, and that evening it was fine and the mountain clear of mist as far as could be seen. In spite of this they may have missed their way and failed to find Camp VI, and in their overwrought condition sought shelter till daylight — a danger that Mallory, experienced mountaineer that he was, would be only too well aware of, but find himself powerless to resist. Sleep at that altitude and in that degree of cold would almost certainly prove fatal. Norton, I know, finds it difficult to reconcile this explanation with the fact that no light was seen on the mountain after dark, and I am well aware it is a potent argument against it. But to me it is by no means conclusive since anything might have happened, in the way of damage or loss of their lantern or flash-light, to have prevented their showing a light. And the same applies to the magnesium flares which we supposed that they carried. In the tent at Camp VI I found one or two of the latter, which indicates the possibility of their having forgotten them the morning of their departure.

The other likely possibility, that many will not unnaturally subscribe to, is that they met their death by falling. This implies that they were roped together, a suggestion that I have mentioned earlier need not necessarily be inferred from their observed movements when last seen. It is at the same time just possible that though unroped they may have been climbing, on the ascent or descent, on some steepish pitch in close order, and the one above fallen on the lower and knocked him off. But it is difficult for any who knew the skill and experience of George Mallory on all kinds and conditions of mountain ground to believe that he fell, and where the difficulties to him would be so insignificant. Of Sandy Irvine it can be said that although less experienced than Mallory, he had shown himself to be a natural adept and able to move safely and easily on rock and ice. He could follow, if not lead, anywhere. . . . They were, of course, hampered by the oxygen apparatus — a very severe load for climbing with, as Mallory had mentioned in his last note to me. But could such a pair fall, and where technically the climbing appeared so easy? Experts nevertheless have done so, under stress of circumstances or exhaustion. Following what we called the 'ridge route,' i.e. by the crest of the North-east Arête, there seemed to be only two places which might in any way cause them trouble. The first was the 'second step,' already referred to more than once. This seemed steep, though negotiable at any rate on its north side. And if it were this step, as I thought at the time it was, that I saw the first figure (presumably Mallory) actually surmount within the five minutes of my last glimpse of them, then we had been deceived as to its difficulties, as at the distance we might well be. The only other part of the ascent that might have presented any difficulty, and probably not more than awkwardness, is the very foot of the final pyramid, where the slabs steepen before the relatively easy-looking ridge to the final summit can be attained. Norton at his highest point was close below this section, and he has expressed the opinion that these slabs, sprinkled with snow, might constitute a considerable source of danger in the case of a slip. But with all due deference to Norton's actual view of this place, from what can be seen of the local detail both in Somervell's photograph taken at 28,000 feet and in Noel's wonderful telephotograph of the final pyramid taken from above Camp III, the difficulties here look decidedly as if they could be circumvented by a nearly horizontal traverse to the right to the actual foot of the ridge of the final pyramid. In any case to a leader of Mallory's experience and skill such moderate difficulties, as these would present, cannot long have detained him, and during the descent such places as the above, and the probable consequences of a slip thereon, would be so impressed upon him, as well of course as on Irvine, that the greatest care and attention would be exercised.

Again, it has been suggested that the oxygen apparatus may have failed and thereby rendered them powerless to return. I cannot accept the validity of this argument, for from my own personal experience, to be deprived of oxygen — at any rate when one has not been using it freely — does not prevent one from continuing and least of all getting down from the mountain. On my second journey up to Camp VI, as related earlier, when I was using oxygen, I switched it off at about 26,000 feet and continued on, and returned, without it. Mallory in his last note to me said they were using little oxygen, and that they hoped to take only two cylinders each, instead of the full load of three each, from Camp VI. But even if later they were using much oxygen, they had both during the previous weeks spent adequate time at extreme altitudes, namely 21,000 feet and over, to become sufficiently acclimatized and not liable to collapse in the event of the oxygen failing. The importance of this factor of acclimatization is discussed elsewhere.

Hence I incline to the view first expressed that they met their death by being benighted. I know that Mallory had stated he would take no risks in any attempt on the final peak; but in action the desire to overcome, the craving for the victory that had become for him, as Norton has put it, an obsession, may have been too strong for him. The knowledge of his own proved powers of endurance, and those of his companion, may have urged him to make a bold bid for the summit. Irvine I know was willing, nay, determined, to expend his last ounce of energy, to 'go all out,' as he put it, in an utmost effort to reach the top: for had not his whole training in another hardy pursuit been to inculcate the faculty of supreme final effort? And who of us that has wrestled with some Alpine giant in the teeth of a gale, or in a race with the darkness, could hold back when such a victory, such a triumph of human endeavour, was within our grasp?

The question remains, 'Has Mount Everest been climbed?' It must be left unanswered, for there is no direct evidence. But bearing in mind all the circumstances that I have set out above, and considering their position when last seen, I think myself there is a strong probability that Mallory and Irvine succeeded.

DISAPPEARED

Even if Mallory and Irvine did reach the summit, they climbed for at least some of the time with oxygen masks, and therefore the question still remains whether the highest summit in the world can be reached without this technical aid, or not. 'Is the world constructed with men in mind, or only "mechanical men"?'

In his book about the Himalayan expeditions during the period from 1921 — 1948, Rudolf Skuhra describes an expedition, almost a decade later, which provided a macabre reminder of Mallory and Irvine's attempt:*

* *Sturm auf die Throne der Götter*, Buchergilde Gutenberg, Frankfurt 1950.

THE IDEA

Professor Odell with a picture of the North Face of Everest; he is indicating the spot where Mallory's ice axe was found.

Nine years later, about 60 feet below the crest of the ridge and 250 yards east of the First Step, Wyn Harris made a surprising discovery — an ice axe! This axe could only have belonged to Mallory or Irvine, no-one else had ever been so near to the crest of the ridge. In all this rock wilderness, chance had led Wager and Wyn Harris to the very tracks of the ill-fated couple. Was this then the site of the fatal accident? Wyn Harris (later) took the ice axe down with him, leaving his own in its place.

No further traces of Mallory and Irvine could be found and so the enigma of their disappearance remained. Since the early fifties Tibet has become a closed country, but Nepal opened its doors to foreign expeditions and so the struggle for Everest was switched to the Southern approaches.

We too after studying the background, evolved our own plan for climbing the highest mountain in the world from the south side. My dreams: an ascent without face-masks.

35

AUSTRIAN ALPINE CLUB

Wolfgang Nairz, 33
Innsbruck,
Leader, mountaineering
journalist for the ÖAV.
Leader, Tyrolean Manaslu
Expedition 1972.
Leader, Austrian Makalu
Expedition 1974.
Hang-gliding descent Noshaq.

The Plan

Overall leader: Wolfgang
Nairz.

Team: A two-man team
(Reinhold Messner and Peter
Habeler) for the South Spur;
4 climbers for the South Ridge,
2 Doctors, 3 Cameramen,
1 Base Camp Supervisor.

Start: End February 1978.

Duration: About 3 months.

Dr Oswald Ölz, 35,
Feldkirch,
Expedition doctor, works for
the Kanton Hospital, Zurich.
Manaslu, 1972.
Makalu, 1974.
McKinley, 1976.

Tactics: Combined climb into
the Western Cwm (partly with
skis). Above Camp III (about
6,600 m.) two separate assaults
on the summit.

Hanns Schell, 39, Graz,
Director of the firm
Odörfer & Segro,
AV-officer, Graz.
Hidden Peak, 1975.
Nanga Parbat, 1976 (first
ascent of a new route).
Five first ascents of 7,000
metre peaks.

Robert Schauer, 24, Graz,
Medical Student.
Hidden Peak, 1975.
Nanga Parbat, 1976.
Kun, India.

Peter Habeler, 35,
Mayrhofen,
Mountain and ski guide.
Tyrolean Andean Expedition,
1969.
Hidden Peak, 1975.
Dhaulagiri, 1977.

1978 EVEREST EXPEDITION

The Goals

First Austrian ascent of Mount Everest.

Attempt on the world's highest mountain without the use of artificial oxygen.

First ascent of the South Spur.

Hang-glider flight from the South Col (c. 8,000 m.), an attempt at the world altitude record for hang-gliding. To test newly developed equipment.

To make a TV film of the climbs, and also to send back progress reports for television news whilst on the expedition.

A book about the expedition to be published.

Franz Oppurg, 26, Wattens, Army mountaineering instructor.
Hindu Kush, 1972.
Andean Expedition, 1974.

Reinhold Messner, 33, South Tyrol,
Leader of the South Spur attempt.
Writer.
Nanga Parbat traverse, 1970.
Manaslu South Face, 1972.
Hidden Peak, 1975.
Dhaulagiri Expedition, 1977.

Helmut Hagner, 38, Innsbruck,
Mountain guide, ski instructor.
Makalu, 1974.
Noshaq, 1974, 1976.

Josl Knoll, 54, Innsbruck, Magistrate's clerk.
Manaslu, 1972.
Makalu, 1974.

Dr Raimund Margreiter, 36, Innsbruck,
Expedition doctor, works for university clinic, Innsbruck.
Tyrolean Andean Expedition, 1969.
Peru Ski Expedition, 1972.
Noshaq

Additional cameramen
Leo Dickinson, 32.
Eric Jones, 42.

Horst Bergmann, 35, Innsbruck,
Motor manufacturer, cameraman.
Tirich Mir, 1970.
Mt. Kenya Rescue Expedition.

37

MOUNT EVEREST 8848·12 m

South Summit 8760 m

LHOTSE 8511 m

*Mallory and Irvine
disappeared 1924*

Camp V 8500 m ▲ SOUTH SADDLE

NUPTSE 7879

▲ Camp IV 7986 m

GENEVA SPUR

THE YELLOW BAND

SOUTH-WEST FACE

Camp III 7200 m ▲

LHOTSE FACE

VALLEY OF SILENCE

Camp II 6400 m ▲

▲ Camp I 6100 m

KHUMBU ICEFALL

▲ Base Camp 5340 m

Overall plan of the climb

Passage	Height difference Distance (approx.)		Time required	Dangers Difficulties
Summit Ridge	850 m.	1.2 km.	↑ 6–12 hrs. ↓ 2–6 hrs.	Strongly exposed to the wind, gullies, steep steps.
		7986 m. Camp IV		
Lhotse Face	1300 m.	2.5 km.	↑ 3–9 hrs. ↓ 1–6 hrs.	30°–60° steep, Yellow Band, Grade III (the most difficult section).
		7200 m. Camp III	↑ 3–9 hrs. ↓ 1½–4 hrs.	
		6400 m. Camp II		
Western Cwm	600 m.	5 km.	↑ 1½–5 hrs. ↓ 1–3 hrs.	Easy in lower section, hidden crevasses frequent. Route-finding problems in mist.
		6100 m. Camp I		
Khumbu Icefall	750 m.	7 km.	↑ 2–6 hrs. ↓ 1–3 hrs.	Dangerous and unpredictable; continually variable. Ice up to 90° Enormous crevasses.
		5340 m. Base Camp		

All estimates after Reconnaissance and preparation of Route

EVEREST WITHOUT OXYGEN 78

In the early days — 1921, 1922 and 1924, the breathing apparatus was far from efficient and the climbers remained unconvinced that its advantages outweighed the handicap of the heavy cylinders. George Mallory and Sandy Irvine, two of the most celebrated and dedicated mountaineers of their day, vanished in 1924 in the summit region of Everest. We don't want anything similar to happen to us. We want to get up and back again without using breathing apparatus.

Apart from our climbing team, all selected to work well together, two British cameramen are coming with us to make a documentary film of Peter's and my climb, for the independent television company, HTV. As it became known in British climbing circles that the two men foresaw filming in the summit region, Leo Dickinson — a small man with an enormous sense of humour — produced a postcard satirising the situation. Don Whillans, a veteran Everester, had remarked, 'What! Leo wants to go up Everest? Don't make me laugh. It's not oxygen he'll be needing then, it's helium.' Eric Jones, known as the Welsh Roadrunner, and Leo, without doubt one of the most successful young mountain film-makers working today, have teamed together over the past few years to produce many memorable films — films on the Eiger North Face, the Matterhorn, and on expeditions in Patagonia, Nepal and Africa. They have taken their cameras in kayaks down the Dudh Kosi, the river that springs from the foot of Everest. These two experienced mountaineers have been friends of mine for several years.

FANATICS, CHARLATANS, CONQUERORS

Further attempts on Mount Everest failed also. In 1935, at a height of 6,500 metres, Eric Shipton found the body and diary of one fanatic who died in 1934 attempting to climb the mountain on his own. Maurice Wilson had first toyed with the idea of crash-landing an aeroplane on the slopes of Everest and then quickly forging his way to the top. When he could not get permission to fly over either Tibet or Nepal, he marched in from Darjeeling, planning to climb from the foot of the mountain.

He was utterly convinced that the power of a man's mind was greater than all the technology of a big expedition, and despite all obstacles, the Briton without a permit to climb, set off. In his diary he had written that

he knew what it was possible for a man to achieve. The failure of all the other Mount Everest expeditions could be attributed to the fact that they were over-equipped, in total and with regard to the individual participants. He had prepared his body to withstand the forthcoming hardships through fasting. After rigorous personal training he hoped to conquer the summit of the world in a single continuous push. He knew that his method of personal training would point the way for the alpinists of the future. . . .

He left Darjeeling on the 21st March letting it be known that he was only making an excursion to the East and would be back in a few days. With the last of his money he hired three porters from Nepal to accompany him. They managed to collect some clothes for him that resembled their own. Disguised as a coolie he travelled through the forbidden land of Tibet. They had one pack-pony with them. It carried the most important luggage. They didn't need much in any event. He was therefore travelling on foot towards Mount Everest, having been forbidden the easier approach by aeroplane . . .

Now on the 29th May he was continuing alone. The way went steeply uphill. His porters would wait for him here. He would make his last attempt. He felt he could almost count off the hours on his fingers until he reached his goal — one way or another.

But Mr Wilson did not attain his goal. He perished on the mountain, like Mallory and Irvine before him, like three dozen men since.

But the fascination of the highest mountain remained. Who did not want to climb it? Even after May 29, 1953 when Edmund Hillary and the Sherpa guide Tenzing Norgay became the first men to stand on its lonely summit, there was no shortage of fresh attempts. But now — since oxygen masks had brought the initial success, they were accepted as a matter of course. All further expeditions relied upon them, and increasingly, the summit of Everest became the cherished goal for 'underdeveloped mountain-climbing nations'. The Indians climbed it, the Italians, Chinese and a South Korean. It was as if a nation gained in some way once its 'heroes' had been to the highest pinnacle in the world. Even today, many people still do associate an ascent of this type with national prestige. Not one of the many expedition leaders have till now themselves reached the summit not all the reports of summit climbs have seemed credible.

One such was the Chinese claim to have successfully reached the summit during the night of May 25, 1960 — conclusive photographs were lacking and experts all over the world doubted the veracity of this claim. The Chinese expedition of 1975 was a different matter; eight men and one woman did reach the summit and for this achievement they used only a limited amount of oxygen, a technique which now proven, may well be copied by other mountaineers.

The Chinese, Tibetans for the most part, had only inhaled oxygen during rest pauses and climbed mainly without masks. They stayed 70 minutes on the summit without breathing from their cylinders. Now we have climbers standing on the summit without face masks, but to reach there completely 'without' has not yet been achieved. There still

Peter Habeler and I determined to climb Everest for the first time without the use of artificial oxygen — 'by fair means' was our motto.

remains a tremendous difference between the man who can make up his oxygen deficit during the night before a summit bid and in the rest pauses after every few steps, and the man who chooses to go completely without additional oxygen from base camp to summit.

Is it really possible to climb the highest mountain in the world without any help from oxygen apparatus? That is the question.

Many doctors don't think so. A large percentage of expedition climbers agree with them. After the West Ridge had been climbed, and the North side, and the South-west Face, as well as the normal route, the problem of a 'fair' ascent still remained, to storm the summit without masks. And I wanted to be the person to do it, together with Peter Habeler; we wanted to attempt to climb Everest 'by fair means'.

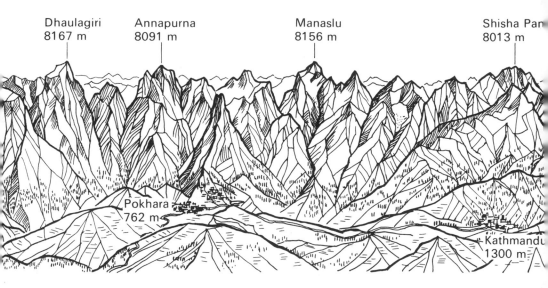

Dhaulagiri
8167 m

Annapurna
8091 m

Manaslu
8156 m

Shisha Par
8013 m

Pokhara
762 m

Kathmandu
1300 m

THE MOUNTAIN

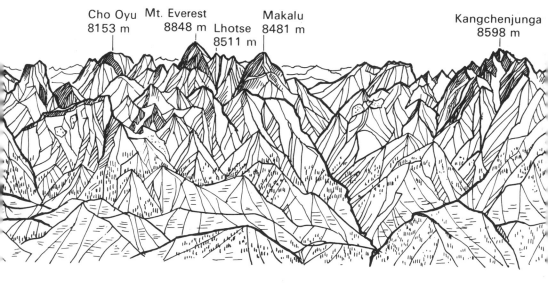

Cho Oyu
8153 m

Mt. Everest
8848 m

Lhotse
8511 m

Makalu
8481 m

Kangchenjunga
8598 m

Cho Oyu
8153 m

Gyachung Kang
7922 m

Pumo Ri
7145 m

Changtse
7553 m

Mt. Everest
8848 m

Lhotse
8511 m

Base Camp

Lobuche

Ama Dablam
6856 m

Pangboche

Kangtega
6809 m

Khumjung

Namche Bazar

Thyangboche

Lukla

Dudh Kosi

The Southern approaches to Everest Base Camp and the classic South-east Ridge Route.

DAWA TENSING'S HAT

'The snow was as deep as a man's hips that year,' says Dawa Tensing and stands up to give an idea of how they had had to break trail every day. Gesticulating with his hands, he bends the upper half of his body forward and takes a few steps as if he is pushing masses of snow away from his feet. His movements run down like clockwork. He knows what it means to climb at 8,000 metres without oxygen, to prepare a trail and to hump heavy loads. He has seen it all. He was there in 1924 when Norton attempted to climb Everest without oxygen.

At that time he had been one of the high-level porters. He was born sometime in the last century; he doesn't know how old he is. Today he lives in the Solo Khumbu. Everest and Ama Dablam are visible over the gable of his house.

The ankle-deep spring snow hurts my eyes as I come down out of the two-storey mud house into Dawa Tensing's small back yard. That is all he has left now. His fields in Khumjung, where he grew up, he has given to his children. He lives here close to the Thyangboche Monastery so that he can pray, look out at Everest and remember the old days. It hasn't always been easy, his life, but it has been exciting. And as he stands talking before me with his hands, his feet and above all his twinkling eyes behind their narrow slits, the images tumble back. He has accompanied more than 30 expeditions and been several times to Everest. In 1953 he was there, under John Hunt, when the South Col route was first climbed. His face looks as if it has been chiselled from granite. He has a single tooth in his upper jaw which fits neatly into a gap in the lower. His white beard is sparse and his grey hair drawn into a knot. He wears colourful Sherpa dress, woven shoes, and as an extra — who knows from what expedition — a pair of ladies trousers.

A great number of letters and pictures are piled around his house, but they are unimportant to him. In his mind the expeditions have all merged

On the way to Base Camp (above), I met the old Sherpa Dawa Tensing. He presented me with his hat and gave me tips for climbing Mount Everest without oxygen masks. Dawa Tensing was engaged as a high-level porter for the expedition to the North side of Everest back in 1924. Since then he has accompanied some three dozen expeditions. I wore his hat in Base Camp and during the climb, as protection against the sun. One day in the Icefall it was blown from my head by the wind and I was unable to find it again. The march-in to Base Camp we took very leisurely: we wanted to acclimatize and to gradually 'grow into' the mountain scene.

In Lobuche (double-page) we camped for the night before we reached Base Camp.

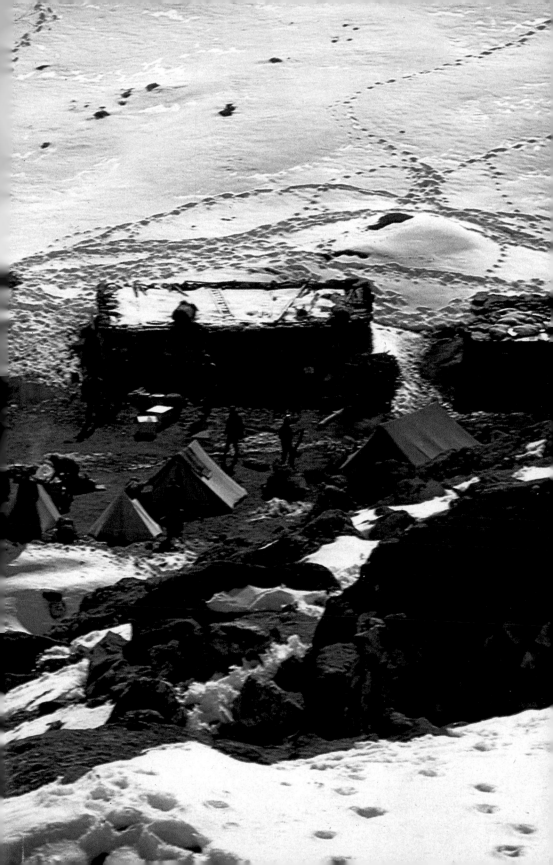

I had been considering the problem of Everest for some years before this Austrian Alpine Club Expedition, to which Peter Habeler and I attached ourselves as a two-man unit. During the march-in, too, we discussed amongst ourselves and with the Sherpas the possibility of climbing the highest mountain in the world without oxygen apparatus. Feelings were divided on this, but no-one saw much chance for a serious attempt. Of course we could only fully appreciate the vast scale of the Icefall and the Western Cwm (seen here, above, from an aeroplane, and, below, photographed from the South Col) some weeks later after we had climbed through them several times.

together and he does not distinguish any particular year and any expedition
leader. But he does remember individual instances and elaborates in minute
detail — standing up and going step-by-step through his garden — what it
is like to be at 8,000 metres or more. I could tell at once that this is a
deeply-ingrained experience. He says we shall have to force ourselves to
eat up there.

'Yes, at altitude it is important to eat even if you don't feel like it — and
above all, to drink. But there's no water and you mustn't suck snow.'

Tsampa is what we should eat, he tells me, and for drink, tea — lots and
lots of tea.

'What was it like on the North side, the Tibetan side that time?'

'Mallory and Irvine didn't come back.'

'Why, do you think?'

'They kept climbing up in deep snow and didn't come down again.'
Pause. 'The wind will have got them, the wind.'

I want to know if he thinks they reached the summit or not. He shrugs
his shoulders. To Dawa Tensing it is not so important whether they got up
or not. They disappeared, that was the important thing.

'It will have been the wind that got them,' he repeats.

I ask him hesitantly what he thinks of our chances of climbing Everest
without oxygen, whether indeed it is possible or not.

'Yes, it must be possible. I have often been to the highest camps without
it, and I have spent weeks on the South Col. All the other Sherpas and
Sahibs were in bad shape after a few days up there, they were sick —
couldn't go any further — came down very shaky.'

The big prayer wheel in his smoky living room is turned by his wife,
his third wife. He lost his first in 1956 while he was away on Everest. His
eldest son was at that time with another expedition, and his wife heard
that both the son and her husband had been caught under an avalanche.
Accurate reports were few and far between in those days. She was dis-
traught, went to the river and threw herself into the raging glacier water.
When Dawa Tensing came home, he found an empty house. His son had
indeed died in an avalanche, and his wife in the river. He married again,
but lost his second wife also.

Dawa Tensing is no lamaist, but he prays a lot and reads Tibetan texts.

We will look in on him again when we come back. He would like to have details of an Everest climb, as he had always wished it.

Dawa Tensing presents me with his hat, an old Gurkha hat. I shall take it with me, at least into the great basin of the Western Cwm. On my return I shall bring it back to him.

'I'll need it again in the summer,' he says, 'against the rain and sun.'

Above the twisted shingles of his roof, a cloud is visible over the summit of Everest, a slender, black pyramid, it rises some 300 metres above the Nuptse-Lhotse Wall. It is unmistakably the highest peak in the whole region. Dawa Tensing turns away as I make to offer him a few rupees as a deposit for the hat. He won't take any money. He wishes me luck and will see me again in the summer. I stand there in the little garden on the damp ground and watch the banner of cloud on the summit of Everest. Dawa Tensing has been close to this summit more than ten times, having approached both from the North and the South. He too gazes up, he has no regrets that he hasn't been to the top. Expedition politics, he says, require a Sirdar like him, as the Sherpa leader, to spend much of the time in Base Camp supervising reinforcements and ensuring that each Sherpa is doing his job.*

As I go past the woodpile heaped in front of his house and shake his hand for the last time, Dawa Tensing says nothing. Then as I turn back to wave, he says, 'Take much care. Eat plenty.' He is reminding me how important it is to force yourself to eat when you are suffering the effects of altitude.

'Come back,' he calls, 'and we'll have a Chang-party in my house. Come back!'

March 21. The huge prayer wheel turns regularly. A wisp of smoke hangs over the roof. Some snow still clings to the north-east eaves, the other side is dry. The little bleached prayer flags flutter in the wind, pointing the way to Everest.

The snow is melting in the midday warmth and water runs in rivulets

---

* *Translator's note:* This is less often true now — the Sirdar is often included in the climbing party. Indeed in 1953 Tenzing was Sirdar to the Everest expedition, and it was always understood he would go high.

along the well-trodden paths. Yak caravans plod through the sludge, bringing food to the high villages and farms and necessary bits of equipment for expeditions. Lost in thought, I wander alone beside the long prayer wall towards the mountains. It is too early for any downy green seeds on the high meadows, and the rhododendron bushes on either side of the track stand starkly, as if burnt, their leaves hanging brown and dusty. But the earth smells of spring.

As I turn Dawa Tensing's hat thoughtfully in my hands, a feeling of calm washes over me. I have been so preoccupied with the prospect of Everest, in my dreams and throughout the journey, that I now no longer know who I truly am — am I this Sherpa who has learned to know Everest from all sides, or am I some crazy European who returns again and again in a desperate effort to find some deeper purpose to his life. With what enthusiasm and what calm acceptance Dawa Tensing had recalled his expeditions! They belong as much to his life as his three wives, or his house here amongst the mountain giants, or the abundant spring snow.

We have now been on the road for a week. We are going slowly in order to acclimatize, making short excursions into the surrounding villages, meeting the Sherpas who have to scratch a living in these barren high valleys south-west of Everest.

I have made up my mind to climb Everest, in much the same way as someone might decide to write a book or stitch a garment. And I am prepared for anything I might have to face on my way to the summit.

It is midday; the main expedition party is well ahead. By now the kitchen has probably been set up, so I will have to forego my meal. But it doesn't matter. I still feel the glow of the golden-green Chang I enjoyed with Dawa Tensing, and although I am still a bit giddy, it has certainly done me no harm.

'As far as Base Camp,' Dawa had said, 'you can drink Chang. Chang — Rakshi — whatever you like, but after that — no more — no alcohol at all. And no smoking either. That is important.'

He repeated this often as if he wanted to print it indelibly in my mind.

As I now scramble down into the churned-up stream bed of the Dudh Kosi, Ama Dablam stands behind me. There are mountains about which, because of their very appearance, no-one asks why we want to climb them. Their colour and their form are so striking and so attractive that the question would seem naive. Every mountain-lover would like to climb Ama Dablam. Every child would understand the challenge of such a mountain, soaring as it does, vertically upwards, its every line marrying together harmoniously on the summit. Why do we climb these mountains? Who can say? Indeed, I don't think I would really want to know the reason, but I often indulge the theory that perhaps it has something to do after all with the fact that we men cannot bear children. Back at home, there always seemed to be a possibility that something, or someone — a desirable woman perhaps — might dissuade me from my intention to climb Everest. Here, the very idea seems strange; here Mount Everest is an intrinsic part of my life; I need no other partner.

Out of the corner of my eye I can see the fringe of prayer flags that I have wound around my hat; at the same time my feet come alternately into view ahead. It is as if they don't belong to me as they trudge up through the oozy mud and pick their way steadily through the stones of the steep slope up to Pangboche. Now and then when I lift my head to peer out from under the brim of the hat to see the way ahead, Ama Dablam looms into view. Then I have a strange, a liberating feeling as if I have floated clean out of myself and am now hovering freely in the air above my head. I am breathing quickly, but I do not lack energy, I am not tired. I feel compelled to keep climbing, climbing steadily upwards with a regular unvarying rhythm on these legs that no longer seem to be my own.

The ragged white prayer flags were presented to me yesterday by the lamas of Thyangboche as a good luck charm after our group had attended a long ceremony of blessing at the monastery. The lamas promised us they would pray daily for our safe arrival, and above all, for our safe return. I wound the prayer flags twice around the dingy green hat to brighten it up. Pangboche is deserted today. Tattered flags of linen, inscribed with prayers, blow in the wind above the dry, painted houses. The fields are flecked with snow, the paths muddy. Mire. Then suddenly, as a dog yelps, a small boy and girl come running and throw stones at a big Tibetan terrier that has bitten their Lhasa Apso. The little boy's forehead and chin

Official postcard of the ÖAV (Austrian Alpine Club) Mount-Everest-Expedition 1978, showing the individual team members.

are thickly encrusted with grime. He certainly hasn't washed since last autumn. His hands are calloused and covered in warts, like the bark of a tree. When he has driven the big dog away, he sidles closer and stares at me with his head on one side as if I am the first stranger he has set eyes on since the hard winter months. I pat his wiry head. Sometimes it seems one has to change skins to be able properly to attune to this country. At last I have broken all ties with my past; I now feel completely absorbed into this land, at one with its people.

Since my last expedition in 1977, since my return from Dhaulagiri, I have not slept much. It was not only the break-up with my wife that upset me, it was as if the very purpose of my life had been lost. Although I am now under no illusions that climbing has any more or any less sense than life itself, still I feel happier again. I sleep well and deeply, I am again in control, objective, as if there were nothing to worry about in my existence.

WHAT IF . . .?

Where the Solo Khumbu Glacier makes a sharp bend to the left, between the moraine slopes and the curve of the glacier, stands our Base Camp. In a shallow hollow two dozen tents are planted amongst the stones. A little cloud of smoke hangs in the air above the camp, for the Sherpas keep their sacrificial fire burning all the time. Hanging on three wooden poles as tall as trees, is a 50-metre line bearing many fluttering prayer flags.

An afternoon in Base Camp. Three dozen people sit in the warm sun in front of their tents. The snow is wet and mushy underfoot but the rocks are warm and dry. On one side, on the low ground facing Pumori, the Sherpas have their tents; on the other, with a view towards Everest, the Sahibs. Between them the Liaison Officer is lying in his tent, moaning, a victim of altitude sickness. Everyone sits around, some on items of clothing, others on the bare rocks, chatting, eating. Now and then one will gaze up into the deep blue sky with an air of expectancy.

Yesterday the first post arrived in Base Camp — newspapers too. Again I felt apart from it all. This feeling of apartness often sweeps over me after I have been travelling for some weeks away from the telephone, the post, the bureaucracy, and from all the restrictions and rules that living together in towns imposes.

I have had to wait so long to realize my dreams that I no longer dare to look forward to them. So finally my climbing has become a game rather than a calling. I am doing something which in the end I no longer dream about.

During the walk in to Base Camp I frequently asked myself why Peter and I should want to climb Everest without oxygen. The reason does not lie in a pure mountaineering or sporting purpose. To be able to explain this I had always to turn back to history and say that in the first 200 years of alpinism, it was the mountain that was the important thing. During this time it was the summit that was conquered and explored, that was the unknown that man attempted to reach by any means, employing any techniques. But for some years now and particularly on my own tours, it is no longer the mountain that is important, but the man, the man with his weaknesses and strengths, the man and how he copes with the critical situations met on high mountains, with solitude, with altitude.

My expeditions have thus enabled me to draw closer to myself, to see into myself more clearly. The higher I climb, the deeper I seem to see within myself. But were I to put all sorts of technical gadgets between myself and the mountain, then there would be certain experiences that I could not feel. If I were to wear an oxygen mask, I should be unable to know exactly what it means to climb at heights of 8,000 metres or more, what it feels to struggle against the body's resistance and to endure the loneliness of being totally beyond the reach of help.

People whose primary objective is to get to the summit may employ any measures, any technical tricks to get there, even if they are intrinsically unsporting. For me, on the contrary, the summit is not that important. If I should be unable to reach it (which after all is more likely than that I should), then I will give up and turn back, be it at 7,000, 8,000 or even at 8,800 metres above sea-level. Even if it were just below the summit. The experiences I should have gained in getting thus far would be greater than any I might gain in pressing on to the summit with oxygen. The march-in, the life here at 5,340 metres on the dead glacier, these have been worthwhile in themselves — to get this far, to have taken part.

On *March 25* our expedition leader, Wolfgang Nairz — we call him Wolfi — had called everybody together in Base Camp for a pow-wow. 'What if something happens? What do we do then? That is the first question I think it's essential we discuss. In the case of an accident, whether we go on or not, really depends on the gravity of the accident. My personal view is that if something should happen to me, the expedition should go on just the same. Now each of you must say what is to be done if it is you that's involved. Should one of you say: "I want my body recovered and buried," we must respect that. We must be fair.'

'Shall I quickly translate that,' asks our Expedition Doctor, Oswald Ölz, known as Bulle.

'Yes please, fine.'

Bulle translates these points into English for the leader of the Sherpas, Sirdar Ang Phu, and for the Liaison Officer.

'The insurance we have covers the cost of bringing a body home. Naturally if someone is lost in the Icefall, how and whether he can be brought down is another question altogether. Please answer in turn, going round the circle.'

'You can bury me where I die and carry on,' I say drily.

Everyone talks amongst themselves and are all agreed, we should carry on.

'The next point to clear up is the actual burial,' says our second doctor, Dr Raimund Margreiter, after a short dispute between Peter Habeler and Hanns Schell on the subject. 'Most of us would want to be buried on the spot, but is there anyone who would prefer to have his body taken somewhere else? If he dies in Base Camp, he can't expect to be taken up to the Western Cwm, of course!'

Only Hanns Schell, a mountaineer from Graz with many years of expedition experience, indicates he would like his body taken home if this didn't interrupt the progress of the expedition, and its recovery did not involve any additional hazard to the others. All this is supposing the worst comes to the worst. Things might not be as bad as that. Wolfi continues: 'Our insurance also covers unlimited helicopter costs. If anyone has an accident, we can fetch him by helicopter quickly. And if he has to go home right away, we can buy a Lufthansa ticket — Miss Hawley, our contact in Kathmandu, has got emergency money in case of accident, and that's covered by the insurance. Expenses to the nearest hospital are covered.'

'That's the hospital in Kathmandu?'

'Just a minute. I'll check. In any case, transport out is covered. It says here: "hospitalisation or return transport in the said country or return transport to the country of domicile." '

'That means back to Innsbruck then, or somewhere in Europe.'

'The insurance will pay either the hospital expenses in Kathmandu or the return flight to a hospital back home.'

'So we don't need to discuss that one — if something serious happens, back home straight away.'

'I need to know everyone's next of kin,' continues Wolfgang Nairz. 'This address list will be kept in a special place in my tent, so that it can be found in emergencies. If anything were to happen, the Liaison Officer has to advise the authorities right away. Miss Hawley would then send a telex to the next-of-kin addresses, which you're giving me now, that is she passes on the news so that in all probability relatives learn of it before anything appears in the press. And while we are on the subject of the press: you all know we have a press contract — I would like to remind you all to keep to the terms of the contract.'

'What's the position with the Dailies?' someone asks, 'we have no contract with the German press, only the Austrian.'

'Let's get on,' Wolfi takes over again, 'should anything happen to me, here in this briefcase — the one with the customs sticker on it — are a variety of documents, necessary for the going-home formalities. Someone would need to take charge of these.'

'I think we should delegate someone to do this,' I suggest, and this is soon done.

'We have been sent a mass of stuff for the expedition,' the leader continues, 'and naturally we must do our bit and provide advertising photographs. We shall need as many of you as possible to pose for the photos on a fine day.'

'The next thing is the film. The post leaves every Tuesday and Friday from Pangboche, so we have to send post-runners early every Monday and Thursday. We must have the post ready the night before. You know that as far as possible, we have to send back weekly reports and interviews to Austria, and Horst will have the job of seeing this is done. But I want to beg you all to give him every assistance and support. If he's photographing a scene, like crossing a ladder, and the shot doesn't work, you should be prepared to stop and do it again. I think we should all do this much if Horst has lugged up all the heavy film equipment. Apart from that every one is free to film or take photographs privately.'

A number of various technical briefings follow, then Wolfgang says: 'We are one expedition, but Reinhold and Peter are a separate unit. We work together as far as advance base, and then the two of them will make up their minds what they want to do. If the Spur proves a possibility they will attempt it; if not they will come and try the Ordinary Route with us, though naturally they will try it without oxygen. I think if Reinhold and Peter are in good form, the attempt without oxygen will be given priority.'

YAK AND YETI

Sometimes I am able to keep from my mind the possible consequences of this Everest expedition. Death is a subject one doesn't dwell upon. But there are other times – hopeless, cheerless times – when despite myself I am beset with misgivings and all manner of premonitions; and sometimes indeed I am so weary with worry that continued existence no longer seems important. The banality of Base Camp conversation and the overall greyness of the surroundings combine to force me into my own thoughts, remembering affection and warmth.

We are still awaiting a large part of our equipment. It is to come up by yak caravan. Since I myself believe the yeti to be more a creature of fable than fact, I don't have the inclination to pass the time in searching for one; and there remains little else to do but sit and wait for the yaks. In my mind our climb is already an unalterable fact and there seems no possibility of withdrawing from it now that the wheels have been set in motion.

In between meal times, the endless conversation drags on.

Saturday afternoon, March 25. In the mess tent drinks are being passed around – some highly-concentrated fizzy glucose drink.

'What's happening Wolfi? It's getting very boring in Base Camp.'
'Will the stuff come up today or not?'
'Not today.'
'How shall we keep the Sherpas occupied?' someone asks.
'If we can't keep to our original plan, then we'll have to amend it.

First of all we'll postpone everything by one day. All of you who've got your own equipment already should start on up so that the Sherpas have something to do,' explains our leader.

'Which way does the route go? Does it still go up where all the ropes are?'

'Yes, for the first section at least. I'm not exactly sure about the second. Maybe we should go further to the right up there', suggests Robert Schauer, who together with Franz Oppurg, has already prepared much of the route through the Icefall.

'The top section will be a bit of a problem', Oppurg breaks in, 'there's been a tremendous amount of movement up there – chasms 40, 50, 60 metres deep – everything has collapsed.'

The discussion on what is the best and safest line to take goes on. The Icefall is the most dangerous section of the whole climb and the route has to be worked out in precise detail. Robert Schauer continues.

'Tomorrow shall we reconnoitre as far as the Question Mark?' That is what we call the barrier in the middle section of the Icefall. 'How many big crevasses are there up as far as you went?' I ask.

'Two.'

'Is that all?'

'The Sherpas should easily be able to prepare the route tomorrow,' I say.

'Cutting steps where it's too steep. And there's one place where you have to jump across from one side of a crevasse to the other. There's a lot of gear left in there from the Korean expedition last year. They banged in wooden blocks for the Sherpas to climb up. But we can take up a small ladder, that should do it.'

'Have the Sherpas got their crampons yet?'

'Yes, but they're still waiting for boots, some of them.'

'Axes?'

'Them too.'

'Rope?'

'They don't have any rope, they'll have to have some from Franz and Robert.'

'Call the two Sirdars over,' suggests Wolgang Nairz. Then, 'We will start tomorrow', he says, 'you 18 Sherpas here now. We start six-thirty and twelve of you have to start work', in simple expedition-English, he begins explaining to Ang Phu, the first Sirdar, and to Dati, the second Sirdar. The job of these two men is to divide up the Sherpas and to liaise between these high-level porters and the team. As so much of the Sherpas' equipment is still missing, it is difficult to do much.

Dati, our second Sherpa-Sirdar.

'Two flights to Lukla were firmly booked for the 21st for our equipment. So it ought all to be here the day after tomorrow,' Nairz pacifies everyone.

'How many tents have we for the high camps?'

'Quite a few.'

'What sort?'

'French.'

'But the French tents are hard to put up.'

'Any tent with the poles inside is harder to erect than one with external poles.'

IN THE ICEFALL

Easter Sunday, March 26. Before breakfast Peter complains of a headache.

'I've hardly slept a wink, and my head's on fire — it feels as if I've had a night on the tiles.'

'Yesterday, I was worried I had a headache coming too, I didn't sleep very well either,' I console him.

65

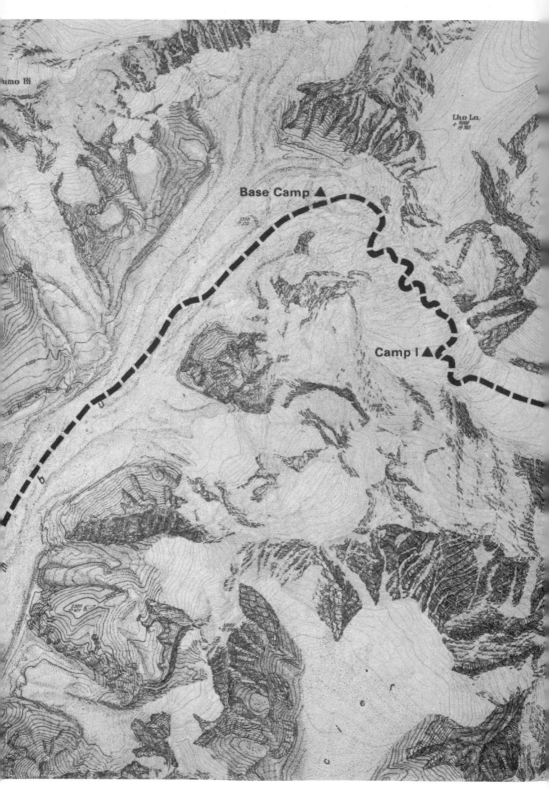

Our route to the summit (section of the Mount Everest Map produced by the German

and Austrian Alpine Club (D/ÖAV) and the Deutschen Forschungs–Gemeinschaft 1957.)

The Khumbu Icefall, an exploded tongue of ice, is the most dangerous feature of the South-eastern approach to the Roof of the World. It stretches from Base Camp to the Western Cwm, which in turn leads to the foot of Lhotse (above). Never in all my life have I been through such dangerous passages as we encountered in the Icefall (below). It took us a week to find a way through this ice labyrinth. With some 50 ladders and more than 1000 metres of fixed ropes, we prepared the route for our porters. These men carried some 18 kilos of material and equipment apiece, through the danger zone. I myself went fourteen times through the Icefall and breathed a huge sigh of relief each time I returned safely to Base Camp (next double-page) from the upper regions.

Eric Shipton, the great British Himalayan explorer, pioneered the southern approach to Everest at the beginning of the nineteen-fifties. Before then, Nepal was closed to outsiders, and climbers had always attempted Chomolungma — as Everest is called in Tibet — from the north side.

The biggest problem in climbing Everest from the South is the Icefall. Still today it presents a big risk factor for each and every expedition. It moves at a rate of about a metre a day and is therefore, continually changing. We too searched long and hard for a safe, viable route. We did not find one. But despite the dangers, the Sherpas toil through this wilderness of ice with their loads day after day. Frequently the route has to be re-sited because a previously prepared section has broken away or been buried under an ice avalanche.

'But it didn't come to anything?'

'No, not really.'

'I think I must have eaten too much.'

'Aren't you coming to breakfast?'

'No — but if you have a minute, can you bring me some tea?'

'I'll send the cook.'

'No, only a cup of tea.'

'Black?'

'I'll be able to get up soon, but I'll stay lying down a bit longer. It's not one of those headaches like I had on Hidden Peak that time, it's a tight pressure in my head. It's the usual thing, I get it every time.' After a pause, Peter continues, 'I was expecting it. Yesterday evening every single bone in my body was aching.'

The next day, Easter Monday, *March 27*, a few Sahibs and Sherpas go into the lower section of the Icefall; they have ladders and ropes with them. We are still waiting for the rest of the equipment which should come today or tomorrow. Then the big attack on the Icefall, planned for today, can really get under way at last.

March 28. Three of us go up into the Icefall — Peter Habeler, Robert Schauer and I. We want to get as high as we possibly can and reconnoitre the route through to Camp I.

My first impression of this labyrinth of ice pinnacles and crevasses is completely overwhelming. I have never in my life been in a more dangerous place. It doesn't do to think too much about it as the dangers at every step of the way, are unimaginably great. The scenery is unique, a jumble of broken shapes; the Icefall is a cascade of ice, continually collapsing in on itself, resulting in a bizarre, chaotic, almost unreal landscape. There are some questions one shouldn't ask, like: What if that serac on the left were to break? What if the great ice wall in the upper reaches of the Fall begins to tilt? Many, many expeditions have passed through the Icefall since 1951 and a certain measure of acceptance has grown up around it There is no other way to approach Everest, and so despite repeated accidents and casualties, the loss of men's lives, it is an accepted fact that some critical questions are simply not posed.

At around midday in a light snowstorm and strong, squally winds, we reach a seemingly endless, unbridgeable crevasse. It appears to split the Icefall from side to side. Despite the onset of bad weather and the first intimations of tiredness, I would love to see around the next corner. This pressing desire for new experience to justify one's own existence! There is life pulsing in the breast, strength swelling in the legs, but a numb emptiness behind the skull, like a hollow behind the eyes, the result of the hours spent searching amongst the strewn ice blocks.

April 1, Base Camp. For five days we have tried fruitlessly to climb beyond the Icefall. Always we are met with this final problem, the huge, transverse fissure where the glacier tumbles out of the lip of the Western Cwm. Can this last bastion be overcome? At 1500 hours in the afternoon, there is a radio link-up between the recce-party and the Base Camp.

'What does it look like?' we want to know from Helmut (Helli) Wagner.

Wolfgang Nairz is on the line: 'I've been up there with Franz, and now we think we know what to do. There's still a couple of enormous crevasses up there, but you can get around to the left and right of them.'

'Great. Can we climb right through tomorrow, then?'

'We'll need to do a bit more work on the lower section, I think,' is the answer. 'There's one spot where I think we should perhaps take a different line as it's so dangerous.'

Then we receive the following information:

'When you get up beyond the last wall, the last great bend, go left, the conditions are not too bad. Franz says the best thing is probably to follow a zig-zag course.'

'Thank God we're through,' says Peter taking over the Base Camp radio.

'Yes, Peter. Robert is here with me and says that it's super over to the left. About 40 or 50 metres from here. I expect we shall be in Camp I tomorrow. We have seen the place, about 30 or 40 metres above us now. From here on it shouldn't be so dangerous.'

'Terrific! Helli — how high are you . . . about? 6,100 or 6,050 metres?'

'I don't know, Manni says about 6,100 — but I don't know if he's guessing or whether he had an altimeter with him.'

'Good, Helli — if we don't speak to you again today, you should now start coming down. Leave the radio up there, please. Probably best to leave it where it was hanging before.'

'We'll do that, Peter. In any case we want to come down over the ice wall, not out round it.'

'Right, Helli. Good luck, watch out as you come down — we don't want anything to happen to you — we'll keep our fingers crossed for you. Till supper time then, Cheers!'

CAMP WORK - CAMP LIFE

A few days later Peter Habeler and I set up the first high camp at 6,100 metres. It's a windy spot. Here in the shadows of the Western Cwm, the Valley of Silence, the blown snow looks blue. I feel recovered now, I have rediscovered my rhythm and am ready to climb the four kilometres up to the second camp at 6,400 metres. Everything around me I regard with a feeling of equanimity — even the stones and avalanches thundering down the sheer sky-high walls to left and right of the Cwm. They, too, belong here.

'Camp II to Base Camp. Come in please.' I call the expedition leader in the afternoon.

'That's marvellous news — to hear you're at Camp II,' he answers.

'It's a bleak Camp II, I'm afraid, but we have plenty of space. We've got our tent up already. It's pretty icy and there's no end of junk lying around from the Korean expedition.'

Wolfgang asks what we plan to do now. I reply, 'We're staying put for the moment. We've overdone it a bit. It was quite a long way and very hard work. We had to make a number of detours and look around a bit before we got here. We had a look at the Lhotse Flank as well, it is fairly blank — doesn't look too easy. As far as we're concerned, we have no option but to settle for the Ordinary Route as well. The South Pillar is green ice. There might still be some ropes on the Lhotse Face.'

'That's good to hear. We'll have to check that out in the next few days.

Column of Sherpas climbing the dangerous Khumbu Icefall.

I expect you've settled in by now, making yourselves comfortable. Are the Sherpas coming down or staying up?'

'They're going back to Camp I. We've only got one tent up with us and just enough food for two or three days. It would be good if a party could come up tomorrow and mark the route. We can start from here and meet them in the middle. Then all of us — Franz, Robert, Peter and I — could come on down to Base Camp together.'

Robert now reports from Camp I, 'I've heard all that. That's all good news. We'll put off till the afternoon fixing the bamboo poles and all the other work we still have to finish in the Icefall.'

'We can do all the rest of the route-work when we go down tomorrow. Can I make a suggestion? First thing tomorrow, we'll get a three-section ladder in position over that gaping crevasse above Camp I, then we'll come on, marking the route, till we meet you.'

I throw in a proposal: 'How would it be if two men came up from Base Camp tomorrow — of course I don't know if anybody is free — and press on up to Camp II, and stay there. If they did that, Peter and I would meet them as we came down. They could then mark the way from below. It's only the first third, or the first half, we're talking about — the second half is easy — it goes straight up hill — there's only a couple of places need marking and we can take care of that.'

'Base Camp here. Robert and Franz can come up right away towards Camp II, marking the route, and we can do the necessary work in the Icefall from down here.'

'As Peter and I will be leaving Camp II, we want to know if anyone else will be coming to occupy it.'

'That's naturally a possibility which we'll have to discuss,' came the answer from Base Camp. 'I can already hear enthusiastic voices round me, so it certainly seems possible.'

'They would need to be fairly strong, of course. It's not everyone could go from Base Camp to here in a single day while they are still acclimatizing.'

In any case, someone says, there's always the possibility that Robert and Franz might want to stay up in Camp II if they feel like it.

'Robert here. This is what we'll do. We'll go up to Camp II, mark the whole route, and this evening we'll give you a detailed account of the stretches in the Icefall that still need working on.'

Base Camp agrees: 'We'll have eighteen Sherpas bring up the stuff for Camp I tomorrow.'

I raise a point: 'Of course, there's still the question of how Robert and Franz will get their personal equipment up here, and their camp gear. They can't hump everything themselves and there aren't any Sherpas at Camp I. We can leave some things of course, but not everything. If we don't want to do things by half-measures, it would be better to wait an

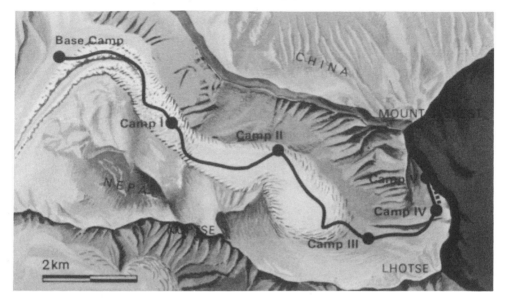

Our chain of camps: Base Camp (5340m.), Camp I (6100m.), Camp II (6400m.), Camp III (7200m.), Camp IV (7986m.), Camp V (8500m.).

extra day and send a new pair, with Sherpas, up from the main camp. Straight past Camp I to Camp II. If we don't have all the stuff we need up at Camp II, we'll be in difficulties and not be able to get any further.'

'Base Camp here. You're saying that really tomorrow only the route should be marked, and the following day a team move up from Camp I with Sherpas.'

'My feeling is it would be much better if a party were to come up to Camp I tomorrow, sleep there, then the next day continue up to Camp II. It means the tent will be empty for a night, it's true, but in one night it shouldn't blow down.'

'Understood. We'll go off and discuss it again, and this evening we'll give you an exact plan of campaign — who goes where when.'

So it is arranged, the next day Robert and Franz will instal the ladder over the big crevasse, and we shall meet them both somewhere and then all go down together.

'Reinhold, have you measured the height of Camp II?' Wolfgang Nairz enquires.

'When we arrived it was exactly 6,400 metres by our altitude meter, at the moment it reads 6,410 metres. Peter's altimeter reads much the same — 6,420 metres. That means we could be as high as 6,500 metres. I should say the first camp really is at 6,100 metres. Here, we are, I should think, some 100 metres below the Lhotse Face, a little to the left of the start of the South-west Face climb. It's the safest place in the whole area.'

'What I'm not happy about, is the weather. I hope it doesn't change suddenly tonight. If tomorrow there are snowdrifts and it's misty, we shan't come down as this section is not well-marked.'

'It's a bit cloudy, certainly,' Base Camp agrees, 'but it doesn't look as if we're in for a sudden drop in temperature. The barometric reading on our Swiss altimeter is still good.'

'Ours also indicates good weather, and we'll leave it at that. We'll sleep here — if necessary we've got food for three days. Peter says — six days if we stretch it out; so we'll have to get down within six days.'

'Okay, don't worry,' the leader promises, 'I guarantee we'll get you out before six days are up. Now, if Camp I has nothing more, we'll close down for now.'

But Robert comes on again and wants to know whether he should take a rope for the first part of the way from Camp I to II.

'Really I think that the bit between I and II ought always to be climbed roped; there are hidden crevasses and it's not without some danger anywhere. Easier, certainly, than the Icefall, but tricky in places. Take one rope with you, 15 or 20 metres. You won't need ladders of course. We found we had to keep fairly well over to the right on the way up because of the crevasses, but there's less danger from falling ice that side too. There are the remains of massive ice avalanches under the shoulder. So turn right there, then higher up move back to the left as the righthand side gets dangerous. I don't believe any more ladders will be needed till we get to the foot of the Lhotse Face. It looks as if you can avoid the first drop by going round to the right. As far as I can remember from when I flew over the area last year, apart from ropes, we shan't need nearly so much equipment higher up.'

Robert has another question for us, 'Is it worth taking skis and skins?'

'Skins — definitely not. It's all ice, sometimes quite hard ice. Peter says

The 1,400 metre high Lhotse Face.

skis might be useful on the way out, in which case keep over to the left. But on the way in, they're only something extra to carry.'

'Okay — we'll leave the skis behind. Just one more thing — Ang Phu is standing next to me. You said there was a Sherpa who wanted to speak to him.'

'Yes — well that's all clear so far. Next radio call 5 o'clock. I'll hand over now.'

The two Sherpas talk with each other for half an hour.

April 2. We have erected Camp II at almost 6,500 metres and set about preparing everything for the night. It is a fearful night, not a wink of sleep. The wind shakes and batters the tent all night long, blowing off the South-west Face and the South Col. We fear at any moment we shall be lying on the bare mountain. The tent will surely be torn to shreds and fly away. Before dawn we make up our minds to climb down to the valley, for the weather looks like worsening and we know that we certainly cannot go down the unmarked Western Cwm in a blizzard.

The next day too is bad, in Base Camp as well. Rest day. The snow-flakes trace messages on the sloping roof of my tent, jumbling themselves with the lines that have come with the post up from the valley. It is a cheerless day, no passing clouds; the mountain stands featureless in a shroud of milky grey mist, but the glacier on which we're camped is still unpleasantly bright.

April 6 — Base Camp, in the Kitchen. Today is the second time I demonstrate a European dish to the Sherpas. It gets very boring eating the same thing ever day — egg and chips every morning and evening, with occasional chinese noodles. I cook a *pasta asciuta*, or as near to it as one can get here at 5,340 metres in a primitive kitchen at the foot of Everest. The Sherpa-cook and I put some yak butter in a flat iron pan, which is being heated over a little fire burning between two huge blocks of wood. Once it has melted, I add some finely chopped onion and garlic; then as it begins to brown, I toss in some bits of bacon fat and later, some chopped sausage. Then some red chillis for flavour and some salt and pepper. I slowly fry this mixture over the low heat. At this height one has to take account of the reduced atmospheric pressure and the attendant lower boiling point. It is not easy to get the onions brown without the bacon overcooking completely. The yak butter smells rancid, but after a while, cooking on the little flame under a low canopy, I don't notice it any more. One gets used to everything. Meanwhile I have put two tins of tomato purée on a big stone beside me so that they can thaw out in the warmth of the fire. With the nights here at minus 20 degrees, everything freezes up. After half an hour, I empty the contents of the tins into the brown mish-mash of bacon, onions, sausage and garlic.

I sit on a crate, my face glowing in the heat of the fire. The kitchen boy puts on more logs. Meanwhile one of the Sahibs comes and takes some hot water for washing, another wants tea.

Suddenly, there's a loud shout outside the stone kitchen. The Liaison Officer who had had to stay down in the valley at the beginning of the expedition because he was suffering from altitude sickness, has come back. He is greeted by the Sherpas in Base Camp with a loud 'Hello!'

It's a fine day outside. Now and then the wind gusts under the cooking canopy, blowing hot ash into my face. I turn round and reach for a piece of toilet paper from a niche in the wall, to wipe my eyes.

My sauce has been cooking over the little fire for a good quarter of an hour, but it still needs another quarter of an hour before it's fit to put on the table in the mess tent.

Meanwhile, one of the Sherpas has brought in a basket of ice; he piles large chunks into a big cooking pot to melt for water. We fetch our ice from the glacier about 200 metres below Base Camp. The Icefall is more docile there, gently undulating like the waves of a lake, and flowing down towards Lobuche — this is our 'spring'.

There is always a lively, colourful atmosphere in the 'kitchen'. It measures some 5 x 4 metres and the walls are made of layers of stones, some as big as a cubic metre. Sausages hang smoking over the fire on a wooden pole, and all the possible bits and pieces the cook and his assistant might need are stored in boxes.

I ask the Sherpas for a mug of hot tea, and at the same time keep an eye on my sauce, which is beginning to thicken, to make sure it doesn't burn. The onions are too dark, I notice. This is probably because they were frozen solid when they went into the hot fat, I think. Ang Phu, the Chief Sherpa, sits now beside me and eats potatoes.

To get the noodles *al dente* at 5,340 metres is a real art. A minute too long and they turn into a soup.

COLLAPSE OF THE ICE WALL

The next morning I am in the kitchen again. There exists an underground atmosphere here beyond the order and tidiness, where men can laugh and where there are no Icefall worries, no talk of summit-at-any-price. I feel at home here. Not just because I like the Sherpas, but also because of the smoke, the smell of humanity, and above all, the fire.

I am making another Italian dish, a *pizza*. Whilst the cook is baking chapatis on a big aluminium plate — specially thin ones, and only a little brown on the underside — I rummage in the kitchen boxes for the things I need — fish in tomato sauce, anchovies, sardines, chillis again, and of course, bacon. There's nothing special happening in Base Camp and no measure of certainty about the blue sky. I'm not waiting for any kind of sign, but I do feel today that I would like something to hang on to, something to take for granted.

Towards 10 o'clock, this *April 7*, I suddenly hear raised voices outside. 'There's a cloud of powder snow gone up at the top of the Icefall.'

This is a sign that an avalanche has come down. Everyone tumbles out of their tents, grabbing binoculars. Anxiously we take turns peering into the Fall. Yes, right, there — near the middle, it all looks quite different. An ice avalanche, about 50 metres wide, come down right over the route. One of the monstrous walls which cross the top section of the Icefall has simply collapsed.

We cannot tell at the moment whether any Sherpas were in the vicinity when the avalanche came down, and now, with our binoculars pressed to our eyes, we anxiously start counting heads. There are seven visible towards the top of the Icefall, all standing there stiffly, shocked. Now we count how many have in the meantime reached the bottom of the Icefall

— six. We breathe again — we are now sure that no-one has been lost. Thirteen Sherpas left for Camp I early this morning.

Tension in Base Camp is running high; the avalanche is discussed excitedly and everyone waits for the Sherpas who were up in the danger zone, to come back and tell us what has happened to the route and whether or not it will be possible to go back into the Icefall.

At last, towards midday, the Sherpas arrive, still a bit pale. They approach the camp like refugees, their crampons in their hands. Nairz goes to meet them and addresses them in simple expedition-English. He wants to know what happened, but his questions come hesitantly, carefully.

'Avalanche? Bad?' he asks.

'Not bad — all OK.'

The Sherpas seem not to be too badly affected. 'I really think it shook us up more than them,' whispers one of the Sahibs.

'What was it like in the avalanche?' Nairz asks the next Sherpa.

'Not bad.'

We cannot understand this composure.

'It either goes one way or it goes the other, it all depends on the will of Buddha, that must be it,' we endeavour to come to terms with their attitude. The Sirdar comes up.

'Hallo, Ang Phu. We are pleased to see you. We were very relieved to see all seven of you coming down.'

'We were lucky,' answers Ang Phu.

'And the ice — did it fall across the route?'

'Only on one side — it's easier now actually.'

We marvel at his calm acceptance.

'Well — it's all right now then,' says Nairz, 'but you were very lucky you hadn't gone up five minutes earlier.'

'Seven is a lucky number for Buddhists,' explains Ang Phu, smiling.

'Okay,' the leader says, then, 'make a big fire today. We'll buy an extra yak-load of wood!'

The Sherpas are delighted. The route, they say, is now better. They are a very remarkable people. Avalanches could do nothing to them.

Wolfgang explains again how it had looked: 'We were watching through binoculars and counting — one, two, three, four, five, six, seven

— then added the six of you who were lower down. Then we knew that nothing had happened.' And to us, he says (speaking German again): 'We have a lot to learn before we can achieve the same attitude to life that the Sherpas have . . . so let us stick to our plan — don't go into the Icefall unless absolutely necessary.'

He asks Ang Phu if there was danger of any more ice collapsing. 'There is one place that's worse than the rest,' answers the Sirdar, 'but I will find a way round it. That's no problem.'

'They are so passive about things,' one of us remarks laconically. Horst Bergmann speaks up: 'Can I switch the subject? Tools. In future, if anyone needs tools, they should fetch them from Robert. They will be checked out and must be brought back when you've finished. Please don't leave them lying about to go rusty — the yeti will get them, he doesn't buy anything new. Incidentally, does everyone know where the red box of tools is kept?'

'Where is it now?'

'In the tool tent up there. Anyone who takes anything out, bring it back immediately after using it.'

But again the conversation veers back to the Icefall, and everyone has an opinion.

'It's easy for the Sherpas. They simply believe everything is ordained from above,' someone says. 'If one of them dies, then it must be meant to happen.'

And another asks: 'Will the Sherpas go back tomorrow?'

'What do you think, Reinhold?'

'We'll have to see how they are in the morning. If they've got over the shock.'

'I don't believe they will.'

'We can't change the route very much up there. To the left, is no good, nor the right either.'

'Unless it's absolutely necessary,' says Wolfgang, 'I'm not sending any-one up there. It's too dangerous.'

One of us ventures: 'Now we've had one hefty avalanche, it will surely be some time before the next.'

'But my point is, that the risk is less if you go less often.' And the

We used wooden bridges to cross some of the crevasses in the Icefall.

discussion continues: 'The risk to the Sherpas is always still great.'

'Our risk is equally great.'

'But just think — if they had been five minutes earlier, then we should all be packing up now, for none of the others would have gone up the Icefall after that.'

Practically every one of our eleven expedition members and the journalists and photo-graphers who accompanied us, fell into a crevasse at least once. But in spite of this, Peter Habeler and I preferred to go up and down the Icefall unroped. Had an ice tower suddenly crashed down whilst we were climbing close by, we could have more quickly leapt to safety without the restriction of a rope. Speed was, in our opinion, the most decisive factor for survival in this unpredictably dangerous territory. We were always extremely anxious as we passed close to these massive serac walls (next double page), fearing how at any moment they could come tumbling down. This was why we moved so fast. Our fastest climbing time from Base Camp (5340 metres) to Camp I (6100 metres) was just under two hours: that for descending the same stretch, 45 minutes.

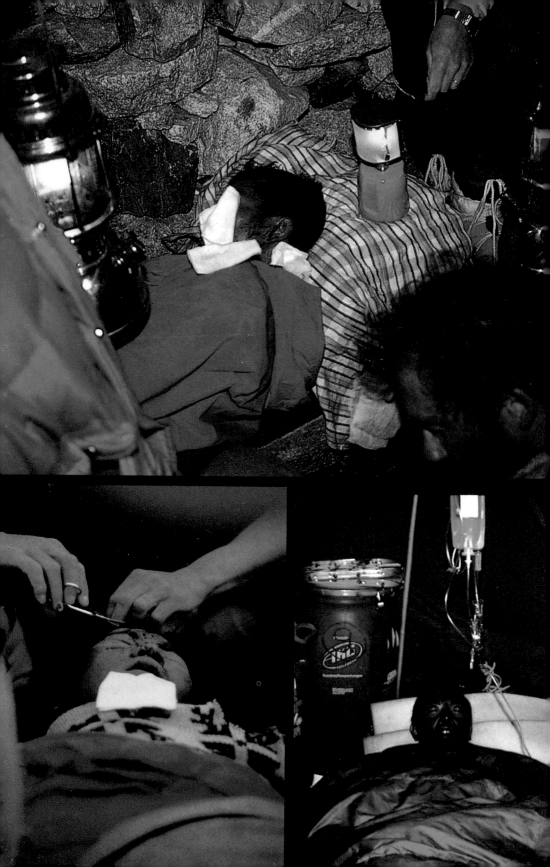

Without the help of the Sherpas, we should certainly never have reached the summit. These tough high-level porters put up with all sorts of hardships and danger to support us. In two months they earn their entire annual income. One of our Sherpas suffered a stroke in Camp II (6,400 metres), three were injured in the Icefall. To rescue these badly injured men from the crevasse was incredibly difficult. One had fallen 50 metres. In Base Camp, which at times began to look like a field hospital, our two expedition doctors, Dr Raimund Margreiter and Dr Oswald Ölz, had their hands full. They treated cuts, frostbite and performed operations, amongst others one for a skull fracture. One Sherpa was lost. The others recovered except for the stroke-victim (bottom right) who remained half-paralysed. Even the man who suffered the skull fracture in his 50 metre fall, recovered in the Hillary Hospital after Dr Margreiter had patched him up (bottom left).

'That I can't say, but I would have tried it without Sherpas,' I answer.
'If seven Sherpas died, none of the others would go with us ever again.'
'That's true. I'm convinced of it.'
'You would have to change things right from Kathmandu on — you would need a helicopter for the Icefall.'
'What we mustn't do at all costs, is to let groups of seven up at once; we should go up in pairs, three at the most, and the Sherpas in threes.'
'We could go singly — or in twos.'
'Only those who are working there or higher up should go through the Icefall at all.'
'I think it's a bit different for us, because we can perhaps evaluate the danger better.'
'I don't think that makes any difference, except you can trot a bit faster through the most dangerous places.'
'The Sherpas move quite quickly all the time.'
'If something starts cracking just above you, I don't think you've got a chance if you're in the way.'
'We were enormously lucky today — it might have been much worse,' I remark.
'The fact is we were too optimistic, thinking the Icefall was quiet.'
'When I think about when Josl and I were up there, how we took our time filming everything, it sends shivers down my spine,' says Horst Bergmann.
'I'd like to know what the Sherpas are saying now, amongst themselves. Chiefly, whether they're prepared to go on or whether they want to-morrow as a rest day.'
'That wouldn't matter. Luckily for the moment we do have enough gear up there.'
'What's most important is that they don't go up in convoys any more. It's a macabre thing to say, but if only one or two get the chop, it's quite a different thing from seven at once.'
'One dead would be too many.'
'There's no way of working it out, you can't predict when another chunk is going to fall off. It could be at any time of the day or night.'
'I am sure it's to do with its being noticeably warmer now; there must

The work of recovering injured Sherpas who had fallen into crevasses and transporting them down the Icefall, was a dangerous and strenuous business.

be a lot more movement in the Icefall; you can see how the whole wall has tilted.'

'And at nights now too, you can feel there are more tensions in the glacier that weren't there at the beginning.'

'It was minus 21 today. Before that it was always 25 or 26 degrees below.'

'7th April, — with seven being a lucky number for Buddhists, nothing could happen today.'

'Seven and six makes thirteen — where does that leave you?' retorts Wolfgang Nairz.

'For my money — the Sherpas are supermen.'

'I'm very struck by the difference between now and when we were on Makalu in 1974. It was much steeper terrain on Makalu and this frightened the Sherpas much more. They don't seem so bothered by these objective dangers, which are indeed greater, as they were with the steepness.'

'They can tell just as well as we can when their lives are in danger — it's just that they're much calmer about it.'

'I don't think they do foresee danger in the same way as us. They simply put themselves in the hands of their Gods. Today has given them more proof that strewing sacrificial rice works — they'll strew even more in future.'

Wolfgang turns to the Sherpa-leader: 'How often have you been through the Icefall, Ang Phu?'

'Altogether? Hundred times — two hundred maybe. This is my fourth expedition to Everest. 1971 I was here with the International Expedition; 1972 with Bonington; 1975 with him again and this is therefore my fourth time.'

'And were there avalanches like this the other times?'

'Oh yes, sometimes. Three times. And closer.'

'You must have a charmed life!'

'Yes, you could say that,' says Ang Phu, laughing.

'Are you a keen mountaineer?' I ask him.

'Yes.'

In the evening Wolfgang Nairz outlines the plan of action for the next day. An air of earnestness settles on the proceedings.

'The day after tomorrow,' he says, 'Peter and Reinhold move up to Camp II; Bulle, Horst and I, we'll go to Camp I. Reinhold and Peter will spend two days trying to push the route up onto the Lhotse Face and, if possible, set up Camp III. Horst, Bulle and I will supervize the transport of supplies from I to II, concentrating on building up Camp II. Reinhold and Peter will stay up working for two days, therefore on the third day, the next team — Frank and Robert — must be ready to take over from them. Whether they go straight up from Base Camp to Camp II or spend a night in Camp I, is up to them.'

Robert asks, 'Can't we leave at the same time as Reinhold and Peter and stay in Camp I?'

'No, that won't do — the earliest you can start up will be the day after them.'

'That means that we'll have to put up another tent then.'

Late afternoon on *April 8* the post-runner arrives. The expedition leader calls everyone together and hands out the mail, letter by letter. We are called in turn and the post for those people in the higher camps was put on one side for them. There are a few letters for me as well. It seems that everyone who might have written, has done so. At first I am delighted, but I quickly lose interest. Such a mass of paper scrawled with meaningless things. The comments and news are repeated from one letter to the next, and they all want answering. I prefer to lie back comfortably in my tent, alone, watching the shadow patterns of the clouds on the thin canvas.

I had plenty of time to prepare for the coming days. Peter and I want to get away by 5 a.m. if we're to get up to Camp II from Base Camp in a single push. We'll need several hours but we ought to be able to make it in one day. Then during the next days we should fix ropes and build Camp III on the Lhotse Face, which rises from the Western Cwm for 1,000 metres up to the South Col. This will be our last spell at high-level before we make our attempt on the summit. Already Peter and I are playing with the idea of keeping going, making an attempt right away if the conditions and weather are favourable, to find the solution to that question that has drawn us here — is Everest possible without oxygen masks?

I have spent a few peaceful days here in Base Camp, enjoying the inactivity and the conversation of my friends. I have even forgotten to take any photographs, it has been so relaxing.

QUITE ALONE

The only person on whose account I could give up climbing is my mother. Previously my wife too, I admit, influenced me in critical situations, but she did not try to dissuade me from going on expeditions. And my mother, also, knows that these adventures are an expression of myself, that I have to undertake them. She is one of the very few people who really understands me. Of course she often worries, but has sufficient confidence in me not to transmit her fears to me. Just knowing she is there, I feel stronger when I am alone, and because I know she cares, death itself does not frighten me.

What I earlier felt as fear, I now perceive as love. As physical as a kind of paralysis or sigh of relief, depending on whether I am approaching a certain point of the danger, or already passed it.

Climbing alone up to Camp III — in unbearable heat with heavy trail-breaking work — I experience a strong sense of reinforced identity, as I nearly always do when I have to commit myself fully.

April 13. I call Peter over the radio from Camp III. He had had to give up a short way above Camp II and turned back towards Base Camp. 'As there's obviously no-one coming up,' I say, 'I suppose I shall have to come down as well.'

'You might be able to stay on you know,' says Peter in reply, 'at any event, I can see some specks approaching your camp, the Sherpas. But whether they are bringing up any more than your personal gear, of course I can't tell from here.'

Earlier, when Peter and I had separated, three of the Sherpas had refused to come any further. The others agreed to stay, but I had to reduce their loads before they would come on. For a while I had climbed with them, then I went on ahead. I wanted to see what lay ahead of us.

I tell Peter that in an hour's time I will know what I'm going to do. If tents, food and stoves arrive, I will stay on in Camp III. Otherwise I shall have to come down.

Robert Schauer and I did almost all the route preparation on the 1,400 m. high Lhotse Face. Each without a partner; hard work at that altitude, between 6,600 and 8,000 metres.

'I can't see them any more,' says Peter, 'there's a bank of cloud in the way. But I have the impression that the porters are continuing in the direction of III. I should think they'll be with you in about an hour.'

'Oh yes, there are two people immediately below me, one is Mingma — he's a very good man — the other is Ang Dorje. I carried up 200 metres of rope, I felt like a Sherpa myself. If I can lay some fixed ropes tomorrow, I shall be happy. Someone else can then carry on to the South Col — it's very hard work to do it on one's own.'

Peter replies that Robert would like to come up but I am of the opinion that he has already done more than his fair share of work, 'I think he should have a rest first.'

'But he wants to come up.'

'I know that, Robert is always willing, and nothing would please me more than to have him in the lead again. He really is one of the best climbers I know.'

I repeat that I want to hang on up here if it's at all possible.

'The weather doesn't seem too good, certainly. If the forecast is good, Bulle and Robert or Franz — whoever's going better at the time — will follow you up and do some work on the route. Afterwards perhaps Helli and his team will take over. He is the ideal man up here.'

If the weather doesn't change, I say, there's no need for anyone to come up, of course. 'It looks very gloomy, but warm, much warmer than before up here. And it's snowing a little.'

April 13, 14.00 hours. I am sitting alone at a height of 7,200 metres, on the spot where the third high camp will be placed. For hours I have been waiting for the Sherpas who are on their way up with the gear for the camp. I must spend the next night here.

I can just make out a black speck far below on the snowslope at the end of the Western Cwm, stretching down, seemingly for ever, in the direction of Camp I. I am not feeling too lonely up here on my own although the mist is closing in. It is snowing lightly but I can still see the summit of Everest, as if behind a veil.

I always feel an air of excitement when I sit beneath the summit of a mountain that I have never climbed before, and one that I am unsure whether I can climb or not. The veil of snow and the wisps of cloud blurring the summit, combine to give this mountain even more of a sense of mystery. The thrill for me is not to 'bag' another 'eight-thousander', but to lift this veil.

The Sherpas come closer. The sun through the cloud strikes the snow slopes as if through a burning glass. It stands high over the finely-chiselled ridge between Nuptse and Lhotse, and occasionally breaks clear of the clouds. In the play of light and shadow, the steep concavity above the Western Cwm appears a vertical wilderness of ice and snow. I am anxious to emulate the stoicism, the powers of acceptance, of the Sherpas, and at this moment believe I really can understand the inter-relationship of it all, and not just that between me and the summit.

A day's march separates me from the next camp.

Some steep passages were climbed with the aid of mechanical 'jumar' clamps.

'Hallo!' I greet the first Sherpa. But he says nothing, merely lifts a tired hand and whistles through his teeth. He stops a while where the fixed rope hangs from its anchorage, staring blankly, fatigue lining his face.

The camp site is as airily exposed as an eagle's nest. As I wait, I watch the fine shreds of cloud chase across the South-west Face and my eyes are caught by a speck of colour amongst the rock and ice — the old tent boxes left standing from Bonington's 1975 expedition. Mingma is still ten metres from the camp site, ten metres that he laboriously puts behind him, slowly forcing his way upwards on the jumar clamps. His feet slip, he stops, coughs and again whistles through his teeth. He gazes across at me and lets out an enormous sigh of relief.

He unclips from the fixed ropes and crosses towards me. He can't take another step, he staggers. His eyes range for a flat spot then he flings him-self down, exhausted, with his head on his unshouldered load, folds his hands across his belly, and is still.

He's out, flat out. Finished. Later he scratches his nose, sits up, throws off his climbing harness and massages his left knee. His dry altitude cough is a typical sympton. He is worn out.

'This place alright?' I ask him.

'Yeah.'

Yesterday he came up from Base to Camp II, and today on to here. It's too much, he says, no-one could do it. His name is Mingma Noru, but we call him simply Mingma.

He shrugs his shoulders when I ask him if it's possible to climb down again today.

'Not possible,' he says.

'Do you want to stay here?'

He doesn't know. Doesn't say anything.

'How are you feeling now?'

'Headache.'

'But you're glad to be here?'

'Only for the money.'

'Do you get a bonus for this?'

'Yes.'

For the climb up to Camp III the Sherpas are paid more than the normal daily hire fee of 35 rupees (£1.50 approximately). To Mingma, that's a fortune. He looses his load from his pack frame, tying the bindings back onto the aluminium frame.

'Mingma, you are supposed to take an empty oxygen cylinder down with you,' I say to him. 'Is it possible?'

'Not possible. Tomorrow.'

'Okay.'

'It's a hard life — in the mountains. You think?' he asks in our simple English. 'Will snow, perhaps?'

'Much, do you think, or not much?'

'Don't know.'

I ask him if there's any risk of avalanches up here.

'No.'

Mingma rummages in his sack. He pulls out a stick of salami, peels it and begins to eat. It's the lunch for two Sherpas, but one has gone back so he gets nothing. Meanwhile I hear Ang Dorje approaching. The snow crunches, he's here. His mouth is smeared with sun cream. It begins to snow harder. He, too, props himself up on his elbows to recover. Mingma continues eating his salami; he doesn't bother to cut it, but bites off chunks. For a few minutes the sun pierces the cloud, like a violet-white ball.

'Are you tired Ang Dorje?'

'Only a bit.'

We put up a little Dunlop Tent, 1·5 metres wide, 1·8 metres long and about 80 centimetres high, inside which the three of us crouch, and cook tea. First we must clear the stove of its crust of ice, but then it burns quite well. Mingma brings in a bag of ice from outside, so that we can keep the billy topped up. We haven't drunk anything since breakfast, are physically drained and the night ahead of us here at 7,200 metres will be a hard one. Harder certainly than any bivouac in the Alps. Added to this, we do not know what the weather will do.

Mingma fiddles with all sorts of pots and containers — first he gets tea bags out of a wooden box, then the sugar, which has got snow mixed in it. We have hung up our wet socks inside the tent. We must dry them out today if they are not to be frozen solid by tomorrow. That would be more than just uncomfortable, it would be dangerous. Frostbite at this altitude would be the unavoidable consequence because of our reduced circulation. I can hardly believe my eyes as Ang Dorje pulls out a tin of bacon and noodles. Such a supper meets with our approval.

I don't seem to be able to speak properly in this position. My brain, apparently at least, is still functioning normally, but I am so doubled up I can't move my diaphragm or my shoulders sufficiently to breathe properly. Getting the tent up has put me in a bad humour, as I couldn't get the poles to fit together. I had to keep thumping them with my frozen fingers till they finally fitted. If I could know for certain that the weather was going to be bad tomorrow, I would retreat to Camp II and Advance Base today. But if the sun does come out tomorrow. I would have a slim chance of going further, I could make a push in the direction of the South Col, to open for the expedition 'the gateway to the summit'.

Mingma smashes the ice with his spoon and puts the pieces into the pot.

He has placed the little cooker inside another pan so that he can catch every drip of the melting ice and not waste any of the precious liquid. Water is so important up here, almost holy. Looking through the tent opening, I see the fine flakes are now falling faster. Not a good sign. Whilst Ang Dorje stirs the soup, I keep my hand on the pot so that he doesn't upset it. Our noses and lips are split and sore, they hurt. Everyone is very thankful that after the many thousand deep and painful gulps of air that were required to bring us from Base Camp to here, at last we have found a dry spot.

I call Camp II on the radio and let them know the two Sherpas have arrived, 'They were very, very tired, but otherwise everything is more or less okay. The barometer isn't good, but perhaps things will look up.'

Things are much the same further down, we hear, it's snowing. Also we learn that the loads are all standing ready packed in Base Camp to come up tomorrow. We are told in detail what there is: 'Axes, six gas cylinders, two petrol stoves, 20 litres of petrol, salt and powdered egg. We haven't got any noodles and rice in camp, we'll have to send down to the valley for some. Franz's boots are packed too, as well as cooking pots and a medicine chest. We only hope that Reinhold and his tent are not blown away in the night.'

Camp II joins in the banter. 'No, he won't blow away, but he might suffocate, if he's sharing the tent with two Sherpas. They probably haven't washed for a while.'

'We can only hope that Reinhold leaves a little hole, at least, for fresh air!'

I gather from the radio contact between the two camps that next day I should begin fixing ropes in the direction of the South Col. 'He won't get far alone, it's true, not beyond the Yellow Band at any rate. It's a long push to Camp IV, from 7,200 metres to about 8,000, that's around 800 metres to the South Col, and it is 800 metres of mixed terrain, rock and ice. It's very steep in places. In any case, Reinhold should make as much progress as possible, and then the next team must carry on.'

'Yes, that's all okay,' I announce, 'I only ask that the next team can come up right away so that there is no interruption.'

'Some time tomorrow we will let you know who is taking over.'

On the Lhotse Face. Here and there we found remnants of fixed ropes from earlier expeditions.

Another weather report is not expected just yet, but various barometers at Base Camp promise improvement; the next official forecast won't be received until about 7.15 tomorrow, after the news. It's important that I know as early as possible whether the snow is expected to stop and whether I can soon get on.

Before we finish our chat, I have another question: 'You mustn't keep it from me if any young ladies appear at Base Camp asking for me.'

'We'll watch out for you.'

'Meanwhile, has the visitor I was expecting arrived?'

'No, nothing yet.'

'Okay, I'll switch on again at 6 — till then I hope the whiff in here won't lay me out! Over and out.'

'Okay, till 6 o'clock then. Out.'

It is warm inside the tent. The two Sherpas are sitting close together, cooking — the tent entrance half-open. They take it in turns. Up here at 7,200 metres, it takes a long time for the ice to melt, and then for the water to finally be warm enough to make tea with. I feel fine at this height. We are squashed in so closely that it is impossible to move, and if we want to lie down, we must layer ourselves like sardines in a tin, two heads one way, one the other. If any one of us has to move, we all move.

THE YELLOW BAND

I sleep well. Long before sunrise one of the Sherpas starts cooking. Then he lies down again and lets the other one keep an eye on the little pot. In the morning we radio Base Camp and despite the doubtful weather, leave the tent. Slowly we start climbing the Lhotse Face, and fixing new safety ropes. Here and there the remains of old ropes protrude from the snow. I follow them and after three hours of strenuous rope-fixing, we traverse left up to the Yellow Band, the most difficult part of the Lhotse Face.

It is now midday and I continue to climb ahead with the two Sherpas carrying the rope. Arriving at the foot of the Yellow Band, I again see bits and pieces of rope left by earlier expeditions and am relieved to know I am still on the right lines. The first part of the Yellow Band I climb relatively quickly; it is steep but has plenty of holds. I am bringing up two lengths of rope behind me, which is unpleasantly dangerous. I crawl rather than climb — not belayed by the Sherpas — up the downward-tilted slabs, which in places are glazed with ice. There is a layer of snow, five centimetres thick, covering everything, so that it is impossible to know for sure whether I have a firm hold under my crampons or whether they will skid off the smooth rock. I know I could slide off at any moment. The only possible belay point on the wide slope, a rock tooth sticking out of the snow, breaks away as I come to test it.

So for half an hour, I pull the 100 metres of rope up behind me, crawling over the slabs, and as I go, I clear some of the snow away from the rocks and ice with my hands, in order to have at least now and then, a little hold for my fingers or a small step to stand in. At around 14.00 hours, at the end of the Yellow Band, our rope runs out. So I let the Sherpas go back down whilst I continue up the shallow basin between the Geneva Spur and the Lhotse Face. I want to reach that spot where the hollow is completely ringed by rocks.

My altimeter registers 7,800 metres, so I must be immediately underneath the South Col and would have liked to press on as far as that. But it is too late and besides, it is snowing so hard that I am not quite clear which is the way to go. I still feel relatively fit, although the strain after every five or ten steps is so great that I have to stop and rest. Since early morning I have had nothing to drink, nor anything to eat, so this tiredness is understandable. All the same I have never felt better at this height. It is the equivalent of being close to the summit of a small eight-thousander. I am convinced now, at this moment, that Everest without supplementary oxygen is possible, if my physical condition, my health holds out.

After every 10 steps at this altitude, I droop my head over my axe, despite the threat that my axe might slide away at any moment. I rest my elbows on the snow only to find my chest doesn't seem to have enough room to breathe, so supporting my hands on the axe, I rest my forehead on my hands. This too proves impossible and my head slips off. No position seems to suit my exhausted frame, as I struggle to draw more breath. I still want to reach the first black rocks at the end of the shallow snow basin to the right of the Geneva Spur. Although as I climb, the rocks get bigger, they still do not seem to get any closer. When I do reach them, I set myself a new objective. But then it is I myself who put a stop to further progress, simply by beginning to climb downwards. At first, I seem not even to notice that I have changed direction.

It is the afternoon when I head back towards Camp III and exactly 16.00

Every time before the Sherpas went into the Icefall they burned sacrificial fires and strewed holy rice. They hoped thereby to appease their Gods and Demons. Despite this we were anxious whenever anyone was in this zone (right, and next double-page). Climbing the Icefall is like Russian Roulette. If one climbs fast, one risks less, but no-one can ever feel entirely safe. The jagged, steeply-banked glacier moves incredibly fast, and in so doing, ice walls and pinnacles tumble, crevasses yawn open, where the day before the surface of the ice seemed set for eternity.

As the route through the Icefall was found and prepared, we feared the climb less. Familiarity dispelled the 'Angst' that accompanied our first reconnaissance thrusts. Only when suddenly an ice-wall, as big as a row of houses, toppled over, did we fully re-appreciate the dangers. Six Sherpas had just passed the spot where this serac fell, covering the whole area with blocks of ice the size of a room. Seven other Sherpas were about to descend when the ground under their feet began to tremble. Like the first six, they had a lucky escape, and then had to find a new route through the debris. It was April 13 and there were thirteen Sherpas. Thirteen is a lucky number in their culture. We had been suspicious of this passage from the beginning, but could find no alternative route. Now with the threatening ice-wall removed, a small portion of the Icefall was thereby made safer.

hours when I arrive and get in touch with Camp II and Base. The others are naturally delighted at the quick progress we have made. Despite the drifting snow, I continue down the face the same day to Camp II. Another night, crammed in the small tent with the Sherpas, didn't appeal to me, nor would it do any good. Down on the glacier Robert Schauer and Franz Oppurg come to meet me because of the crevasse danger. They escort me back to Camp II, from where the next day I return to Base. Peter and I want to rest up and prepare ourselves for a summit assault.

We are now so well advanced with the route preparation that we — Peter and I — can launch the first attack. We do not need to take much with us for the last bivouac. What we do need is a little more than a week of relatively fine weather, and luck. Neither of us dare fall ill, neither must lose his impetus. The commitment to see it through to the end, to endure the exertions, the loneliness, the exhaustion, concerns us both. If one is genuinely determined to go for the summit, it is often as if one's skin becomes thicker — one even seems to feel the cold less. For my part, I will climb till I drop.

April 16, Base Camp. Today early, on waking, I hear a bird's voice singing in the sky. The morning sun is warm with a hint of spring about it. No frost crumbles onto my face as I turn over in my sleeping bag. It is obvious I am not in one of the high camps any more.

At Base Camp much has changed; the snow has melted from around the tents, and the stone terraces that we built in front of our tents are already warm. Wolfgang Nairz and Horst Bergmann have assembled their hang-gliders and the Sherpas are gazing at them wide-eyed, like an eighth wonder of the world. They test everything once more. The Sherpas and the local farmers who bring up the wood from the valleys, seem both amused and astonished at these strange birds. But will the two men succeed in floating down from the South Col, as they hope? Such a flight is not merely a question of wind and the ability to concentrate. To trudge with these gliders to a height of 8,000 metres will be no mean task.*

Peter and I discuss a possible assault plan. Peter, who till now has only worked on the first 200 metres of the Lhotse Face, returning to Base

---

* It was not possible for the proposed hang-glider flight to be completed.

Camp a day ahead of me, is nevertheless convinced — as I am — that everything is sufficiently ready on the mountain, the route provided with fixed ropes, ladders and camps, that, given a fine weather period and after basic recuperation in Base Camp, as a two-man team, supported by a few Sherpas, we could now launch our first attack.

Now, in the afternoon, it snows again. The fine, even sound on the roof of the tent is like a monologue. I lie under the light Gore-tex fabric and gaze at all the bits and pieces I have strung to the middle pole: my altimeter, headband, a marker flag from the Korean expedition last autumn, goggles. Despite the light gusts of wind I have the comfortable, homely feeling of being well-cared for. At the prospect of the attempt which I know will demand the utmost from me, I am tense with anticipation; I know that it can perhaps mean the end for me, but I no longer feel that the whole enterprise wants of good sense, as I found myself thinking a few months before. I am living objectively now, intensely. Yet in the back of my mind clings the desire that this expedition should have no end, that this ambition of mine could stay with me forever in my dreams, wherever I go. Everest-without-oxygen, as the eternal Utopian ideal. I have the presentiment that through success, something will be lost forever — and that not just a mere personal fantasy.

BURIED ALIVE

Night. As I lie completely motionless in my sleeping bag I have the feeling I am out in the open. Safe, yet in vast, unending space. Only when the wind rattles the fabric of the tent do I realize I am lying here in Base Camp in the cold. Sharp as a knife, the wind makes an incision between my feelings and my consciousness.

When I awake I have to touch my warm skin several times to prove to myself who I am, where I am, in order to be able to believe in myself.

When the glacier on which we are camped, snaps under its tensions, it is like wood crackling in a fire. The ice groans and spits.

Today, *April 17*, Robert and two Sherpas have pushed up further on the Lhotse Face. The way is now clear to the South Col. It is snowing very hard down here. There was thunder and lightning half of the night and every hour or so, I had to sit up and shake the snow from my tent to save it from crushing in on me. Despite the sudden drop in temperature, Peter and I hope to be able to break from Base Camp on the 20th and make the first thrust for the summit. And this for me not to be able to say I have 'done' Everest but in order 'to be' up there.

April 18. Till late into the night yesterday, we sat all together in the kitchen — Ang Phu, a few Sahibs, Sherpas and I. Whilst the kitchen boy and the cook washed up the things from supper, we heard the weather forecast. It was not good for today and so we did not plan anything special.

This afternoon Ang Phu suddenly came back from the Icefall, distraut, completely beside himself, and reported that his companion, Dawa Nuru, had fallen into a crevasse whilst he was trying to fix new ladders across it. This news was a tremendous shock to us, even though we had known from the beginning of the expedition, since we first studied the Icefall, what a fearfully dangerous place it was. Every expedition can reckon on some mishap there. The Icefall is several kilometres long, and about one and a half kilometres wide; it moves at a rate of about a metre a day. That is uncommonly fast. It is not seldom that it happens that a whole section of the Icefall simply crumbles in on itself, massive crevasses loom open, hundreds of metres long, great teetering towers of ice, shudder and tumble to pieces. That first time the great wall of ice fell from the Western Cwm, thirteen of our Sherpas had had a lucky escape. This time we were not so lucky.

'There is no point in taking up a rescue party,' says Ang Phu; the crevasse it appears is terribly deep, bottomless. Another Sherpa who was there on the other side has climbed on up to Camp I because he didn't have the strength to jump back over the chasm to join Ang Phu and come down to Base with him.

So now we wait for radio contact with the higher camps to learn what they are doing. It is hot today. A cloud hovers over the lower section of the glacier throughout the middle hours of the day, and the sun burns on the craggy white surface of the Icefall.

One Sherpa was lost without trace in the labyrinth of ice. Lost for ever. Two others were rescued from deep crevasses.

'How have the other Sherpas taken it?' comes the question from the upper camps. 'Presumably, they won't want to go on now — or don't they all know yet.?'

'In Base Camp they do. And the Sherpas in Camp I will know by now, too, because the other Sherpa who was with Dawa Nuru has gone up there. Ang Phu had to come down to Base because at the moment the spot is impassable, and can only be made safe again from above, I understand.'

Hanns Schell from Camp II comes on and asks again whether there is any possibility of getting the man out.

'Not a chance. Ang Phu himself had a look at the place and he says it's such a deep crevasse that you can't see or hear anything. There's not really any sense in going back to search.'

'So what happens now?'

'Ang Phu was very shaken-up when he came down, but after about ten minutes, he was more or less ready to get on with the day's business. He says that the Sherpas should be allowed to rest tomorrow and then the expedition should go on.'

From Base Camp comes the instruction that Robert, Franz and Josl should stay in Camp I today, and tomorrow climb down and safeguard the passage again.

'Understood.'

'What about us in Camp II,' asks Schell, 'should we come down too?'

'No. I've got Ang Phu on the line now. I think only the Base Camp Sherpas will have the day's rest tomorrow. We don't know about higher up until he's spoken to the Sherpas up there. We may have to give these Sherpas a rest day tomorrow too. Otherwise carry on as usual.'

A WHISKY BOTTLE FULL OF BLOOD

One morning Oswald Ölz sits apathetically on a rock outside his tent. His eyes are glazed, his arms hanging limply from his shoulders. When he does speak, I can hardly understand what he says. This is not the Bulle, our Expedition Doctor, that I know, not how I remember him from Manaslu or Makalu, or from McKinley where we succeeded in making the first ascent of the Wall of the Midnight Sun. He is a wreck. What has happened to him? Two days ago he made very fast time down from Camp III, getting to Base Camp in a single day to operate on a Sherpa who had been injured in the Icefall. Now he himself seems to be nearer death than life.

In the tent entrance lies a whisky bottle full of blood. Shortly after completing the operation successfully, Bulle took blood from himself. His haematocrit had risen to around 63, and by drawing off some of his blood and replacing it with an infusion of plasma, he had hoped for an improvement. But he became weaker and is now completely listless. We prescribe oxygen and after a few hours he begins to think clearly again.

'So — thinning the blood isn't the answer, the cure-all?' I ask.

'No there must be more to it than that,' is his answer, 'someone dilutes the blood of a couple of students, without any control group, and then launches a theory on the world — a theory, in fact, which is very rocky on its legs — like I was yesterday.'

'I won't let you dilute any of my blood at altitude!' I say.

A few hours later Bulle explains the problem in more detail. 'During acclimatization,' he says, 'the body produced more red blood cells, thereby raising the oxygen-carrying capacity of the blood. An effect of this rise in the number of blood corpuscles is a rise in the haematocrit, that is the percentage of the blood that is cellular as opposed to fluid. In a man who usually records 40–45 per cent, it can rise to over 50 per cent. But if it climbs above a certain critical figure (which we haven't pinpointed exactly yet, but is probably over 60 per cent) the result would be that the blood gets so thick that it cannot circulate as it does under normal conditions, through the fine blood vessels, the capillaries. The oxygen supply to the tissues therefore decreases even though the capacity is there for carrying more oxygen in the blood. The tissues starve even though they are surrounded by a surplus. This thickening of the blood is naturally speeded up if a person doesn't drink enough liquid. It was these facts that gave rise to the theory of haemodilution, as it is called, blood-thinning. If the haematocrit climbs above a certain critical level, then blood is withdrawn and replaced with plasma or a plasma-substitute. Two German expeditions postulated that this would increase a climber's potential for going high and guard against altitude sickness.

All climbers before setting off for the summit lowered their haematocrit by blood-letting and plasma-infusion. Taking account of the good performance of these climbers, who were all using oxygen in any case, and account of the fact that they seemed to suffer less from altitude problems and were not frostbitten at all, it was concluded that this method was beneficial. But these conclusions are, however, scientifically absolutely inadmissable because there was no control group.

During our expedition we have continually monitored our climbers' haematocrit-value and on average a rise of 20 to 25 per cent has been noticed. The haematocrit value measured, therefore, between 50 and 60 per cent — figures over 60 per cent were only found in conjunction with marked dehydration.*

Our conclusions, therefore, are that even after long periods above 5,000 metres, no excessive build-up of red corpuscles ensues that would warrant haemodilution. A dangerous thickening of the blood can be avoided by simple self-discipline, in this case by taking in sufficient liquids.

* After the return of climbers from the summit of Everest, this figure of 60 per cent was not over-stepped, and none of the climbers suffered troubles which could be attributed to hyperviscosity of the blood.

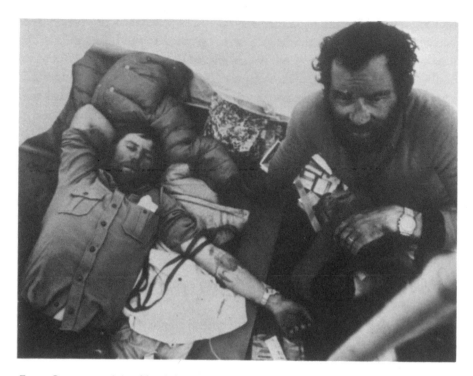

Franz Oppurg receiving blood-thinning infusion under the care of Dr Oswald Ölz (right). These two were the only ones to experiment with haemodilution, both with disastrous results.

April 20, Base Camp. In the four weeks that I have been in Base Camp and above, I have hardly done any reading. Much of the time I was working in the Icefall and then up on the Lhotse Face, but there were also days in which I did nothing but simply savour the moment. I would lie in my tent in the early morning until the first warmth of the sun licked away the frost that hung in fine crystal threads from the tent roof. I listened to the bird-song outside and heard the cracking and grumbling of the glacier above and below me.

Today I sit, having had my customary wash, from sunrise to midday on a sunwashed stone between the tents and boulders, lost in daydreams, absorbing the peace and solitude — until the kitchen boy's call that it is lunch time rouses me from my reveries. He serves to remind me how time passes. I feel much better for spending my mornings like this, than in doing something; to me it doesn't seem like time wasted, more like a gift of time.

For a long while in the afternoon I sit with Robert Schauer in the tent, chatting.

'Are you writing an intimate diary?' I ask him, 'one with your impressions and feelings — like for instance what you experience when you go through the Icefall? One with all the scandal?'

'I write a few lines each day, that's all.'

'And what do you write about?'

'Only what's happened. A summary of my impressions.'

'I think you can lose a lot by writing a summary. In the end all you have is a distillation of impressions, but the most important experiences aren't there — your most profound perceptions get lost.'

AT DEATH'S DOOR

All evening long, the storm forces fine snow dust through the seams of the tent. There is a layer a good ten centimetres thick on our sleeping bags. It is enough to drive one to despair. True, it's a relief suddenly to be under no further obligation to press on, to be able to forget one's goal, not to feel anymore what it was one wanted, not to remember who one once was.

Peter Habeler and I had made up our minds to climb the highest mountain in the world without using oxygen apparatus, yet here I am now sitting fast with two Sherpas on the South Col, the saddle between Everest and Lhotse almost 8,000 metres high unable to go up or down.

Yesterday Peter was ill, his stomach was upset and he remained down at Camp III. But the good weather lured me on. I closed my left eye and blinked. The idea of attempting a solo ascent gradually took hold of me as an exciting thing to do. Now I no longer believe it possible. Neither to reach the summit without oxygen, nor indeed to make one more climb using it. I have no faith in myself and the idea of 'Everest by Fair Means' that I have nurtured for years, now seems to be merely presumptuous. If I get out of this one alive, I will give up climbing. If I can only come through it — just once more!

With two Sherpas I had come up from 7,200 metres to find a suitable place from which to launch my eventual solo attempt. The three of us managed to reach the South Col and there put up a roomy tent, where Mingma, one of the Sherpas, immediately crawled into his sleeping-bag. The other, Ang Dorje, is now helping me with the cooking, and at the same time, desperately trying to control the wildly flapping tent from the inside. The storm raging outside keeps battering the loose fabric against our heads and I am frightened that at any moment the tent will be torn to ribbons — and us along with it.

Yet, a wonder indeed, the tent holds till early morning; then it begins to rip. Blasts of snow and hail are hurled in at us. Where are my goggles? Where is the cooker? I delve for the reserve tent and ask the Sherpas to help me put it up. Up here, with the wind at 200 kilometres an hour and a temperature of 40 degrees below, we shall be lost without shelter. And it is out of the question to climb down.

True to my basic principle of no-technical-tricks, I have not had the foresight to bring any oxygen up to the South Col. Had I done so, the Sherpas at least could have pepped themselves up with it after a night in the 'Death Zone'.

Mingma is still lying perfectly motionless, there is no response from him at all when I shake him. I try shouting, but he only gasps apologetically, 'Power is gone,' and curls up again like a kitten. He no longer believes in survival. He has withdrawn into himself and no longer resists death. We shall all perish — Mingma, Ang Dorje and I — here on this highest pass in the world, on the border between Nepal and Tibet, this natural wind-funnel on which I have put my tent of my own free will.

The Sherpas are no more or less heroic than I, but they do believe in Fate and abandon themselves to it. They are not sacrificing themselves to an ideal, nor yet for one another. They know fear, as I do myself, but they no longer resist it.

I must get this second tent up. I do want to come out of all this, I do want to survive. One more time. So Ang Dorje and I climb out from the chaos, under the torn canopy, and try in the lulls of the storm, to erect a new tent. But over and again the gusts of wind get under the slack fabric and blow it up like a balloon. The tent is almost ripped from our hands. The storm drowns our cries; we cannot understand each other from as little as a couple of metres apart. We have to keep turning out of the wind to rub away the snow which is clogging up our eyes. Once I can see the utter ridiculousness of our situation, I relax a bit. Even towards death. It is too late for anything. The storm builds up into a hurricane. My skin feels as if it burns. The first blue-white tinges of frostbite appear on my finger tips and the end of my nose. I am chilled to the marrow although I am wearing a complete down suit.

At last, after an hour, I crawl into the second tent. It sways, it flaps, but it holds. It holds, and I burst into tears.

Mingma moves in. Whilst I arrange the foam mattresses and set out the ice-covered sleeping bags up on them, this crazy notion of mine of wanting to climb Everest, seems more nonsensical with each passing minute. It is time for the radio link. The apparatus is a single clump of ice.

Camp III comes through, but they don't tell us anything we don't already know — we talk of the hurricane raging around the South Col. Two or three hours later, I speak to the other camps again.

'Ang Dorje,' I report, 'is doing very well, but Mingma has been laid up since yesterday. He says he's not ill, we keep giving him water. We mustn't let him get altitude sickness.'

'Can you hold out the night?'

'Yes, we must. If the tent goes again, I'll try and put up our other reserve, that is a Gore-Tex-Nippin-Spezial, but if that should prove unsuccessful, I don't know what we shall do.'

'We hope it won't come to that, Reinhold. We'll keep the radio open so that you can always call us.'

'It's alright — survival is my big forte. I'm not too worried. If the weather improves, we have a chance of making it, but if it doesn't we may have a couple of days then — curtains.'

'I understand. Let's pray the weather gets better.'

'It's the Sherpas I worry about constantly,' I say.

'Yes we all want to see you down, of course, but it sounds as if it's desperate that the Sherpas don't stay up much longer.'

'Okay — I'll wait for your weather report.'

How slowly the lonely hours pass when one's life is in danger. It seems like an eternity until the evening radio link-up.

And then Camp II comes on with the report that better conditions are promised for early the next day, but that in the afternoon it will get cloudy and bad again.

'Then we are saved!' I shout back, 'we can get down! I'll tell the Sherpas right away!'

Our condition is very bad, 'We haven't drunk anything for a long time. You must help us if we can't get down under our own steam.'

'Yes, of course we'll help you. Tell that to the Sherpas. We are all thinking of you up there. We can imagine what it must be like.'

'I believe the Sherpas pray. They entrust themselves to higher powers. For them, it helps to know that their lives are not totally their own responsibility. They sustain themselves with that. . . . This tent nearly takes off when the wind blows, it must have a speed between 150 and 250 kilometres. And it's minus 50 degrees. The tent flaps so noisily that we have difficulty understanding each other.'

'Yes — I do hope that tent holds out.'

How close death still is. Yet I am not becoming apathetic — the rattling of the tent keeps us alert. But if it goes, we are lost. There's another problem as well.

'What must I do if one of the Sherpas turns funny? Can you ask Bulle at Base Camp what I should do if one of them goes berserk?'

Soon the required information comes through: 'Bulle says on no account give any drugs — better to shout at him, or if necessary dot him one, so that the shock quietens him down.'

'Alright. I have never known such cold. When I put up the tent, there was half a centimetre of ice all over my face, and after half an hour it was impossible to see or do anything any more. If you stood upright, the wind blew you right over.'

Now I am alone again with the two Sherpas and the wind outside. If only there were someone else on my own wavelength. As I creep into my bag, I know that my venture is both impossible and senseless. I stare at the wall of the tent through which the snow is sifting and think — No! I will not give up. We have got to get down.

Mingma is again lying perfectly still beside me, giving a fair imitation of being dead. I have to pinch myself as well, to make sure I am still alive. All my deliberations are very slow. I have the greatest difficulty in speaking. Later, back in Base Camp, when I play back the tape I made up here in this storm, I don't recognize my own voice, neither its pitch nor its pace. It is so incredibly slow, it sounds as if I am dying.

Before night falls — the second night here in the Death Zone — I go outside the tent again and check the outside poles. My fingers freeze onto the aluminium. I remain outside in the storm for a while, waiting, for — I am not sure what. Perhaps just for the cheer of a narrow blue stripe on the horizon. But the world around is relentlessly grey. Nothing but cloud, snowdrifts, storm. Our plight will be hopeless if it is not better in the morning.

I pull myself together. Even though the wind keeps blowing out the flame of the gas-cooker, we must not give up. We must drink — all three — drink enough so that none of us perish in the night.

By next morning, the wind has eased; through the blanket of cloud, we can see blue patches in the sky. We can go down! Mingma is onto his feet in an instant, and Ang Dorje soon after him. Before you could say, 'Jack Robinson', the pair of them are off and away, heading down the mountain. They plunge through the drifts of snow towards the Geneva Spur in the teeth of the wind.

Now I'm on my own, and so very tired. My body doesn't seem to respond any more, my legs fold up underneath me and I simply sit down — and stay down. Then I rouse myself again. I must radio, it is time.

'Camp IV here. We've had the hurricane all night. I haven't slept at all keeping a watch-out. But I could sleep now. The tent held.'

'I was wondering how you managed. How are the Sherpas?'

'Already on their way down.'

'Good — while you're waiting for the sun to come up, get everything together, and then come down. What's the wind doing at this moment?'

'Still quite strong, but I can stand up. What's new down there?'

'Not much. We were all thinking of you and hoping you were sur-

Ang Dorje, our strongest Sherpa. He was with me during the two nights I was storm-bound on the South Col.

viving the night. Now we'll keep our fingers crossed that you get down okay.'

'Who's left in Camp III?'

'No-one. All the Sherpas were so tired that they wanted to come down.'

'That's okay, but if there's no-one there. . . .'

'We had to pull back the Sherpas, otherwise when we want to get going again in a few day's time, they won't be able to do anything.'

IMPOSSIBLE

I remove the tent poles so that the tent collapses flat and I pile empty gas cylinders on top of it so that the wind can't blow it away. The South Col is littered with the old oxygen cylinders of earlier expeditions. I weigh down the tent entrance as well and check again that the zip fasteners are shut.

I have spent nearly 50 fruitless hours in the Death Zone, without sleep, without a single peaceful moment. Every instant I feared for my life. I have aged years in these hours.

A cheerless, sunless day; no driven clouds. The steep pyramid of Everest looms mistily out of the grey sky, seemingly endlessly high. Its storm-scourged summit looks the very essence of inaccessibility.

It has grown a little lighter; the sun must be lurking somewhere behind the clouds, but it doesn't come through. The storm continues to ferment above the South Col. I take my rucksack out of the tent. The Sherpas have already vanished. I try and call after them but they don't stop. They are in flight. They are frightened.

Clumsily in my mittens, I attempt to disentangle the aluminium poles of the two tents and lay them down. I drag several of the empty oxygen cylinders that are lying about, out of the deep snow, and put them onto the flattened tent. Our camp looks forsaken. The West wind tears at my down clothing and continually flings crystals of ice into my face; in a matter of seconds they form a fine coating. My whole face is clogged and taut and my eyesight very much restricted.

The wind swings round, coming from the South, up from the Western Cwm and not from Tibet as I would have expected. I grow weary of struggling against it as on weak, tired legs I lurch across to the Geneva Spur and climb up onto its crest. I turn round to look back at the grey tracks, leading away in the direction of Tibet. Above me, the dark ice leading up to Everest and to my right the dome of rock that is the Spur. It conceals Lhotse from view.

I squat down and again call after the Sherpas who should be waiting. Useless. Sitting here, exhausted, I am not despondent that nothing was achieved this time. Not sad, simply infinitely weary. The idea flits through my mind that I could equally well have climbed off down to the East into Tibet. It would have made little difference. The feeling of depression, dis-orientation that has dogged me for months, washes back over me. My curiosity has died; but I am well aware that only I can pull myself out of this isolation, the answer lies within me. Through activity and objective self-recognition.

I struggle back onto my feet and try to keep my balance against the storm. I move out across the slabs of the Geneva Spur towards the Lhotse

After my first summit attempt, during which I was pinned fast on the South Col (almost 8,000 metres) in a snowstorm, a bridge gave way as I was returning through the Icefall, pitching me into a crevasse. I had been climbing down the Lhotse Face (next double-page, with the tents of Camp III in the lower right of the picture), amid the Western Cwm, and was infinitely weary. After a rest at Camp I, I didn't begin coming through the Icefall until 6 o'clock in the evening. Once the sun has gone down, the snow becomes harder and the risk of avalanches less. I was alone and, in my exhaustion, a bit absent-minded. Suddenly the aluminium ladder slipped under my feet. I was left dangling on the hand-rope which I happened by chance to have caught hold of. I was able to swing across to the other side of the crevasse and crawl out onto firm ground. The bridge had to be repaired the following day.

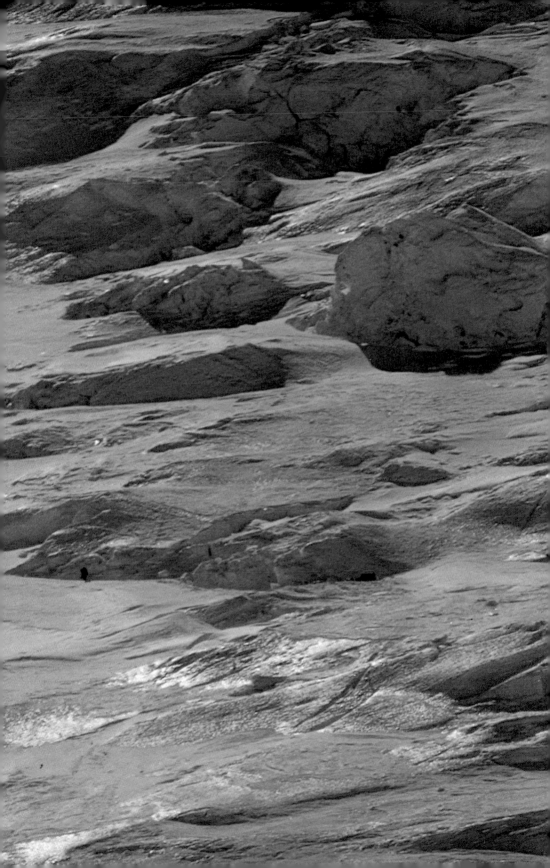

Camp II was rarely as romantic a place as it looks in the lower picture. Mostly it was cold in the tents with hoar-frost building up on the sleeping bags and the inner side of the fabric walls. Frequently icy winds swept through the campsite, which was situated at 6,400 metres at the foot of the steep South-west Face of Everest. We mostly occupied ourselves with thoughts of the morning's climb (above). Ploughing through knee-deep snow: the tired, stiff movements on leaving camp: and the scorching heat just before midday — the anticipation of these we already felt the night before, prior to blowing out the candles having drunk our last cup of tea. Despite all these discomforts, I would not wish to dispense with the memories of either the cold, stormy nights nor the back-breaking work of trail-blazing. They all contributed to the reward I sought — to strip away all complications and come to closer terms with myself.

Face. From the top of the Spur, where the fixed rope begins, I can see below me the two figures of the porters wading through the snowdrifts. They don't turn round at my shouts. When I do get down to Camp III, I find Ang Dorje has waited for me; Mingma has carried on down.

I lower myself slowly, almost jerkily, down the rope. Frequent fits of coughing interrupt my progress, when I simply lean into the face, gasping, snatching a rest. I am unutterably tired, and I begin to feel twinges of pain in all those parts of me insufficiently protected against the weather — the tip of my nose which is lightly frostbitten; my fingers, particularly my fingertips which have turned bluish-white; my whole face is raw.

For two whole days I climb downwards, following the fixed ropes, leaping crevasses; I cross slopes heavy with snow and stumble in the remorseless midday heat down the Valley of Silence, the Western Cwm. I pass all the places where weeks before we worked to prepare a route, where we fixed ropes and built bridges to make the passage easier for our heavily-laden porters. But now, I have the feeling that I have never been here before in my life — have I lost my memory? All night long in Camp II I am overwhelmed with depression.

On the evening of *April 27* at 18.00 hours I am in the middle of the Icefall. The sun is going down as, alone, I pick my way through the pinnacles of ice. Having a rope here would mean little since one can hardly belay oneself. If a whole section were to collapse, as it did that time our brave Sherpa was killed, there could be no escape. Fatigue and the spectral rays of the setting sun seem to get in the way of thinking clearly; I weave my way through the fantastic shadow patterns that mottle the mountain in the evening light.

Suddenly I notice that the ladder in front of me is only hanging loosely on its ropes. I am a bit dubious, but it must have borne the others, I tell myself, so it will hold for me. I take two steps into the middle of the bridge, until I am right over the yawning hole, when the ladder suddenly jerks clear of the lip of the crevasse behind me. It drops away, plunging me into the depths. With one hand I manage to cling to the hand-rope, and dangle like a pendulum in the jaws of the crevasse. The ladder crashes against the other side of the crevasse. I swing my legs and try to reach the rungs of the ladder with my toes. Hand-over-hand I swing gingerly over to the ladder, and once there, claw my way up it and flop over the lower rim of the crevasse into the snow. I don't immediately feel the shock of this experience, it is only in the evening back at Base Camp that it hits me, and I notice that the arm on which I was hanging, will hardly move. I tell the others that the ladder has collapsed so that someone can do something about it first thing the following day, making it safe so that the expedition can proceed as if nothing had happened.

Even several hours after arriving in Base Camp, I am still not myself. I am completely shattered, burnt with the sun, drained by the altitude, chilled by the cold. All the same, I am quite relieved that none of my friends proffer sympathy. It helps me to cling to my dignity and regain my self-composure. And gradually — even during that first night — things settle down in my mind and I again begin to wonder if I really should abandon my plan. The old ideal — though not yet seeming positively tenable — is at least creeping back into my subconsciousness. Vaguely at first, but then with greater urgency. The dream wants to become reality.

EVERYONE WANTS TO GO TO THE SUMMIT

As Peter and I are recovering in Base Camp, another team attempts Everest. It's a disquieting feeling to know someone is three and a half thousand metres above you. Base Camp itself is a good 500 metres above the height of the summit of Mont Blanc. The Lhotse Face is as high as the biggest alpine faces. And the summit ridge that starts at a height where the lesser eight-thousanders finish, is itself 800 metres high, almost as high as climbing the Matterhorn. All this is very hard to comprehend unless one is experiencing it for oneself.

At midday on *May 3*, the summit party of Robert Schauer with Ang Phu and Wolfgang Nairz with Horst Bergmann, reach the top. Everyone is naturally quite pleased about this success, but the general feeling is not one of euphoria amongst the other team members. Everyone feels that his own summit chance has been diminished, since for this first attempt, all the gear and — more important — all the Sherpa forces were employed.

That at least is how it seems at the moment. It may be hard to understand, but up here anyone who has aspirations to reach the top cannot help but feel some envy towards those who do. And at the moment, this includes us. Apart from Bulle, we all combine our satisfaction at the first success with a certain amount of anxiety. Can *we* still do it? We try and keep such anxieties from our conversation, but if it should really come about that we no longer have any chance of success, then there would inevitably be a measure of criticism of the expedition leadership. We would need then to be able to blame this misfortune upon somebody or other.

Peter and I left Base Camp in splendid weather and climbed up to Camp II. It was fearfully hot and we felt noticeably less fit that we did earlier on. Now, in our tent, we are sorting out the food for higher camps. We are determined to have another go at the summit even if the Sherpas do refuse to help us.

Also up here are Dr Raimund Margreiter, Helmut Hagner and Hanns Schell, waiting to make their three-man summit bid. After the first summit success, which had lessened the chances of the other team members — our conversation was tinged with envy and ambition. Hanns Schell comes into the tent; he has just been in touch with the summit party over the radio. 'So — all four of them got up,' he announces, 'it took them four hours 20 minutes from Camp V. Very hard work, they said, a lot of deep snow. Robert had to break trail for about three quarters of the way. Now they're back at Camp V and coming down.'

'What's on the summit? Is the Chinese Maypole still there?'

'They didn't say. But they spent about an hour up there, then two hours getting back to camp.'

'What time did they leave?'

'I didn't ask.' Ang Phu has left an oxygen cylinder with over 1,000 PSI, on the South Summit. His second one.'

'Did they have a good view?'

'I forgot to ask them that either. I should think so, if they sat up there for an hour.' Then, 'Robert said that the going was not good, much steeper than he had expected, not just the Hillary Step. There are a lot of places, apparently, where you need to use a rope.'

'And they're on their way down now — are they still using oxygen?'

'It takes three cylinders each, apparently, from South Col to the summit and back.'

'That's the end of my part of this expedition,' says Helmut Hagner, sadly.

'What have they left in Camp V?'

'Wolfi said something about mattresses, otherwise he didn't say. They were only on for a short while as they wanted to brew some tea then get on down.'

'They have probably still got some strength left. Things seem to go much easier with oxygen.'

'I wouldn't have thought it made that much difference.'

'Everyone that uses it, says it does. If they had to use a couple of old cylinders left at Camp V, as well as what they took with them, it means they didn't have enough in the first place, and wouldn't have reached the summit if they hadn't found the extra. They were lucky. We ought to be able to get up now — Bulle, especially.'

'Josl's going well too — he deserves to go, he's stronger than most.'

'Oh, with oxygen, he'll do it easily.'

'Well now we can only hope the Sherpas will carry up our stuff.'

'And if they won't — what then?'

'No chance.'

'Well, I wish you success, as always,' I say to Manni, Helli and Hanns.

May 3 — Camp II, evening. The wireless link between the summit party back on the South Col, and Camp I has finished. It was an exciting day today — the big success, the triumph. Four of our members have reached the summit! But on the other side of the coin, we have one desperately ill Sherpa, who had to be brought down to Camp I, wrapped up in a waterproof sheet. He has had a stroke. Bulle, our Doctor, came up from Base Camp with Josl and Franz to take charge of him and supervize getting him back to Base Camp in the morning. Ourselves, we lie here, poised as it were, between Base Camp and summit — caught in the many discussions the second summit party have with the first. Yet Peter and I don't concern ourselves much with these discussions, since we are planning to climb without oxygen at all — and ours is therefore quite a different ball game.

Gusts of wind tug at the tent and although I have taken something to help me get to sleep, I can't seem to drop off tonight. I am uneasy — fearful, even. Next to me, Peter breathes deeply — a special sort of deep breathing that indicates he is struggling for air. We are not particularly high, well within safe limits, but already I comprehend what it means to be without the help of oxygen equipment, to be climbing heavenwards without a breathing mask to fall back on. Perhaps that is what is worrying me, and perhaps too because by the light of the moon, all the difficulties, the dimensions and the exertions involved, always seem to be doubled. I keep imagining the slopes above, recalling the harsh nights I spent stormbound on the South Col. It would be an easy thing to climb Everest with oxygen — this I know because Horst and Wolfi were far from their peak condition and still did it in good time and fine style. I know that perhaps it will turn out to be completely impossible without oxygen and no-one can prophesy in what state someone would come back from the summit. . . .

I had been much easier in my mind on the last attempt. More resolved. More resolved not only in my attitude to chance it, but also in my determination to carry on till I reached the end of my resources. But then, also, I was far more strongly convinced that it could be done. Now I am frightened, so frightened it won't let me rest. I toss from side to side, worrying my head with questions I cannot answer, questions no-one can answer. Not even someone who has climbed Everest before.

It is uncannily quiet. The roof of the tent above looks like the keel of a boat, and I have the strange feeling that I am sailing among the stars. Luckily, we have left the tent entrance open a little, so that we can get sufficient oxygen in this starved air. I can hardly believe how warm it has grown here at Camp II at 6,400 metres; it is so warm that it is uncomfortable. I would like to undo my sleeping bag and take off some clothing but, know that I would pretty soon get chilled if I did. I go on fidgeting from side to side, and the worry never leaves me, the madness of my scheme, and above all the unreality, the insubstantiality of it all, the feeling of not-belonging to anything, not even to myself.

May 4. In the morning begins the business of transporting the half-paralyzed porter down to Base Camp. We have a chat with them before they go.

'I hope the Sherpas help you — it looks like being a lengthy business.'

'We're going to need some help with this heavy man, certainly.'

'In the meantime, this is what's happening here — Helli, Manni and Hanns have set off; how far they'll get they're not sure. It depends on the weather. In any case, we are alone. Here at II, and will stay here till the others are at Camp III, and the people from the South Col get back here.'

'Yes, that's okay. It's a bit selfish, I know, but I hope that the Sherpas that are left can be persuaded to carry some oxygen up to Camp IV so that we have a chance later.'

'Josl, there isn't a single Sherpa left,' I say. 'It's going to be very, very difficult for the second group too. I must say they are trusting to luck rather. The Sherpas that came down are tired, and they are climbing down to Base Camp. How long they intend staying there, we'll have to see. But I don't think any oxygen will be carried up, nothing will be!'

'Hmmm.

'Yes — that would be fine. Although I rather think they would sooner have a week's rest, than a couple of days. I think they have more or less made up their minds — they've got one team to the summit and are not interested in any more. But we shall see.'

'Perhaps some of them have got personal ambitions for the summit — that would be in our favour,' says Josl.

'Did you leave before the post yesterday?'

'Nothing came up yesterday — I reckon it should show up sometime today. We'll let you know.'

'We'll be going without Sherpas too. We have none, as I said. Perhaps we'll try to motivate someone or other, but it will be difficult. If nothing comes of it, we'll still try alone. We're not very optimistic any more, I must say. The whole thing seems to have taken an unhappy turn,' I say to Josl.

'Yes,' agrees Peter, 'it's a real swine, how things are at the moment. In retrospect — I can only say it would have been a lot better if you hadn't been up to the South Col.' The others would then have had less chance

The evacuation of the half-paralysed Sherpa was a lengthy and incredibly difficult operation.

of a summit success certainly, but someone had to build up the camp.

'It's there for our benefit too,' I remark.

'It was on the Lhotse Face, that I felt most alone — they all kept very much to themselves there, even the indefatigable Robert. No one once said — it's not fair Reinhold — let me take a turn at going ahead and preparing the route. But of course, if the weather had stayed fine, we would both have had the first chance.'

'Yes, you were a day ahead of me, but I could have come on to join you,' says Peter, who at that time had turned back.

140

'You've only got to wait, Wolfi will say — so why then was he in such a hurry? We have held back long enough, we have waited ten days.'

I have just finished speaking with Wolfi in Camp IV, over the radio. It was our first conversation since his summit climb, and during the course of it he himself conceded that it was no hard thing to climb an eight-thousander with oxygen, and that such a climb should not be esteemed too highly in itself.

Bulle, who had supervised the transport of the critically ill Sherpa down the mountain, reports from Base Camp.

'There's no-one here yet from the South Col,' I tell him, 'they are somewhere between Camps III and II, but going slowly without oxygen. And the team at Camp III had a lot of snow to contend with — it's snowing here now quite badly. I think we're in for a spell of bad weather. If it's still bad tomorrow, they'll come back here, but if it's fine they will move on up to the South Col. Helli says he has spoken to Ang Phu in any case and there's not much hope of any Sherpas going up again to the South Col, or beyond.'

At last Wolfgang Nairz reached Camp II. He enquires how things are with everyone.

'There are mixed feelings,' I tell him, 'naturally everyone is pleased at your success but there is also a strong feeling of gloom — we don't think anyone else will get up.'

'Why? Because we did, you mean?'

'Yes — because all the resources went into your attempt.'

'But we carried all our own gear up!'

'It was a mistake for Ang Phu to have gone with you. It ought to have been one of the other Sherpas.'

'If we hadn't all carried 25 kilos each — which would normally mean three Sherpas — we should never have reached the summit. That's a fact.'

'Sure,' I reply, 'but the next team haven't a hope now of getting to the top.'

'They've got everything they need. We've done all the preparation. All they've got to do is get going.'

The first summit party called so heavily upon the resources of equipment and Sherpa strength, that the following teams felt their chances of success to be diminished. The Sherpas were unwilling and unable to help further.

It is understandable that everyone is now thinking of his own chances, and that Nairz, as leader, is coming in for a lot of criticism from the others who would like to climb Everest too.

'And what about us?' I ask.

Without the help of Sherpas to transport the heavy oxygen cylinders, a summit succes would not have been possible for the other members of our expedition. After the firs group had climbed Everest, most of the Sherpas refused to haul further loads up the Lhotse Face

'It doesn't affect you, because you don't need oxygen anyway,' Wolfi consoles us.

'That's not quite true,' I return. 'The Sherpas do have an important part to play for us too. If I haven't got any porters and have to lug up 20 kilos myself, it's a poor lookout. That's the logic of it,' I explain.

'The Sherpas will back you up — those that can,' Wolfi declares.

'That's not what Ang Phu seems to think. He told me he thought the Sherpas were tired and wouldn't want to come up again. That's what he said.'

'What he told us was, that he'd do his utmost to see that the Sherpas kept on working, fully.'

'What clothing have you left up there?' I ask.

'Everything — wind suit, gaiters.'

'And what's the reserve oxygen situation.'

'There's just one cylinder on the South Summit. It'll get you down to the South Col.'

'We won't need it.' I say dryly.

'You can't be certain of that. Just suppose — you stagger back to the South Col in a fine old state and mutter, "It's all up — and before I freeze to death up here, I'm going to take some oxygen!"'

'He's right,' Peter agrees with the Leader. 'If it turned out like that, it would be false pride not to use it.'

'Is there any food up in Camp IV — and gas?'

'I'm not sure about Camp III, but there's plenty at IV and V.'

'And what's the route like?'

'Steep, it's a very steep slope.'

'Are there many cornices between Camp V and the summit?'

'Yes.'

'Dangerous?'

'Only the Hillary Step. It really is loose and rotten there.'

After this long and exciting discussion, we again call up Camp III. Manni comes on and wants to know if the summit team have arrived with us.

'Yes,' I reply, 'they've just come. Naturally they're in very good spirits. It's still snowing here. We have more or less given up the idea of coming on tomorrow. There is scarcely any hope at the moment of getting hold of any Sherpas because Ang Phu is not there to persuade them.'

'We'll try and reach the South Col tomorrow.'

'Understood. We've got some interesting details for you. There's a lot of gear up there and Horst had prepared it all for you. All you need is good weather!'

'I'm not so optimistic as that — but let's hope anyway.'

'Okay — when would you want to make a start in the morning?'

'Between 7 and 8.'

'Good — then we'll talk again at seven.'

THE FIRST SUMMIT SUCCESS

Now, therefore, Wolfgang Nairz, Horst Bergmann, Robert Schauer and Sherpa-leader Ang Phu, have their summit triumph under their belts. The first group of the Austrian Alpine Club Expedition, to which we had attached ourselves, has climbed the route we prepared as far as the South Col, and from there they placed a fifth high camp at about 8,500 metres from where they made their summit burst. They first began to use oxygen at 7,200 metres, except for Robert Schauer who did not switch on his set until 8,000 metres. This was, therefore, a classical Everest ascent, the 22nd since Hillary and Tenzing first stood on the summit on May 29, 1953. More than 60 people have been there since, and all with oxygen apparatus.

Now in Camp II, Robert tells me his impressions of the climb:*

'The actual dimensions are crazy — incredible. The vast scale, the altitude, the highest point of all mountains. A magical goal, a goal demanding so much awareness and concentration.

It was important to me that I kept right out in front, and that all the little unknowns that still existed despite all the literature — that these decisions were left to me. I simply wanted it that way. Even when we

---

* From an authentic tape transcript.

were down in the Icefall, searching for the best route, I was just bursting with enthusiasm. You couldn't have held me back even though it was so dangerous working in the Icefall. And I was thrilled, too, when I found the way up into the Western Cwm and saw the route clear to Camp I. We set off for Camp III on *April 30*. The weather was perfect, but in the afternoon it changed again. This seemed to be the pattern every day and it didn't bother us at all.

The decision on who should go to the summit was a bit awkward at first. I knew that Wolfi and Horst hadn't done any of the work in the Icefall — and also I had seen Wolfi once turn back long before he got to Camp III because he was feeling so wretched (but he wasn't well-acclimatized at the time). A lot of people had wondered about whether he ought to be in the summit team or not, and I had the feeling that I could become the draught-horse, so to speak, for this climb.

I thought, I don't want to go as far as the South Summit and then find that Wolfi or Horst couldn't go any further because they were feeling too weak. So I looked for someone else to join us, someone who could help carry for us, as well as carrying his own gear, and that was Ang Phu. He is a marvellous goer, technically, if a bit unorthodox. I noticed that going up and down the summit ridge — it took him a bit longer to size up a situation and he was a bit slow. But his safety lay in his slow pace. My attitude was that if Wolfi and Horst found they worked well together, or if they had to turn back, then I would still have Ang Phu with whom I could press on.

The nearer we four got to Camp III, however, and then on to Camp IV, the clearer it steadily became that stamina would be no problem. They went marvellously, and the way we all got on together took me very much by surprise. I was soon delighted that I was going with these two. It was apparent they were not likely to fall back and leave me in the lurch. What if they were in better condition than me, I then thought, if I dragged behind, would they then abandon me! I worried about that but my worries were unfounded as it turned out. We all got on marvellously well, and all showed concern for each other.

On the South Col where the climate is relatively harsh, there is a cold wind blowing constantly. All my movements (I didn't use any oxygen

Robert Schauer, one of the most experienced expedition mountaineers of today, prepared the route on the Geneva Spur, and was first on the summit.

As the weeks passed, we developed an instinct for how the weather was going to develop. Of course we still checked our altimeters (which were also barometers), but more important for decisions in the mountains remained the colour of the sky, the first clouds on the horizon, or even just the smell of the air. On both my summit attempts rainbow-coloured clouds whirled over the Lhotse summit as I climbed the upper reaches of the Western Cwm (next double-page). The first time this cloud formation signalled bad weather. The second time, on May 6, I didn't believe that the weather would again change for the worse. It would have spelt final defeat for us. I simply admired the way the clouds welled up and then dissipated, regarding their patterns to the right of the Geneva Spur as an impressive natural spectacle, and went on believing in good weather. Peter Habeler and I finally decided to go only once more through the dangerous labyrinth of the Icefall (right), and that on our descent, hopefully from the summit.

On May 3, the day that the first two ropes of the ÖAV-Expedition reached Everest summit, long discussions took place in Camp II, our Advance Base Camp, On the one hand we were delighted that Wolfgang Nairz, Horst Bergmann, Robert Schauer and the Sherpa-leader Ang Phu, had been successful, but on the other hand, the other climbers felt cheated of their chance of getting to the summit since so much equipment and Sherpa support had been expended on these first four. As the returning team arrived in this camp, another group was already on their way towards the South Col. Peter Habeler, for a short while, wavered from our original plan and wanted suddenly to attempt the climb with oxygen, since the returning climbers all felt there was little chance of success without it. But he came round again to our plan, and we were both then resolved to climb as high as possible, even if not to the summit. In any case without oxygen apparatus. The bottom picture shows Peter at a height of around 8,200 metres. In the middle background one can see the two yellow tents on the South Col, our assault camp.

between Camps III and IV, nor in Camp IV) became increasingly clumsy. But at night if you use a sleeping set, your spirits pick up, you begin to think, to re-enact, all the things that have happened during the day — recross the Yellow Band, which is quite hard, go into the gully leading up to the Geneva Spur, and then that long, marvellous traverse, up the right-hand side of the Col, when you gradually see Everest rising up on the other side — it's quite overwhelming.

'After the South Col we climbed up to where we wanted to establish Camp V, at 8,500 metres, at the very beginning of a 500-metre long couloir. This turned out to be right on the South-east Ridge and a very exposed spot. It was quite late when we started off that day because we were still having problems with our oxygen equipment. I developed an unreasonable hatred for the whole business — we had spent so much time in Base Camp testing cylinders, adaptors, masks, gauges, regulators and had only sent up the cylinders that functioned best, simply to find at 8,000 metres that the apparatus didn't work at all. The cylinders were not good until we had attacked them with a pair of pliers. We were able to use some American cylinders we found up there and that was naturally a tremendous advantage. We spent a lot of time deciding which flasks we should, and which we shouldn't take. It all became a dreadful nuisance. I packed one flask and set aside another I wanted to use as a sleeping cylinder in Camp V, and then I just gave up.

When we got a bit higher, I began to film with a borrowed camera. It's a tremendous effort just to operate it at this height, especially wearing thick mittens and with ice blowing into your face — but all keen, I had kept the camera in a side pocket of my trousers so as to be ready to start shooting as soon as a suitable subject presented itself. What happened? This super camera, specially designed for just such conditions as these — what did it do? It was useless, the motor would not work, I would have liked to throw away the films and the camera at the start of the steep gully, but I thought to myself — I might be able to get it working again up in Camp V if I warm it up and tinker with it. Technology seemed to be letting me down! I was so disillusioned by it all that I resolved in future to trust only to my own skills and strengths and understanding. I would then know exactly how far I could go.

I had now started up the couloir, in which before me, four Sherpas had made a track. I soon climbed it although I was carrying some 25 kilos in my rucksack. Being the advance party, we naturally had the disadvantage of having to bring up a complete camp in our rucksacks. Two tents, cookers, pots and pans, sleeping bags, mattresses as well as reserve equipment and cameras, films, food, etc. Also, of course, it was important that we had climbing gear with us — ropes, harnesses, carabiners, ice screws. We didn't know what conditions might be waiting for us.

Something that happened up there I will remember for a long time. After a relatively long spell of trail-breaking, we had worked ourselves into quite a good rhythm when our Sherpas, as we came out onto the ridge, discovered the remains of a Korean camp. Immediately they dropped their loads and started off down. And there we were, suddenly, the four of us, completely alone with our axes and a half-blown-away tent. We had to force ourselves to make camp here. I would much sooner have sat down and fallen asleep and not moved till next morning — it was a question of forcing oneself to pick up a shovel and axe, and start hacking out a flat platform for a tent.

Ang Phu and I finally moved into the Korean tent, in which we found some food they had left behind, including seaweed. I was very sceptical about this at first, because in fact it just looked like a sheet of black paper. Ang Phu shoved a couple of sheets under his nose and sniffed, and rolled his eyes with delight. I thought I ought at least to try it just once, so I did and in fact the leaves tasted quite excellent. Of course they weren't very filling. We then brewed up plenty of tea. That too was an effort, of course, melting enough snow. Ang Phu and I got on very well together. Wolfi and Horst had put their tent two metres above us. It was very small and they were as cramped up there as Ang Phu and I were, squashed in the other little tent.

We began making tea at 5 o'clock the next morning. The sun was already shining on the ridge and as we opened up the tent, our sleeping bags began to steam. They had got very wet in the night and so of course had lost a lot of their insulation value. I had been quite cold although I wore all my clothes inside my sleeping bag. Still, I slept quite well and that was very important with the long, strenuous day ahead. We cooked, ate a little, for we had little appetite, but drank plenty. Dressing began with the boots that we had put in our sleeping bags overnight so that they would not freeze solid. Then the overboots and then we went outside where a fresh wind was blowing up from Tibet. It was important not to take off one's gloves under any circumstances; our mittens were frozen rigid, so fastening crampons was a tiresome business. We checked the contents of our rucksacks, and then again, so that we didn't forget anything.

And then we set off.

Wolfi and Horst started half an hour ahead of Ang Phu and I. They had indicated that they wanted to establish the first part of the route. First of all it was relatively flat, then it followed a steep slope up for about 200 metres, leading directly to the South Summit. But by this time we had caught up with them and took over the lead up the steep buttress. Horst told me he was having problems with his oxygen set. It was losing pressure very quickly and something about it was not functioning properly.

I tried to go without oxygen when working on the route. I wanted to know what my rhythm was like, and how strong or weak I was without it. My rucksack weighed between 12 and 16 kilos, and to carry it was such an effort for me that it took all my strength and all the oxygen in my muscles, simply to thrust out my chest to take in air, and then to let it out again. That made me think, I can tell you. I became frightened in case the set might suddenly stop working. The other thing I noticed without it was that I felt withdrawn, as if in a trance. Later, on the summit I felt this even stronger. I believed I was floating half a metre above the ground and weighed several kilogrammes lighter. I could only manage 30 or 40 steps without oxygen, and they cost me so much strength, that the possibility of my climbing Everest without oxygen, didn't even enter into the question.

Ang Phu and I climbed on a short rope. As we went up, I would stop and bring him up on the rope, at the same time gazing around at our immediate surroundings. It was an overwhelming sight! For example, Lhotse, with all its 8,511 metres, one of the highest mountains in the world, was lying *below* us, and also, far away, we could see the huge massif of Kangchenjunga. We saw Makalu, and to the North, a swarm of four, five, six-thousand metre peaks, which at this distance looked no more than sugar icing on a cake. And then the glaciers!

The summit of Mount Everest with the Chinese survey pole just visible on the horizon.

The South Summit itself was quite a milestone for me. From there it looked as if the going would be more or less level, in actual fact it is still quite a tiring climb up to the Main Summit. Ang Phu and I set off in front, with Wolfi and Horst following.

Just above the South Summit I was suddenly made aware of a very human, very urgent, call of nature — which I dared not deny. It was no easy matter up there stripping down to my shirt in the strong wind, but my dungarees gave me no other option. I don't know what Ang Phu made of it all — for him these eternal snows are the resting place of his Gods!

Horst had begun to film with his 16 mm. camera. I said I would go ahead with Ang Phu — if we hung about we should get very cold. I always look for a rational reason to get in front. There was this unquenchable force within me to get on with this last, wonderful part of the climb. I believe this section of the route must be more beautiful than anything I have ever seen before in the mountains. It gave me an indescribable feeling to negotiate this ridge, and however dangerous and difficult it might be, I would still not have let anyone else go in front.

Ang Phu and I began the short descent from the South Summit down into the little notch, from where the lovely ridge leads on up to the Main Summit. At first the visibility was a bit poor, some clouds had gathered round the ridge and the light was dim and diffuse; the sun didn't break right through. Despite this it was quite warm and a light, fresh wind came up from the Chinese side of Everest.

Then I began, very slowly and cautiously, to tread the ridge, which to start with was quite sharp and my crampons kept stripping the snow from the rocks. This was rather unpleasant for the rocks were very smooth and there was a constant danger of slipping off them. I tended therefore, more and more, to apply myself to the snow, the hard firn, of the knife-sharp ridge, and after a few difficult passages, I brought Ang Phu up after. We used a longer rope for this bit so that we had a certain amount of play, about 20 metres; that was enough to allow an ice axe belay — the only way to secure the second man coming up at the same time as safeguarding the first.

Despite all the difficulties and dangers, on which we had to concentrate, we found plenty of time to just let the impressions soak in. I don't know how it was with Ang Phu — he hardly spoke at all unless the rope was running out and I should take a stance, or if he was starting to follow up. But for me, this traverse along the knife-edged ridge, exactly on the border between China and Nepal, was something quite wonderful.

Far below us, we could see the little tents of Camp II in the Western Cwm, also the Nuptse Ridge at around 7,700 metres, continuing round to Lhotse and to the steep flanks that plunge down into Western Cwm. And then the South-west Face of Everest, which in its upper section, does not appear to be all that steep. To the right, that is to the North, is the Chinese Flank, a snow and ice face steeper than the South-west Face.

At the start of the Hillary Step I again let Ang Phu catch up. He was able to climb quite quickly in my tracks. Then slowly I began to attack the Hillary Step. I had noticed a rock rib on the lefthand side, broken by a couple of improbable bands of snow, and to the right, a 50–60 degree steep slope of hard snow, rose sharply. The snow was rotten, unpleasant. I had to take great care not to overload the steps, I had taken such care to fashion, otherwise they would have simply collapsed. To avoid this, I tried to steady myself with my ice axe rammed deeply into the snow on one side, and on the other would plunge my hand deep into the snow. It was very hard work even though I had turned up my oxygen flow to the maximum. The necessary concentration and the physical effort was very heavy on oxygen, and after every five or ten steps I would need to rest over my axe for a few minutes, my eyes closed, and my head on my forearms. As I recovered my strength, curiosity about what happened further on, would grow until I could move forward again, one foot in front of the other, rhythmically, moving only one extremity at a time — left hand, then right foot, and right hand, then left foot — and soon I came to the top of the Hillary Step, 20 metres or so above Ang Phu, who had belayed me. I had hoped to see the Chinese Tripod by then, but sadly it was still some way off and besides there were clouds gathering round the summit, obscuring the view.

Slowly I ploughed forward, thinking all the time of the cornice which could break off at any moment. The snow texture up here was quite different to that on the Hillary Step. The first part of the ridge had gone easily, we had moved quite quickly from the South Summit to the Hillary Step, but now it seemed as if we were progressing at a snail's pace only. And the cloud, which was getting denser all the time, seemed to carry the ridge away into the distance. I could no longer make out the end of it, I thought it would be like other summits I have climbed, when one suddenly finds oneself on top without really realizing it. But here, just where I could have wished it like that, it was the reverse. There was no summit. The ridge stretched away further and further into the mist. My thoughts were now centred entirely on this ridge, and as a result I was going along it almost hypnotically. It was simply grandiose, but I couldn't grasp it.

And then finally reached the last hump on the ridge, from where I could see the three-legged aluminium survey pole put up by the Chinese. It twinkled a little in the sun, but even so was difficult to make out properly.

Now I recognized the last part of the climb, the last 20 metres to the summit. I could remember seeing pictures just like this; I was absolutely sure now that there were but a few steps to the summit. Even so, I didn't trust myself to think that in a few moments I would be standing on the roof of the world. It was too overwhelming, especially since we were also the first of our expedition to reach the summit − Wolfi and Horst only arrived some 20 or 30 minutes later. Horst miraculously filmed our climb. I waited two metres below the summit to let Ang Phu catch up. Just before we stepped up onto the top, I took some pictures − the highest point was exactly at eye-level, and it was this short stretch of ridge with the base of the tripod, that I photographed. Then I put my arm round Ang Phu's shoulders and said to him: "We must go up together." For me it was the happiest moment of the whole expedition when we both stepped onto the summit. We hugged each other and suddenly, like a little child, I began to cry.

I could see Ang Phu's face for he had taken off his mask, as I then did also, and we could see our emotions mirrored in the face of the other. It was not necessary to say much, indeed it was not necessary to say anything, one had only to look into our faces. Ang Phu murmured to himself gently and prayed. He prayed for us, for himself, and for everyone in the world. At that moment I believe he was the happiest Nepali alive, the happiest

Sherpa, for his Gods had suffered him to enter their kingdom and he knew he was welcome there.

The tripod just behind me, was humming gently in the wind, yet I heard nothing except the music that had seemed to accompany me throughout my climb. It was a very rhythmic music, baroque music. I have tried to recapture the melody since but it is impossible, the theme has gone for ever. I heard this music on the summit, softly accompanied by vibrations in the air. There was nothing else to hear except the light wind, just this singing in my ears which doubtless had something to do with the pulsing of the blood, but it didn't seem like that to me, it seemed to be the vibrations of the mountain I was experiencing.

Ang Phu continued his prayers, but with a few interruptions. Once he stood up, turned himself in the direction of Base Camp, then back again towards me, where behind me was the highest spot, and then he sat down again, crossing his legs. He was getting a bit agitated and I couldn't understand why. Something seemed to be distressing him and I asked him why he didn't just sit quietly and relax. Everything was alright, he told me, but he was just very excited because this was for him the greatest moment in his whole life and he found it impossible to sit still.

Through the mist we saw Wolfi and Horst approaching. They were coming very slowly, stopping for a short pause after every few steps, and looking upwards. Wolfi took photographs, whilst Horst, behind him, filmed, and it was not long before they were both standing next to us. We embraced each other, endorsing how happy we were, and how lucky to be all up here together. And I began to howl again, as also did Wolfi and Horst. They took off their masks and we could see each other.

Then we sat down and we hardly exchanged a word. Once our pulses and breathing had calmed down a bit, we set about the tasks we had set ourselves, slowly. We had said we would take photographs on the summit, and for me this was a tedious exercise. I think if ever I am in the same position again, standing on a big mountain, I shan't bother with photographs.

I was fairly subdued much of the time on the summit, for after a while without oxygen, one's features gradually begin to distort. I felt as if I had some sort of muscular cramp, and I couldn't close my mouth any more.

It was like when you lie in the sun too long, and my lips began to tremble violently. I couldn't account for it and I was a bit disturbed by it all.'

FAILURE

'It is impossible. There's too much snow,' Helmut Hagner is reporting from Camp III. Asked if any trace could be seen of the prepared route, Helli replies: 'Hardly at all. There's scarcely a hope of getting at the rope on Lhotse Face. And if it snows again, that's definitely the end.'

'Why didn't you give one of the Sherpas an oxygen set and send him on ahead?'

'None would go. We thought about letting the Sherpas go without their loads, but there is so much powder snow, that even the third in the line would still not have had any tracks to follow. The snow is waist-deep, we were wading in it up to our middles. We'll have to give up.'

We speak of the weather problems and I try to persuade them to continue with their climb. I have the feeling that this is their last chance, and of course also hope they will tread a trail for us. Helli, Manni and Hanns, who are so worn out, are scarcely less experienced or less strong a party than the first summit team.

So why should they fail?

Peter and I make plans. We will only have a chance if we send a Sherpa off early in the morning ahead of us.

'He needn't carry anything — just break a trail for us,' declares Peter.

'Yes, and only as far as the South Col.'

'We have to go tomorrow.'

'And if we get away quite early, I can't imagine why it should not succeed.'

Helli, Hanns and Manni have returned to Camp II. Downcast. They all feel envious of the successful team.

'Was it cold up in Camp III?' I ask.

'No, I wasn't cold personally, even when there was ice on the inside of the tent. But I didn't really sleep at all.'

'This is a crazy situation.'

'But *you* can still do it at least — hopefully,' they encourage me.

'It would have been really good to have had you in front of us. We could have followed a day later without oxygen. It would be less risky that way.'

I have another chat with Peter who is still convinced we ought to take a couple of oxygen cylinders with us. He still hesitates, unsure whether now to attempt the climb with or without breathing apparatus.

'We only want to take some for emergencies,' I say.

'You deteriorate all the time up there. It could suddenly be too late.'

'If we have good weather and don't let ourselves get daunted by the problem, we shall do alright,' I declare.

'But suppose we have to sleep in Camp V, and then the next day we are kaput, what then?' asks Peter later.

'Then we go back. But I have the feeling that the three today were beaten because they were not strong enough, not fit. There's a lot of snow on the route, sure, but they had a chance.'

'Without doubt.'

Taking everything into account, we still had hope.

'Our friend the wind is whistling well up there,' says Peter before falling asleep.

TO BE OR TO HAVE

Our own spirits had been dampened after the success of Wolfi, Horst and Robert, and the Sherpas were unwilling to support a second summit bid. Added to this, Robert Schauer from Graz — who is a very tough mountaineer indeed had found that when he took his oxygen mask off just below the South Summit, he had been out of breath at every step; he was convinced that it would be impossible to climb Everest without oxygen. Wolfgang Nairz, too, reported that he was overcome with dizziness when he took his mask off for only a few minutes on the summit.

These findings from the first Austrians to have ever climbed Everest, seemed to demoralize Peter. From being so resolute before, he now began to waver and suddenly to think in terms of an attempt *with* oxygen. Better to reach the summit with it, than not to do it at all, now seemed to be his feeling on the subject.

'How will it look,' he explains, 'if Josl — who is a pensioner — gets up and I don't? Most people won't understand the difference. With or without oxygen — it's all the same to them. It's only the summit that counts.'

I can appreciate that, but for me the summit is not so important. I stick to my original ideal of 'Everest by fair means', but can understand how Peter now feels. I give him my support — even in trying to find a new partner. I don't want to climb with him, or anyone, who is breathing oxygen from a cylinder. I don't want any help nor anyone to show me the way.

Peter now starts looking for someone to climb with, and because of the Sherpa situation, this means a partner from Base Camp. Bulle could come up and make a start with Peter the next day, or the day after. But I will make my attempt alone, without oxygen. I realize, of course, that my chances of reaching the summit are now much slimmer, but I still want to go as far as I can, and in any case, to go without oxygen.

Josl Knoll and Franz Oppurg are not very enthusiastic about the new turn of events. They feel that Peter is thrusting himself forward. 'He has done nothing to help us,' they say, 'he has just played the "Star".' They feel he should be an ordinary climber and have no more opportunities than the others.

I explain the position again, and Bulle is convinced. Josl disagrees because the new plan doesn't comply with the original precepts of the expedition. Then the whole situation changes again as it becomes known that Manni, Helli and Hanns are now climbing down. The three in Base Camp decide that they would therefore like to stick together and make their attempt as a single team right away.

Peter is furious. No one will go with him. Obviously it would be best even for him to climb with a partner, but who could keep up with him? To describe Peter as an average climber is a wild understatement. I am no longer irritated by Peter's hesitation over our attempt, but by these prevarications coming up over the radio. I can see Peter is boiling mad. Now he wants to prove that he can also do without them, and so he says, 'I'm coming with you, Reinhold — to the summit!'

It's true his decision was taken partly out of stubbornness, but also he saw a faint glimmer of hope. Again he went along with my plan and pledged he would stick it out whether we reached the top or not.

For my own part, I had not come to Everest because I had an ambition to climb it at any price. My desire was to get to know it, in all its magnitude, its difficulty and harshness, and I was determined to foreswear the summit if I couldn't reach it unaided by breathing equipment. As I have said, modern oxygen apparatus has the effect of reducing the height of Everest to around 6,000 metres. If I want this experience — I don't have to go to Everest at all. But if I do want to experience Everest's unique sheer bulk, then to be able to feel it, sense it, I have to climb without any technical tricks. Only then will I know what a man feels like being there, what new dimensions it opens up for him, and whether he can thereby learn anything new in terms of his relationship with the Cosmos.

CASTING ADRIFT

May 6. I am climbing up the Lhotse Flank on my own. My trunk sways from side to side as I mount the fixed ropes. The heat is unbearable. The sun is hidden behind whirling clouds, that blow up from nothing, then just as quickly disappear. Early this morning I decided to set off in the direction from which the wind was blowing. I always prefer to head into the wind rather than have it behind me, and sometimes need the smell of it to show me the way to go. Contrary to all the indications, I firmly believe that the fine weather will hold. I read each change in the cloud formation, each variation of the wind, as a good weather omen! Up here, the clouds taste different from the fresh air, and when the wind blows, everything becomes sterile. That is the only thing I have against this wind. Supported by three Sherpas, Peter and I today climb up towards Camp III. We feel fine, in good form. Although the new snow makes the going heavy and we can expect to find the camp snowed up, we are full of confidence.

Tomorrow we will move quickly on up to the South Col. As a safety precaution we do take with us the two French oxygen cylinders, that a Sherpa has carried up. Should one or other of us become ill, or suffer a brain haemorrhage, as has been prophesied for us, we have the satisfaction of knowing that oxygen is available on the South Col. But we don't expect to touch it and will leave it intact in Camp IV for the next summit party.

Setting-off days, like this, used to be such a strain for me. Physically wearing. Somehow, to leave all one's ties behind is harder for me than the actual climbing.

The next day too, climbing up from Camp III to the South Col, I am aware only of humdrum monotony. I don't mean that the climbing itself is boring, or that there is any sense of compulsion about it. Indeed through it, I do find a deepening perception of myself.

On the Geneva Spur I catch up with Dati, who, climbing, without a load, has led the way this far. If, after a short breather, I begin to feel waves of futility, I have only to go on a bit further. Effort for me at this altitude represents the means of rescuing each step, each drawn breath, from my sense of pointlessness – life up here is reduced to concern for myself mostly.

After three and a half hours I am up on the South Col. Peter Habeler and I settle ourselves in. We brew tea all afternoon as if drinking alone could substitute for the lack of oxygen apparatus. And in between, we doze for short periods, but always wake gasping for breath. Our lives now depend simply on our breathing faster and more deeply.

In the evening, our three Sherpas having long since returned down, Welsh cameraman, Eric Jones toils into camp. He will film us from the South Col. Now everything is ready for the critical day. The weather is fantastic and when, at 18.00 hours, I step outside the tent again after Base Camp had radioed to say that good weather was forecast, looking out to the West, I can see every peak silhouetted against the setting sun.

For me, It seems as if all my wishes, all the hopes inside my head, are beginning to distil into reality. I feel that deep inside I have all the reserves of energy that my curiosity and ambition could call for. All the criticisms that were levelled against our 'lunatic' attempt, no longer trouble me. I have been poised for a year now, ready to venture to the outer limit of my existence. Peter and I have known each other for fifteen years and we have perfect confidence in each other's mountaineering ability. That does much to set one's mind at rest.

'What day is it?'

'7th May,' answers Peter.

'7th May, 1978, South Col, 8,000 metres. Both together in the tent, about 8.30 in the evening,' I talk in clipped telegrammatic phrases into my miniature tape-recorder. Peter has left his behind in Camp III and listens to me.

'The bottom of the tent is stiff with ice, the cooker hums, and we are waiting for the last cup of tea, which we shall drink without sugar. . . . Peter, tell me, do you think we shall get up tomorrow, to the top?'

'I don't now. We'll get as far as Camp V for sure.'

'Maybe as far as the South Summit,' I say, 'but for the rest, it's in the lap of the Gods.'

'From here to the summit looks frantically far to me.'

'That may well be. But look at it this way — to the summit is another 800 metres, to Camp V, 500 metres. Today we climbed from an altitude of 7,200 metres to 8,000 metres, that is we climbed 800 metres — we knocked that off in a very short time and in far from favourable conditions — there was an incredible amount of new snow and a lot of fresh trail-breaking to do. I am positive that we can reach the South Summit.'

Peter considers this. 'True,' he says, 'that would not be any further than we did today, but it's all very much higher.'

I asked him whether he thought this made much difference.

'If we are going as well as today, and if we can make up our liquid deficiency, it should go all right. I'm optimistic in any case.'

'It will depend very much on the wind.'

'Certainly,' Peter answers, 'if the wind gets much stronger, we won't have the slightests chance.'

'What are your feet like — cold? Mine are.'

'Yes, like lumps of ice, right up to my knees.'

'Rub them together, that's what I do.'

'We must keep wiggling our toes.'

'Do you think this mountain of snow in the tent will be enough for early morning tea, or should I go and fetch in some more?'

'I think it should be enough. If you bring in any more, we'll be icebergs ourselves by morning.'

'You don't notice the lack of oxygen so much when you're lying down, do you?' I remark.

'No, that's because you're passive, not doing anything.'

'But everything you do do, like sitting up for instance, it makes me so, so tired. If it's no better in the morning, I don't know how things will turn out.'

'Pity we haven't got any more sugar, nor any more tea.'

'We slipped up there. Shall I make the water hot, or will lukewarm do?' I ask Peter. I'm making coffee.

'Don't make it so hot that we burn our tongues on it.'

'I'll leave it on a bit longer, and then I'll turn off the stove, otherwise we'll burn up all the oxygen.'

'We mustn't do that — we must be sparing with the air in here.'

'Wasn't it a marvellous evening tonight! Tremendous atmosphere — like a dream!'

'But it was bloody cold. It was at least 35 degrees below outside the tent today. You can never get yourself warm up here.'

'Well — it's a roomy enough tent. Even for your mice!'

'I won't have you say anything against my mice — they bring me luck.'

'Are you taking them with you tomorrow, or will you leave them here?'

'I don't know yet.'

'What is their significance? One for your wife and one for your little son?'
'Yes.'

'When I get to the top, shall I bury a couple of photos that were sent to me in Base Camp by some young ladies? They are not much use to me, I shall leave them up there.'

'And I shall photograph my two mice on the summit, but I won't leave them there, they come home with me.'

'The water must be warm enough by now,' I break into our fantasies.

'It's scalding my hands.'

'The whole thing would be simple, if we were using oxygen.'

'But we do agree to go on unless things get too bad.'

'Well I'll tell you this much — I'm turning back before I start going out of my mind!'

'Me too!'

No-one cares for the prospect that they might become a cabbage.

'If I notice any symptoms that could mean brain damage, I'm calling a halt.'

'If our speech gets affected or we notice any disturbance of balance or anything like that, then we must certainly turn back.'

'But if we haven't gone very far and it's only one of us that is affected, then the other ought to go on. Personally, I would very much like to get higher than Norton did in 1924.'

Peter's ambition is revealed in these words.

'So — more than 8,600 metres then?'

'Heights were a bit vague in those days.'

'And the North ridge cannot really be compared with this side.'

'Wolfi says that it's very steep near the top on both sides.'

'Hey — look at us! What would a housewife say if she could see all this gear and food mixed up with snow and ice — ice all over everything! She would go crazy.'

'Not only housewives. There are plenty of other people who think we are mad too.'

'Okay — true. But on a day like today when everything goes right — you feel well, you get a stupendous view — that all adds up to something really beautiful. Not to be missed. When I was coming up the Geneva Spur today, I fancied I could hear sounds — not music exactly, but a murmuring and humming, like being in a big empty church at night. Have you heard the mountain singing like this?' I ask Peter.

'No — I prefer to sing myself.'

'I don't sing much myself, but I enjoy listening,' I reply.

'Didn't you think I sang well at Camp I?'

'Yes — very well.'

'I soon gave it up as we got higher. I won't be singing any more till we are back in Base Camp.'

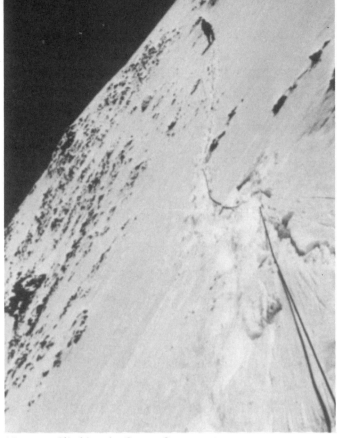

May 7 — Climbing the Geneva Spur.

'You only have to pay attention. There are places where the mountain emits sounds — not really a tune and no rhythm, just an even sort of humming.'

'Like lamas praying?'

'Yes, something of that sort. Perhaps they learned their singing from the mountains.'

'Let's hope there's no wind tomorrow,' Peter brings the converstation round to another topic. 'That's my biggest worry.'

'So long as it stays within limits and you can keep your face clear of snow and ice, it'll be alright. My feet are my biggest worry.'

'My toes have been ice cold today', Peter complains.

'I have difficulty with my left foot, because there aren't any toes on that one. It's not so easy to wriggle the stump. We spent a long time in the

Welsh climber, Eric Jones, a very experienced mountaineer who accompanied Peter Habeler and me to the South Col, from where he filmed our return to camp after the summit climb.

shade today. Would you like another mouthful of coffee? It's not hot any more, I'm afraid. Doesn't it get cold as soon as you sit up to cook, even though you only have your shoulders out of the sleeping bag.'

'I can't work out why it took Eric so long today — eight and a half hours from Camp III to Camp IV. The normal time is about six hours.'

'Yes, and we did it in three or four today. It's hard to imagine how cut off we are now — you can see how easily something could happen.'

'You can't expect any help from anyone here. If you can't keep going yourself, you're a goner.'

'A retreat down the rocks of the Geneva Spur would be far from easy.'

'I made my will before I came,' I say half-seriously.

'What I'm saying is — the Rock Band is dangerous.'

'The first time I was here, it was easy compared to today. But you could see what would happen with a little snow covering the smooth rock underneath. It calls for great care.'

'We haven't drunk our four litres today.'

'Ugh — it tastes horrible,' says Peter as I pass him the mug.

'But we must drink, Peter. The wind's getting up again.'

'It's worse higher up.'

'It can be an advantage if it blows the clouds away, but it's hard work fighting against it. If it doesn't snow in the night — I don't think it will — we'll leave early in the morning. I think we'll have a fine day tomorrow.'

'How about a beer before turning in?'

'Beer? You're joking! What I wouldn't give for a good cup of tea!'

'Well, if not beer then, how about a Glühwein at least.'

'Now, that would be nice. I could swill four litres of that with no trouble at all!'

'I've still got some strength left in my legs,' says Peter.

'Me too.'

'But I did have a terrible headache — I saw everything double.'

'This isn't the best place to start our climb tomorrow — the ideal would have been to have had a tent 200 metres higher. We could still have slept almost as well.'

'The night up here without oxygen will set us back.'

'Well we won't get any better, certainly, but I doubt if we'll deteriorate.'

'I don't know, Reinhold, I think we will. We're bound to. You can't sleep at 8,000 metres and expect to wake up just the same.'

'The last time I was here, after that night when the tent ripped, I got up and worked satisfactorily,' I say. 'I didn't even blow my top when Mingma wouldn't help me.'

'What was the matter with Mingma, was he sick?'

'I don't know, depressed more likely.'

We make another drink. As Ang Dawa said, we must drink plenty.

'That tastes bitter.'

'Frightful. But then it's not tea, just tepid water. Horrid.'

'We ought to try and get some sleep. I'm going to take a tablet.'

'I'm quite comfortable at the moment.'

'This really is quite a roomy tent.'

'I'm shivering again', I say and a minute later:

'I've got a cough, and pains under my left ribs. I had them yesterday as well, but not so badly.'

'They'll go away.'

'We'll have to carry heavy rucksacks tomorrow, as we must carry up reserve equipment and emergency food to Camp V. It wouldn't be a good idea to sleep at Camp V, I don't think, certainly not on the way down.'

'We'll be much faster coming down than going up. There will be no holding us back.'

'Now we must get some sleep.'

'Goodnight!'

But a little later we talk again.

'Hey! I can't do up my sleeping bag, the zip's frozen.'

'Do you always sleep with your hat on?'

'Yes,' replies Peter, 'always.'

'I never do.'

'You've got a thicker mop of hair.'

'That's why I wear it long.'

'I have to keep my hat on, otherwise I'd get headaches. Besides, you're head's always outside your sleeping bag. I couldn't get to sleep if I was too cold.'

'Obviously I have very good circulation in my head. It rarely feels the cold.'

'Well mine is delicate and I have to take care of it.!'

'That's understandable. Headaches are the only thing that bother you at altitude.'

'But I always manage to get rid of them — till now at least. Sometimes they're so bad they make me cross-eyed.' Peter says, 'then I can't talk or anything. But it only lasts half an hour then it goes away. I don't know why exactly. But it doesn't seem to affect my condition in any other way, I can still go on. I find heat hard to cope with, as well. If it gets up to 40 degrees or more, I start having trouble.'

'Heat does for me too. I've had it very hot on Nanga Parbat, on Hidden Peak too, and on Manaslu.'

The South Col completely covered in snow (7986m.). On the skyline our two tents.

'It's an advantage when there's two of you. Two is the ideal partnership — even if one or other gives out, it can usually still move.'

'At high altitude, a fast two-man team is the best safety factor.'

'That's obvious.'

'But you mustn't go so fast you have nothing in reserve for an emergency.'

'You have to know your capabilities.'

'We haven't done a lot together, but the things we have done have all been "Big Deals".'

'We've done some very fine things together, very fine.'

'If we go on talking much longer, we'll use up what little air there is left in this tent.'

'Goodnight!'

May 8. Shortly after 3 o'clock I begin to brew up some coffee. The huge lump of snow, as big as a man's head, that's been lying in the tent all night, I now break into pieces and put into the billy. It takes a long time before the water is warm. We drink in turns.

Still lying in our bags, we put on two pairs of socks and our inner boots. I try to warm up my stiffly-frozen outer boots between my legs. Dressing oneself at 8,000 metres is a protracted, breath-consuming struggle.

Between 5 and 6 o'clock we are finally ready. I am wearing silk underwear, then a fleecy pile undersuit, over that a complete down suit, with double-layer boots and gaiters of strong insulated neoprene; in addition, three pairs of gloves, two hats, storm goggles. In case of emergency, I have another pair of gloves, another hat and some more goggles in my rucksack.

Other than that I only carry the barest essentials — a length of rope, cameras, altimeter and a miniature tape recorder.

The hoar frost that crumbles off the inside of the tent, and the fact that my sleeping bag is rigidly frozen and my beard encrusted with ice, these things worry me less than they did. For the six weeks since we have been in Base Camp and above, these have been the facts of life and we have learned to live with such discomforts.

As Peter and I leave the tent, a squall of sleet hits us in the face. No! It can't be true — the sky is overcast, and there is only the barest strip of blue in the western sky. A sharp wind blows from the West and all the valleys are filled with mist. We are horrified, at first sight it looks as if we are beaten. But then, in the certain knowledge that we won't get another chance, I resolve that come-what-may, I shall still go as far as is humanly possible.

Peter still hesitates and I do my best to encourage him. 'We can always turn back if it gets too bad,' I say.

When one, like he, has a wife and child to consider, these decisions are very much harder to make. In one's subconscious mind a barrier of apprehension builds up quite naturally. It was the same for me when I was still married. But since I have been on my own again, I feel much easier in my mind when confronted with life or death situations. I just direct all my concentration towards the immediate problem — there is no before or after in my mind. I have nothing to lose except my own being — and I still live.

Despite our light rucksacks, we only make slow progress, then our pace quickens as we cross the crevasse-torn icefield. From the top of the ice, with the summit pyramid rearing directly in front of us, we can see for the first time Makalu out to the East, a massive granite peak. A huge fish-shaped cloud shrouds its summit. It is snowing there already and above us too, the wind is plastering everything with snow. The blue stripe on the horizon has disappeared. Endless emptiness of sky.

The snow beneath our feet is hard, and the teeth of our crampons bite into it well. But in this rarefied air, we have to frequently pause and rest. Higher up, where the drifting snow lies knee-deep, we frequently take to the ridge of rock, which, although it offers more difficult climbing, spares us the heavy work of breaking trail.

We converse in sign language. Every time Peter scratches a downward-pointing arrow in the snow, meaning 'We should turn back,' I reply with another pointing upwards — a discussion without words.

After four hours we reach the fifth high camp, which for us is only a staging post. Through an occasional break in the clouds, we can see the summit of Lhotse, which is level with the height at which we are now, and the sharp, finely-detailed ridge of Nuptse. We brew tea. Again I dictate a few impressions into my tape-recorder.

'Peter and I are at 8,500 metres in the last camp. Considering the conditions, we have reached here quite quickly but the weather is extremely bad. We don't know if we'll be able to go on or not. The snow is so deep, the work of breaking trail so back-breaking that we can't see very much hope of success. We are now trying to melt some snow to drink. Earlier today, when we saw that the weather was not as good as we had hoped for, we didn't bring our sleeping bags with us. We confined ourselves to the barest essentials so that we could move as quickly as possible. But now we are faced with a dilemma. To sit it out here and bivouac is a risk we should only take in the direst emergency. To go on — for we are still quite early — is an equally chancy business. Looking across at Makalu, sometimes wearing its cloud, sometimes clear, I sit inside the tent drinking my tea, and feel a little better. When we are climbing, talking is out of the question, dictating too, it would be too exhausting. We need every last bit of oxygen. It's practically certain we can't reach the summit. But we

On my first attempt, there were bare rocks on the South Col, but on our successful bid, there was more than a metre of snow in places. The tents were crushed under the weight of the snow.

could perhaps get a bit further. We'll try anyway. We are both in good heart and spirits. Even if this frightful weather should finally thwart us — we would still like to go a bit further.'

'Peter, what's the weather doing at the moment?' I ask from inside the tent.

'Still bad.'

'Is it snowing?' And without waiting for an answer, 'do you still want to try and get a bit further?'

'We can but try.'

'If we can keep up the speed we've been making and the snow is not too deep, we perhaps have a chance of getting as far as the South Summit in three or four hours. To get any further than that won't be easy.'

TO THE ULTIMATE POINT

After half an hour's rest, we continue our cautious way. Our climbing gets even slower. The snow is hard on the Chinese side, the East side, of the ridge. But soon we have to cross back to the Nepalese side when it gets too steep on the other. Frequently, we are wallowing in knee-deep snow. The steep rock spur to the left of the Hillary Route looks impossible, but we cross over to it nevertheless, and with the help of the points of our crampons, climb gingerly up the ledges. After every few steps, we huddle over our ice axes, mouths agape, struggling for sufficient breath to keep our muscles going. I have the feeling I am about to burst apart. As we get higher, it becomes necessary to lie down to recover our breath.

I am convinced now that we can reach the summit. There is still mountain in front of me so I keep on climbing. Automatically now, without thinking very much about it. We don't put the rope on until we're on the South Summit. A little later it pulls taut, and I turn around to see Peter taking off his rucksack. He wants to climb unfettered. I fumble in my rucksack for my camera and film him as he storms up. In front of us stretches an enormous snow ridge, the most beautiful ridge I have ever seen. Enormous cornices overhang it on the Tibetan Side. Towards Nepal, the angle is easier. The main summit still seems to be enormously distant. I tell myself – so far as my condition and concentration allows – that distances are deceptive at altitude. The thin air makes everything seem a long way away.

There is still my axe in my hand as a balancing aid. For hours without ceasing I plunge it into the snow or slide its point along the surface of the hard snow. It has become essential to my support. If I had no axe, I should simply fall down. As I anticipate reaching the summit, I dare not look ahead any more for I don't want to know how far there is still to go. Some of the time I feel full of purpose and self control, in the face of the storm; but at other moments I am filled with despair and try desperately to clench my teeth despite my wide-open, gasping mouth. The storm chases along the cornised summit ridge. Peter and I, trying our hardest to be

178

cautious in our movements, seem nevertheless to be unusually clumsy, and completely exhausted with the effort. There is insufficient air for talking in the summit zone, and as if we had pledged ourselves to silence, we continue our sign-language with the points of our axes in the snow. Each buffet of wind, hurling sleet into my eyes, leaves me more awkward than ever.

Apathy mingles with defiance. Is this the weather we must contend with all the way? Peter seems to be scribbling in the sky with his axe. I watch carefully and finally laugh as he reaches the end. In the South, Ama Dablam has broken clear of the clouds. it is bathed in sunlight. Perhaps the weather will yet hold.

I climb down into the notch that separates the South Summit from the Main Summit, and with a wary eye for the edge of the cornices, gingerly advance. Immediately below the Hillary Step, the most difficult pitch on the summit wall, I stop. Peter catches up; then I climb the steep step, resting three or four times on the way. Once up, we alternate leads. From the South a stiff wind blows crystals of ice into our faces. Between photographing and filming, I sometimes forget to pull my goggles back over my eyes.

Now, shortly after midday, and at a height of 8,800 metres, we can no longer keep on our feet while we rest. We crumple to our knees, clutching our axes, the points of which we have rammed into the hard snow. We are no longer belayed to one another, climbing quite independently, but each aware instinctively of the other's presence and confident that he is making no mistakes. The harmony of our partnership has grown up over the years through a repeated sharing of delicate situations. Now neither of us has any doubts about the other.

Breathing becomes such a strenuous business that we scarcely have strength left to go on. Every ten or fifteen steps we collapse into the snow to rest, then crawl on again. My mind seems almost to have ceased to function. I simply go on climbing automatically. The fact that we are on Everest, the highest mountain in the world, is forgotten — nor does it register that we are climbing without oxygen apparatus.

The only thing that lures me on is that little point ahead, where all the lines come together, the apex, the ultimate. The exertion now must be terrible, and yet I am insensible to it. It is as if the cortex of my brain were numb, as if only deeper inside my head is there something making the decisions for me. I don't want to go on. I crawl, I cough, but I am drawn on towards this farthest point as if it were some magnetic pole. Perhaps because to be there offers the only solution. My mind is disconnected, dead. But my soul is alive and receptive, grown huge and palpable. It wants to reach the very top so that it can swing back into equilibrium.

The last few metres up to the summit no longer seem so hard. On reaching the top, I sit down and let my legs dangle into space. I don't have to climb any more. I pull my camera from my rucksack and, in my down mittens, fumble a long time with the batteries before I have it working properly. Then I film Peter. Now, after the hours of torment, which indeed I didn't recognise as torment, now, when the monotonous motion of plodding upwards is at an end, and I have nothing more to do than breathe, a great peace floods my whole being. I breathe like someone who has run the race of his life and knows that he may now rest for ever. I keep looking all around, because the first time I didn't see anything of the panorama I had expected from Everest, neither indeed did I notice how the wind was continually chasing snow across the summit. In my state of spiritual abstraction, I no longer belong to myself and to my eyesight. I am nothing more than a single, narrow, gasping lung, floating over the mists and the summits.

Only after I have drawn a couple of deep breaths do I again sense my legs, my arms, my head. I am in a state of bright, clear consciousness, even if not fully aware of where I am. In the instant that Peter joins me and flings his arms around me, we both burst into tears. We lie in the snow, shaking with emotion. The camera is cast aside. Our tears express everything we feel after such a concentrated effort of will, they are our release.

We lie next to each other, there on the summit, lost to oblivion. And so we remain for some while, up to our necks in drifted snow, mouths open, recovering. When I do stand up, Peter stares at me as if he wants to impress my face on his memory, as if indeed he doesn't recognize my face at all.

Standing now in diffused light, with the wind at my back, I experience suddenly a feeling of completeness — not a feeling of having achieved something or of being stronger than everyone who was ever here before, not a feeling of having arrived at the ultimate point, not a feeling of supremacy. Just a breath of happiness deep inside my mind and my breast. The summit seemed suddenly to me to be a refuge, and I had not expected to find any refuge up here. Looking at the steep, sharp ridges below us, I have the impression that to have come later would have been too late. Everything we now say to one another, we only say out of embarrassment. I don't think any more. As I pull the tape recorder, trancelike, from my rucksack, and switch it on wanting to record a few appropriate phrases, tears again well into my eyes. 'Now we are on the summit of Everest,' I begin, 'it is so cold that we cannot take photographs. . . .' I cannot go on, I am immediately shaken with sobs. I can neither talk nor think, feeling only how this momentous experience changes everything. To reach only a few metres below the summit would have required the same amount of effort, the same anxiety and burden of sorrow, but a feeling like this, an eruption of feeling, is only possible on the summit itself.

Everything that is, everything I am, is now coloured by the fact that I have reached this special place. The summit — for the time being at least — is the simple intuitive answer to the enigma of life.

There is no sense of triumph, no feeling of potency, only of being, and of thankfulness towards my partner. Everything else is forgotten in a wave of happiness. For a short while all reason is lost and emotion holds sway; my feelings have taken over and will no longer be resisted. Peter and I don't speak; we take a few photographs. All at once Peter feels a tightness in his fingers, just as he had done earlier on the Hillary Step. Cramp? Or might it signify something much worse? He remembers the Sherpa who a few days earlier had to be carried down the mountain half-paralysed following a stroke brought on by exertion at great altitude. Peter grows very uneasy and wants to get down.

He starts back alone, without the rope. I see him reach the South Summit whilst I am still talking into my tape recorder. I unpack a film cassette and, instead of throwing away the wrapping paper, I toss the film over the edge. Only as it disappears do I realise what I have done. I take a second cassette from my rucksack and load it into the camera. After so much concentration, I am again overcome with emotion. I take a deep

Peter Habeler and I took turns to break the trail. Seen here close to the high Ridge Camp (V), which we did not use.

breath, then I drop everything back into the rucksack, one thing at a time — recorder, cine-camera, still-camera — I tie the spare batteries onto the Chinese summit emblem and squat down again. I am no less aware than I was, but I am now able to think about the business of going down.

It is only early in the afternoon, but the light gives the impression that it is already evening, and I feel as if I have been sitting on the summit for a long, long time — a few hours even. And yet I am still reluctant to leave; descent, it seems, was not any part of my plan at all. In all the preparations I made for this climb — and they stretch back over several years — I have always only concerned myself with getting up, or at most, with being on the summit. I have never given a thought to going back down again. I have now to summon every last ounce of resolve, and make myself stand up and leave this place.

I say to myself — 'Now, you must climb down, but slowly. Take care on the Hillary Step. Remember how exposed it is, so go carefully! In a few hours you will be down where the air is richer, and then it will go a lot easier.' I force myself to look ahead, to look down, so that I can climb down. Then with one last touch of the length of rope and the batteries hanging on the tripod, I set off after Peter in the hope that he is waiting for me on the South Summit.

Despite myself, I turn around just a few steps below the top, almost sad to be leaving. I feel I belong sitting there and regret that I must depart without going back just one more time. There are fine scratches in the snow where Peter went down, the marks of his crampons. Unlike the ascent, I now seem able to think as I go. When I pause to rest, I have no difficulty in keeping on my feet, and can stretch and breathe deeply. Sudden realisations come to me — looking at the Nuptse Ridge, swimming in mist, I am struck with a deep sense of loss. It dawns on me that this is a sad day for me. Something irrevocable and final has taken place. My long-cherished dream is gone. The mountain from which I descend is now but a shattered illusion. . . .

I look back along the summit ridge, I see the footprints in the snow, I feel the axe in my right hand. All these things belong to me; all these things are part of me. I reach the South Summit half an hour after Peter, but he is no longer there. He must have been desperate to get down. As I plod slowly on through the deep snow, letting one foot fall in front of the other, I can see the marks of a slide away to my left on the steep 50 degree snow slope. The tracks disappear somewhere in cloud. And I realise with a jerk — for logical thought has now returned — that that East Flank falls away for 4,000 metres and is riven with crevasses. Once past the South Summit, it remains only to go down. Down, down, one step in front of the other, face to the valley, trampling the snow, planting the crampons, unwavering concentration — but down. That is all that is left. I take one last look back at Everest summit. I have really climbed it after dreaming about it for so long. I experience a little thrill of pride.

There is no trace of Peter, in fact hardly anything to be seen even of our ascent; it would seem to be a totally different mountain from the one we climbed; that has seemingly vanished into the mist. Yet I feel Peter is still close, as if the mountain and Peter and I, were one. Unthinkable to have one without the others. As I peer ahead for a sight of him, I realise how our friendship has grown. I am not annoyed that he did not wait. Only concerned for him.

Just below the South Summit, I see the slide marks again, just like those disappearing into the mist on the Chinese side of the ridge; but the possibility of a catastrophe is not yet in my mind. I think only how close death

On May 8, between 1 and 2 in the afternoon, Peter Habeler and I reached the summit of Mount Everest. We photographed each other beside the summit tripod (right), the surveying pole put on top in 1975 by a large Chinese expedition. Since then, the top of the pole on which a flag had hung, has broken off. The nine Chinese who reached the summit did so with a minimal use of artificial oxygen. During rest-pauses they took doses of oxygen, as their film shows and as also is described in their report and book. Peter Habeler and I were the first to go from Base Camp to summit without once breathing oxygen from a cylinder. The next double-page shows Peter Habeler at about 8,800 metres (large photo) and after the Hillary Step immediately below the summit, with Lhotse in the background.

A tiny triangle, Everest rises above the mighty Nuptse-Lhotse Wall. I attempted this wall unsuccessfully in 1975, At that time I was not able to get a direct view of the highest mountain in the world. I only really saw it in 1977 during a flight over the Everest summit — at that time about 9,000 metres without oxygen and without ill-effects and got an idea of its scale. After the expedition's first summit success with oxygen and the climbers were back in Base Camp celebrating (below: in the centre Expedition Leader Wolfgang Nairz, near him Sherpa-Sirdar Ang Phu and Horst Bergmann films in the foreground Robert Schauer) Peter Habeler and I still doubted our chances. We knew that the Englishman, Norton, had forced his way to 8,600 metres without oxygen way back in 1924. But what we didn't know was whether people could still survive higher than that. We knew we would need to be fast, in any event, if we were not to come back with some brain damage. We put our confidence in our light equipment, the condition we had built up over the years, and instinctive climbing sense.

still is to me. I follow the ridge down, keeping to the right of the tracks, almost proud of the apprehension that prevents me from following Peter's example and sliding down on the seat of my pants. I look forward to catching him up and hearing from him the story of his bizarre descent. Again I have the conviction that he is the only person who could have shared this experience with me. I need not feel too concerned on his behalf. Peter does not make mistakes.

Here now I have discovered how alone I am. Loneliness seems to be reaching out and enveloping me from all sides. There is nothing but emptiness far and wide. The great sky above me is formless, with no scurrying clouds. Just above the spot on the ridge where the fifth high camp is situated, the slide-marks suddenly end. Peter must obviously have crossed further over to the right onto the South-east flank, and continued his glissade down this too, to the South Col. Tramping past the deserted camp alone, I nod to myself, as if to convince myself 'You have really done it.'

I frequently stop to wait for the mist to blow over. Then below me I can make out two yellow specks, the tents. Nothing else. Though I cannot see him, I am sure that Peter is in the camp already, or if not, will soon be there.

When I am tired, I simply plump down into the snow. At long last, within me, I feel a tight concentration of joy at our success. And this pleasure spreads and grows and seeps through everything as I sit there in the snow, oblivious of my tiredness. At last a mountain on which I don't 'anticipate'. Content to do only what I really do do. Even 100 metres below the summit I was still thinking ahead, anticipating that I would soon be up there. Now I no longer plan; now, it is only the here and now that matters. Beyond that, I cannot think nor yet do I wish to. I have no doubts that I can reach the camp, but I don't allow myself to think about it yet — what little there is to think about, that is, like crawling into a warm sleeping bag.

I am so tired that I can't hurry my thoughts along. I cross the last snow slope above the South Col like a sleepwalker. Whenever I sit down to rest, I automatically look at my watch but I don't register what time it is. Now, with the last few steps to the tent, I have the feeling of having done something once that I will never more achieve again. The tents offer a sense of security that is quickly lost in the desolation of the South Col. Only inside the tent does it really feel safe. Peter is there, and Eric too. As I crawl into the tent and see Peter, I feel triumphant: we have done it!

And we shall climb other eight-thousanders without oxygen also! I am now so overcome with happiness that I even forget to pause for breath. My excited conversations over the radio with Base Camp are only occasionally punctuated by deep intakes of breath.

And in between I turn to Peter: 'Tell me again what you thought after the Hillary Step, when you were no longer yourself?'

'After the Hillary Step, it was no longer me that was climbing — it felt like someone else on the steep face, climbing for me.'

'Peter — If we left between 5 and 6 this morning, we must have been on the summit at something like 1 or 2 o'clock. It must have taken us eight hours to do the climb. You came down in one hour — that is crazy, really crazy! I took an hour and a half, or an hour and threequarters.'

'Shall we sleep in the same positions as last night?'

'Yes, yes that's — fine.'

'I don't need to cook so much today.'

'Tell me — this morning, did you believe we'd do it?'

'I wasn't a hundred per cent sure.'

'When were you absolutely sure, then, that we would?'

'On the South Summit.'

'On the South Summit I began to shoot more and more film. For a long time I didn't know if it was you I had in the picture, or a crevasse, the wind was blowing so hard. There was just this black blur and a wild storm. It looked tremendous. Did you notice?'

'I didn't notice.'

To start with, we are both in incredibly high spirits, euphoric. But as the evening progresses my eyes begin to ache, and Peter's ankle, that he knocked earlier, starts to swell badly. My eyes get dimmer by the minute and the pain becomes excruciating. My first fear is that I am going blind. We have been warned that nerve damage is not infrequent at altitude, and irreversible brain damage possible. But then I feel as if I have sand in my eyes and realize that I am merely snowblind.

191

There follows a fearful night. I have the feeling that in place of my eyes, there are now just two gaping sockets. I keep sitting up and pressing my fists into my eyes, weeping and crying out. The tears help to soothe the pain and Peter comforts me as if I were a small child.

The descent the next day, *May 9*, from the South Col down to Camp II is a nightmare. Snowblind, as I am, I stumble behind Peter. I cannot see more than a metre in front of me.

On *May 10* we stagger back into Base Camp like a pair of invalids. We are still, according to our friends at least, out of our minds.

Our undertaking, we know, could just as easily have turned out very differently. We don't think about that. In the Death Zone, success and disaster run as closely together as storm and lull, hot and cold.

Of the seven times I have attempted an eight-thousand metre peak, I have only four times reached the summit. Nowadays I appreciate that — as in all true adventure — the path between the summit and the grave is a very narrow one indeed. That there is no way of telling in advance which way it will finish, doesn't mean that life up there is any more significant than elsewhere, but it is certainly more intense.

AN EIGHT-THOUSANDER, A HOSPITAL AND A WINE CELLAR

'Congratulations, Bulle! You made it! Bravo!'

'High time you did!' We all congratulate the third summit party. It pleased everyone that Bulle, our expedition doctor, had now also reached the summit on *11th May*. For Reinhard Karl, a student from Heidelberg and photo-journalist to our expedition, there is also much friendly sympathy, but Bulle's success thrills me as much as my own.

'It was obvious you'd get up, it was only a question of how and when.'

'We had terrible conditions, such deep snow. We didn't think we'd ever do it!'

'I didn't believe it until we were at Camp V; then I saw we would have enough oxygen,' Bulle's broad face creased into a grin.

'How long were you on top?'

'I can't say: I was coughing so much I couldn't breathe. I only used one and a half cylinders as far as the summit and back,' says Reinhard Karl, who led most of the climb.

'How anyone can climb it without oxygen is a mystery to me!'

'Yes — 8,500 metres is one thing, that I can imagine, but not the rest.'

'No it's a complete mystery to me — you only have to take the apparatus off for three or four minutes on the summit and you're clapped out.'

'You get dizzy.'

'Wheeze like a cow!'

'Did you have any trouble with your masks?'

'None at all.'

'We came down by the steep rocks, half an hour it takes from the last camp back to the South Col.'

'Tell me, Doctor,' I imitate a reporter, 'what are your ambitions in life?'

'An eight-thousander, a wine cellar . . . and a hospital!'

'The eight-thousander you have already, the cellar won't be long.'

'It must be deep underground so that I can keep wine for twenty or thirty years. And each year I will drink to celebrate the eight-thousanders.'

'Did you see Peter's slide-marks?'

'No, but I can imagine it. I wouldn't glissade down from the South Summit myself.'

'Perhaps it was an effect of the altitude — a certain diminution of brain function.'

'Or fear — "quick! quick! out of the way!"'

'Come on, let's all get down to Base Camp and eat something sensible.'

'This morning when we started, it didn't seem so mad then. But I had this terrible feeling — I certainly didn't feel we could do it, but I wanted to put everything I had into getting as high as possible. I knew it would be a very hard day and would demand my utmost. In fact, it went better than I expected,' recounts Reinhard.

'We were on the summit at midday, and by three o'clock were back on the South Col.'

'We were delighted when we heard.'

'It's only really hit me tonight, once I got back to Camp II.'

'It's like re-running a film, everything that's happened, everything I saw, and so on.'

'You were concentrating too much on the summit up there, I expect.'

'That's right — that's all I was thinking about, getting there. Photography was the last thing — it didn't interest me at all.'

'It was the same with me — everything took second place to getting up.'

'I didn't really come to till we got back to Camp II. It all went so quickly. I can remember changing the oxygen cylinders, that was at 8,600 metres. I remember saying to myself, "My God, here I am at 8,600 metres — it doesn't seem possible." It was as if I was in a trance, I changed the cylinders and then I remember being on the South Summit and seeing the Main Summit and I thought: "Now we've only got to trot along there — it won't take long." And we did. We climbed up this Everest and the summit wasn't anything special, there were these last slopes and then we saw this Chinese tripod-thing and realised: "Now we are up".'

'What did you leave up there?' I ask Reinhard.

'We brought your stuff down — the yellow rope. Me — I left crampon straps behind.'

'I think it's hilarious that whatever you leave up there, the next person brings down again! Did you leave my batteries hanging on the pole?'

'Yes.'

'We took photos for the family album — "Me on top of Everest". It's a great thing to have been there, but a bit of an anticlimax in a way. I was like that after I'd climbed the Eiger North Face, too, disappointed.'

'That's because you've lost your goal — it's no longer there in front of you. Isn't that it?'

'Yes, that's it exactly. You have put so much into it — read everything, dreamed about nothing else. Then climbing down over the South Col, I suddenly thought, "My God, you were on Everest!" It all went so smoothly, nothing went wrong, no frostbite, nothing. It was like clockwork.'

'We've all been lucky.'

'It's almost unbelievable how smoothly it's all gone.'

'Hello! How are you?' the Sherpas greet Bulle, their Doctor-Sahib.
'Fantastic!'

'I could eat a horse! There was nothing left to eat at all in Camp II.'

'Success will change your life! Your mother and father are probably at
this moment being besieged by reporters wanting all your baby pictures,'
someone ribs Reinhard.

' "Little did he then know, that one day . . ." that's what it will say under
them in all the papers!' jokes another.

'Something like that perhaps,' replies Reinhard Karl. 'Our summit climb
was very stylish, anyway. Bulle was ahead on the ridge because I was
having difficulty with my set. And he waited for me a couple of metres
from the top, then we climbed up to the summit arm-in-arm.'

'I must have something more to drink, before I can eat anything,' says
Bulle before going off to take a look at his patients.

'Are you all recovered — all okay?'

'I've only got the 'flu — I won't bother you with that,' replies Hanns
Schell.

'I've got some fairly strong "phantom-pains" in my toes,' I put in, 'I
don't usually feel anything in my amputated digits, that's something new.
No swelling — just a dull ache — there — where there's nothing but air.'

'How long have you had them? And your snowblindness?'

'In Camp II, the night after coming down. I took a painkiller and slept
alright. About 5 next morning we were on our way and it was much
better. I still can't see anything sharply.'

'Practically everyone has had trouble with their eyes.'

'Because we had the wrong sort of goggles?'

'We've got 95 per cent absorbent glass, but what's the good of that if
we don't always wear the glasses.'

'We came down slowly, like that time on McKinley,' Bulle continues,
'I knew it would never happen again, that this was the highest mountain
I'll ever climb, I thought I would enjoy it and come down slowly and
comfortably.'

'The view from the South Summit down the East Face is pretty impressive,' Reinhard cuts in.

'I told myself not to think about the cornices or anything — just to climb.'

'But always keeping far enough over to the left.'

'Well — it wasn't always possible to see them properly because of the mist up there.'

Bulle still feels the need to talk.

'The Hillary Step — for twenty-five years I've read what a nasty spot it is, but it's a joke really.'

'I can't imagine how some people can need twelve hours to reach the summit from the last camp.'

'And climbing the broken rock is not that easy with 10 or 15 centimetres of new snow on it. You need to have considerable alpine experience. It couldn't be done by a numbskull,' Peter asserts.

'No — this certainly isn't an easy mountain.'

'Well it's a steep one, anyway.'

'And what about your world sensation — Everest without oxygen?'

'The news has already gone all round the world,' smiles Peter.

'When you think about it — I was like a patient on a heart-lung machine when I was on the South Summit. It's true — with the cylinders turned on!' says Karl.

'And did you really get dizzy on the summit, Bulle?' I ask.

'No more than you would expect after pumping your body full of oxygen and then taking off the mask.'

'There was a storm on the South Col this morning.'

'A bad one?'

'Yes, tremendous squalls.'

'We can't know exactly how Franz and Josl will stand it. It's their first time up there and it's blowing pretty strongly.'

'Bulle, what struck you as the hardest bit?' asks Peter.

'Above Camp V it was clear that we would have some trouble since I would have to climb vertical ice pitches,' Reinhard answers right away.

'And you know, with two cylinders on your back, you don't move very fast either,' Bulle adds.

'We changed cylinders at 8,600 metres, when we were back on the

Reinhard Karl, one of the best German rock climbers—a photographer and a student. He became the first German to climb Everest.

rocks. Out to the left, that was quite good.'

'You should try the Habeler-Method of descent, that speeds things up a bit.'

'I think the Habeler-Method will go down in mountaineering history.'

'Only to be used in thick mist,' laughs one.

'We collected rocks,' Reinhard relates, 'I was getting anxious and said, "Come on, let's get down", but Bulle just said, "Look at the rocks", and starts taking off his rucksack. I beg him to come on down, I was getting cold.'

'That's the lack of oxygen,' says Oswald Ölz.

'Bulle, when you were up on top, did you have your mask off a lot of the time. How did it affect you?'

'You became slower and slower.'

'That's what comes of withdrawing the oxygen suddenly.'

'You have an uncontrollable urge to put the thing back on and be able to breathe again, to hear the comforting sounds of the valves as they let out a stream of life from the cylinder.'

'The big difference is between 8,000 and 8,500 metres. Between 8,500 metres and the summit, you gradually come up to the critical limit.'

'The critical level is over 9,000 metres in my opinion', I say.

'Bulle and I always maintain that Hermann Buhl would never have used oxygen, ever!' I am utterly convinced of this.

'Buhl had extraordinary endurance. He would have kept going till he dropped.'

'You mustn't forget, Buhl was on Nanga Parbat. Several people have done that without oxygen since.'

'Fifteen perhaps.'

'I don't care.'

'But look at what he did on Nanga! 1,300 metres of altitude in a single push. I still think that to get to 8,000 metres on Nanga is harder than 8,500 on Everest.'

'Because it's climatically more difficult, do you mean, or what?'

'No, it just is. The higher the mountain, the easier it is to get to a certain height.'

'Psychologically, or why?'

'I don't know why, exactly, I just feel it is so.'

Meanwhile we are all very worried about Josl Knoll and Franz Oppurg, who are making the final attempt on the summit.

'They've got enough gas.'

'I did tell them they were on their own completely. All the camps are depleted now, they daren't make any mistakes. They should always try to radio at the usual time — that way we'll keep in touch with them.'

'Franz looked tired to me,' says Bulle.

'Did you tell him that it's difficult to come down from the South Col without oxygen,' asks Nairz anxiously.

'I told him to always have it with him.'

'They have enough oxygen,' Reinhard says.

'For night-time as well?' Wolfi nods. Our minds are set at rest.

'Not that they're likely to slip, but the traverse is not so easy.'

Reinhard Karl (left) and Oswald Ölz reached the summit on May 10. They made use of the oxygen cylinders Peter Habeler and I had left on the South Col in case of emergency.

'I very nearly flew down,' says Reinhard.

'I lost my footing once, it wasn't so bad,' someone adds.

'Bulle, are you going to have some visiting cards printed now, for the hospital or your practice? "Bulle, Dr Oswald Ölz, Conqueror of Everest".'

'Plus — "Honorary Lecturer".'

'Plus — "Professional Vorarlberger".'

'Sure!' Bulle guffaws loudly.

'Kilimanjaro — he didn't manage, but Everest — yes!' Someone says.

'He didn't have oxygen that time, that's why,' Wolfi laughs.

'He was in Nairobi beforehand and spent all night on the town,' someone chaffs.

'I have yet to climb Aconcagua,' Bulle adds.

'We'll have a fortnight's holiday in Mendoza, where they have the tenderest steaks in the world and marvellous wine, and we'll take time off to nip up Aconcagua in between,' says Nairz.

Bulle praises his partner, and Reinhard is enthusiastic about Bulle.

'I must say it went well. When Bulle was tired, I dragged him along.'

'But when it came to evening, Reinhard just climbed into his sleeping bag and wouldn't do anything. He didn't melt a single lump of snow. Never mind,' Bulle turns to Reinhard, 'I did it for you in return for all your hard route-finding.'

'It boils down to the fact that a climbing partnership has to work in harmony, just like a marriage.!'

'It couldn't have worked better!'

'Perfect harmony, that's the thing!'

'When one of you is feeling weak, the other takes over.'

'You were freezing all the time. I could have spent another two hours on the summit, but you kept saying — "Come on, let's go now, come on",' says Bulle ruefully.

'How long did you stay on up there, Bulle?'

'We came down together — once I managed to prise Bulle from the stones, we both came down together.'

AN EMPTY VOID

It is several days since we have been back in Base Camp. The atmosphere is much more relaxed although the last summit pair are still somewhere between the South Col and the Summit. Sometimes when I wake at night, a feeling of emptiness sweeps over me, the emptiness that is all that is left after my dream of climbing Everest without oxygen, has been realised. This hole, this ache, has not yet been replaced by a new dream, a new ambition. Also, I begin to be haunted by everyday worries. I know that in a few weeks we shall be back in Europe, back to civilization.

May 16. The last summit team of Franz Oppurg and Josl Knoll return. Here in Base Camp there is an air of decampment already. Josl Knoll who is a 54-year-old pensioner with a bad leg, was unable to get to the top, he had to give up at 8,500 metres. Franz Oppurg climbed on alone. 'On the steep slope I was struggling madly through the new snow,' says Franz Oppurg, the effects of the strain still showing in his face.

'Wasn't your oxygen set working properly?'

'I don't know if I was breathing wrongly, or whether I had it wrongly adjusted. But I took an incredibly long time getting up to Camp V,' explains Josl Knoll, who was robbed of the summit only by a defect in his oxygen apparatus.

'What a shame!'

Everyone is very sympathetic.

'Thanks to this stupid gammy leg, I have no feeling in my stiff foot.'

'In Camp V it must have been grim without a sleeping bag?'

'Franz sat up all night in the tent, wearing his mask.'

'Wasn't there room to lie down?'

'No, he had the mask and kept it running at setting "1" all night.'

'Didn't you have sleeping sets?'

'He had the big mask, and I just sat there.'

'Without oxygen?'

'I tried the sleeping mask first of all. But I had the cooker standing between my feet, and it was on. It was very unpleasant for the warmth of the cooker was drawn up right over me. The tube kept falling out as often as I repaired it. So, I gave up and said to myself — sleep without it, it won't matter. And I didn't notice any real difference whether I was breathing the sleeping oxygen or not. So mostly I didn't bother with it. That's how I sat — all night long.'

'No oxygen.'

'That's more or less what it amounted to. In the morning I felt fine sitting down. But when I crawled out of the tent, everything just span round. I realised something wasn't quite right but thought I would probably pick up alright once I took oxygen again. My set was simply iced right up. I wanted to connect it, but there was no oxygen coming through. I didn't know why. I tested the mask and tubing, switched on — nothing. Completely iced up. Then I looked at the regulator. If we had had an expert with us, I expect it could have been made to work.'

'We've only got two experts in the whole team — Bulle and Horst.'

'And Bulle only gave me the one set.'

'It seized up before when we were going to the South Col. Even though I had a 3,000 PSI cylinder, when I was just above the Yellow Band, the stuff ran out.'

'Was it a French cylinder?'

'Yes, a three-thousander. Just above the Yellow Band it went — nothing! No more oxygen at all! When I met Bulle, I had used 1,000 PSI — and I thought to myself — Careful, I must go easy so that I can manage on the remaining 2,000.'

'Had the gas escaped somehow?'

'Probably. But what could I do up there? I tinkered with it, then I struggled on. I had never been at altitude before, Franz was well ahead, although at first he had been much slower than I. Then, at the beginning of the Geneva Spur, where the route goes amongst the rocks, it happened to him too. His oxygen gave out. He was a bit ahead, as I said, but he didn't go any further, took off his rucksack and sat down and waited till I caught up. It took me two hours to reach him. We asked ourselves what we should do. Do you know what, I said, I'll leave my rucksack here, go up to the South Col, fetch two cylinders and sets, come back and our problems will be over. So I toiled up to the South Col, into the tent — and couldn't find any connecting pieces. There was nothing for it but to pick up two cylinders and climb back down. While all this was going on it had got bitterly cold, and dark too. That must have been when I connected the apparatus up wrong — it didn't work at any rate. Luckily, however, I've got Bulle's set in my rucksack, so I get that out and connect that up and all goes well till I get up over the Geneva Spur. But on the last bit, where the fixed ropes are, I could feel I wasn't getting any more oxygen again. So now I crawl up without it, just like before. It was about 10.30 when we finally got to the tent.'

'That's terrible!'

'Yes — so at 10.30 we got up to the South Col, found new oxygen and cooked, all without incident. We slept soundly that night, didn't take any sleeping pills, didn't have any headaches. The next day we said: "What shall we do now? Rest first and then in the afternoon go up to Camp V and bivouac there. That should be possible".'

'Reinhold had already told us that it was quite snowed up and that we should have to dig it out. So we went up to Camp V, it took us about four hours.'

'Was your apparatus functioning then or not?'

'I didn't have any problems. I thought to myself, I'm going quite comfortably, so long as I don't make too many demands on the oxygen. Then ten metres below Camp V, the oxygen ran out. In the morning this wouldn't be a problem, but it had already grown very cold. I continued using the sleeping set. I thought I might yet be able to recover, but without oxygen at this altitude, it's simply not possible. In any case, I had to say goodbye to the summit.'

'Sleeping is no problem, I know that from the South Col, but in the morning one needs longer to get going again.'

'I simply wasn't getting any oxygen to get going on. I fished all the ice out of the mask and the tubing. I tried to find the fault, but I didn't get any air through at all.'

'And after that, what happened?'

'After that, we said to ourselves — Franz should now go on alone. It

When Peter Habeler and I climbed down from the summit (right — descent over the Lhotse Face) we were not then fully aware what we had achieved with this mask-free ascent of Everest. In our fatigue, there was no sense of success. Added to this we were both suffering — Peter from a damaged Achilles tendon: I with snow-blindness: we both also had light frostbite on our fingers and our noses were peeling. We knew that our push to the topmost point without the aid of oxygen sets, would provoke discussion since most climbers and almost all doctors had prophesied utter failure. That it caused such a world-wide sensation, I suppose can be traced back to the fact that we have broken some taboo. In the Middle Ages we would have been burned as heretics, today we are greeted with disbelief, for as long at least until we can produce evidence of our climb, or until mask-free ascents become the rule.

When the evening glow has died from all other summits, the last pinnacle of Everest remains rosy (preceding double-page). It is this topmost pinnacle that surpasses all other mountains in the world. The human dimension has always interested me on my expeditions, and so too with Everest and my hopes for an oxygen-free ascent. Edmund Hillary and Tenzing Norgay, who reached the summit on May 29, 1953 (presumably the first to do so: Mallory and Irvine disappeared after their summit bid in 1924) did so with the application of such aids as were available to them. Their ambition was to stand on the summit: mine was the adventure towards spiritual and ethical self-examination. We both succeeded — Hillary with his Everest summit (above): I with a new measure of myself. Therefore there can be no jealousy between us. Hillary was one of the first to congratulate Peter and me (below, standing between me and Peter Habeler, right).

would have been more sensible to have stayed at the South Col and recovered properly, then to have got started early the following morning and gone on two cylinders. I hadn't had any trouble until I got to the fifth camp. We climbed in quite normal time, were in good form and had no problems generally. Probably it was the night. Ah well — nothing can be done about it. What's past is past.'

'Josl, it's past for us too. We missed our chance as well,' says Manni, who is still bitter because the summit was denied him.

'I'm glad to be safely down again,' Josl says and adds:

'The Gods were against me, even from the beginning.'

'Once I left Camp V, I knew I would get up,' burst out Franz Oppurg, his eyes still shining with the excitement.

'You can never be quite certain one can do it, when you are dependent on a piece of apparatus. But I was fairly sure. It wasn't so different from the Alps. There are hundreds of ridges like that in the Alps.'

'And how did you feel on the summit?'

'I was in good form, I didn't feel very much at all, thanks to the oxygen.'

'Did you take any pictures?'

'I took a round of panoramic shots, and I got a bit cross with my camera in so doing; it was fairly iced up. Honestly, it didn't feel very different than if I had done a solo climb in the Alps.'

'Perhaps it hasn't really hit you yet?'

'Well, I was perfectly aware that I was standing on the highest spot in the world, and that I was alone . . . but I was very controlled about it.'

'Did you cry?'

'Well, yes, a little. But I've always tried never to let my feelings get the better of me.'

'Were you able to see any of the lower mountains?'

'Oh yes — it was very clear, just windy, very windy. It was like a dream, and it wasn't cold either.'

'I'm very pleased you got up — you deserved it', I say to Franz who had worked hard throughout.

'Well I must say that towards the end I had rather given up hope and didn't think I stood a chance. I was so often ill during the expedition, I had

Franz Oppurg climbed alone to the summit from 8,500 m., where Josl Knoll had to stay behind because of a defect in his oxygen apparatus. The picture shows Peter Habeler below the South Summit.

a lot of trouble with my stomach. Even on the day we left here, I had to stop to be sick.'

'And did it get easier further up?'

'Oh yes, with oxygen, and it also gave me a boost when we met you coming down and knew that you had made the summit. I found my strength after that.'

'Bulle was certainly very pleased with himself!'

'Yes it bucked me up too.'

211

'Everest is no easy mountain. It is not easy,' says Franz reflectively.

'But all the same, it is not hard, is it?' I put in.

'No — but it can suddenly turn very nasty.'

'Too true! If you get a storm at Camp V or on the summit ridge.'

'And the temperature drops abruptly to minus 40 degrees.'

'This is the first time you've been on an expedition — how do you feel about it. You're an extreme climber — do you like expedition mountaineering or would you rather. . . .'

'I wouldn't want to go on another expedition of this sort. I have often said I wouldn't go on an expedition like this again, when you are reliant on apparatus or on outsiders, like the Sherpas.'

'In Nepal the Sherpas are so pleasant. I wouldn't like to climb an eightthousander here without Sherpas. I'm happy to let them carry the equipment for me as far as possible.'

'Would you prefer to go on a small expedition to a relatively easy route, or rather go to some fierce virgin wall, something like the Eigerwand but three times as big?' I enquire.

'The last would suit me better.'

'I believe that difficulties at altitude over a level of 7,000 metres or so, are more of a decisive factor than oxygen equipment.'

'Sure. But then it's up to me.'

'Annapurna South Face or Lhotse South Face could leave you standing. You really can't rely on being able to climb properly at 7,500 metres. It can take five hours to climb ten metres, and if you make some risky move that doesn't come off, you are morally finished. At least, that's how it is with me.'

'Yes, it's quite possible. Was that your experience on the Lhotse Face?'

'I am quite sure that in the case of all the big faces that have defeated us, it wasn't the lack of oxygen apparatus that turned us back, but simply the height of 7,500 metres. It's encountering technical difficulties at that level that does it.'

'It's the Gasherbrum Wall that attracts me like mad,' Robert Schauer joins in the conversation.

'More than the K2 Pillar?'

K2 with the South Pillar in profile on the right. This is my next big objective. Robert Schauer will be a member of my team, but Peter Habeler won't be coming this time.

'Personally, the K2 Pillar doesn't appeal to me like the Gasherbrum IV Wall.'

'It's the Lhotse Face that interests me. But Lhotse is 8,511 metres high, and that's too much.'

'Coming back to the Gasherbrum Wall, I have seen a possible line on it. It goes up the righthand side, and then crosses to the left.'

'That would be something for a young four-man team. I've seen the face; it looks too broken for me', I say.

'Can I ask you something, Reinhold? Have you got permission to attempt Nanga Parbat this year?'

'Yes.'

'Will you try the South-east Ridge?'

'I'm not sure yet,' I answer.

'A new route?'

'Yes, a new route, in any case.'

'The ridge is too steep but so too is the Diamir Face.'

'Will you go alone?'

'On the face, yes.'

'When?'

'July, August. I've only got the permit for six weeks. I didn't really expect to get it, it was a long time ago I applied for permission.'

'And you won't try our route?' asks Robert, who knows Nanga Parbat well.

'Perhaps on the descent.'

'I take my hat off to you.'

'I must have had just the right conditions. It's a question of luck naturally. I must have caught a long spell of good weather.'

'Apart from the weather and the other objective things, how do you rate your chances?'

'Less than fifty per cent.'

'Less than fifty, you are still a realist, then!'

'I'm a great realist. If the weather were continuously fine, then I would give myself more than a fifty-fifty chance.'

'The biggest risk is one of mental collapse, I imagine.'

'Risky — at any event.'

'Nanga is the only eight-thousander you could comfortably attempt alone because it doesn't start with any crevasses.'

'True.'

'If I had known I'd get up Everest, perhaps I shouldn't have applied for permission for Nanga. I didn't really expect to get it.'

'You'll have to get started again fairly soon then,' Robert says not without some envy.

'Have you got anything planned for this summer?' I ask Franz Oppurg.

'I'll probably go on a guide's course.'

'On a military course?'

'You'll be promoted right away!'

'Something I would really like to do this year is the Rochetta Alta di Bosconero.'

'That's a beautiful route.'

'But it needs to be dry.'

'People say, you haven't a chance if it's wet.'

'People say a lot of things.'

'There's another possibility to the right of that, the Strobl-Kante. It is harder, but not so fine. It's variable — only hard in the middle, at the beginning and the end it's easy. The face has class throughout, and it's very beautiful.'

'Are there any in the Dolomites that aren't!' Franz is looking forward to a summer of climbing.

'You know what you should do, the Burel. Have you heard of it?'

'Is it a ridge route?'

'A face. A beautiful, concave face. It faces the sun and it's the second highest face in the Dolomites.'

'How high is it?'

'1,400 metres altogether, but the bottom section is easy. You have to start climbing through a stream. Higher up the face is crossed by a fifty-metre roof. Above the roof it's broken and messy. It's not beautiful, but it is a wild wall.'

'Who has done this route?' Franz asks eagerly.

'Italians the bottom, Poles the top.'

'And where is it, which part of the Dolomites?'

THE MOUNTAIN

'In the Schiara.'

'I must say I like it round there, the whole district is very, very lovely.'

'Asia — I like better!'

So, after achieving one ambition, each builds a new dream to fill the gap left behind. I hope I can always find enough new dreams.

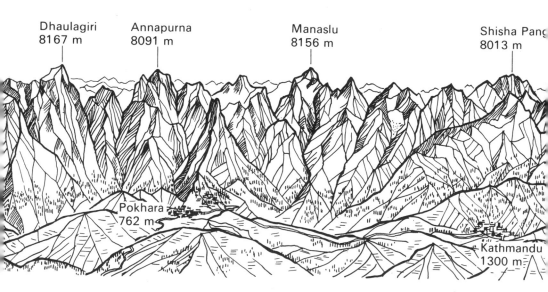

Dhaulagiri
8167 m

Annapurna
8091 m

Manaslu
8156 m

Shisha Pang
8013 m

Pokhara
762 m

Kathmandu
1300 m

EVEREST
CHRONICLE

Cho Oyu
8153 m

Mt. Everest
8848 m

Lhotse
8511 m

Makalu
8481 m

Kangchenjunga
8598 m

EVEREST FROM
THE NORTH-WEST

Summit

South Summit

South-east Ridge

South Col

North-east Ridge

Norton Couloir

Hornbein Couloir

North Ridge

North Face

West Ridge

South-wes

North Col

Rongbuk Glacier

Lho La (l

THE 14 ROUTES OF EVEREST

1 1953 British Expedition: first ascent by E. Hillary and Sherpa Tensing Norgay via South Col and South-east Ridge; the same expedition made first ascent of the South Summit.

EVEREST FROM THE EAST

South Col

South-east Ridge

Summit

North Ridge

East or Kangshung Face

t Shoulder

Western Cwm

Khumbu Glacier

2 1950 Chinese Expedition: North Ridge route (disputed).
3 1963 American Expedition: first traverse West Ridge/South-east Ridge as well as two summit ascents by the classic South-east Ridge route.
4 1975 British Expedition: fist ascent of South-west Face.
5 1979 Yugoslav Expedition: entire West Ridge.
6 1980 Japanese Expedition: first full ascent of North Face.
7 1980 Polish Expedition: South Pillar route.
8 1980 Reinhold Messner: solo ascent via a new line on the North Face without supplementary oxygen.
9 1982 Russian Expedition: route over the South-west Pillar.
10 1983 American Expedition: first ascent of the East, or Kangshung Face.
11 1984 Australian Expedition: North Face and Norton Couloir.
12 1986 Canadian Expedition: West Shoulder route.
13 1988 American Expedition: Second ascent of East or Kangshung Face, by a line to the left of the 1983 climb, leading to the South Col, and then to the summit by the original route.
14 1996 Siberian Expedition.
- - - - - (concealed route)

EVEREST CHRONICLE

(Geographical location of Mount Everest: 27° 59′ 16″ N., Latitude 86°55′40″ E., Longitude.)

1590   The first known sketch map of the Himalayas, drawn by Father Anthony Monserrate, a Spanish member of the Jesuit mission of the court of Akbar.

1705–   The first sketch maps of southern Tibet and the Himalayas are
1717   produced by Chinese lamas.

1733   Jean Baptiste d'Anville, the famous French geographer compiled a map of Tibet, basing it upon the measurements and observations of the Jesuit missionaries from China. It was published in Paris as 'Atlas of China' in 42 sheets.

1749   The Survey of India discovered and fixed a high peak in the Himalayas by means of observations taken from the low-lying jungle plains of India. The peak was known as Peak XV.

1803   Charles Crawford produced the first map of Nepal.

1849–50 Peak XV observed from six separate (174–190 kms. distant).

1852   The computations of the Survey indicated that Peak XV measured 29,002 ft (8,839.81 metres), higher therefore than any other known mountain.

1856   Various names were put forward for Peak XV – among them Devadhunga (Throne of the Gods) and Guarishankar (gleaming white bride of Shiva), finally Andrew Waugh, the Surveyor General of the Survey of India at that time, suggested the name Mount Everest, commemorating his predecessor Sir George Everest. This name was approved and adopted by the Royal Geographical Society in Britain.

1880–   New measurements were obtained from closer stations, includ-
1905   ing from the hills around Darjeeling, resulting in corrections

being made to the height. In 1905 Sir Sidney Burrard's calculations produced a height of 29,141 ft (or 8,882.18 m.).

1904 Col. Waddell and Sarat Chandra Das heard the name Chomo Kankar applied to Mount Everest by Tibetans in Tibet.

1906–7 C. G. Bruce, T. G. Longstaff and A. L. Mumm began preparations for an expedition to Everest in 1907 but political difficulties thwarted the attempt.

1907 An officer of the Survey of India, Natha Singh, who was allowed to survey the Nepalese slopes of Mount Everest, heard the name Chholungbu applied by Tibetans to Mount Everest.

1909 Sherpa Bhotias, who live high in the Dudh Kosi valley of Nepal, told General Bruce that Everest was known to them as Chomo Lungmo.

1920 Sir Charles Bell, the British Political Agent in Sikkim, visited Lhasa and received an official sanction from the Tibetan Prime Minister for an expedition to Mount Everest, and in the sanction the mountain's name was given as Chha-mo-lung-ma. This, as also does Chomo Lungma, translates as Goddess Mother of the World. Other documents of around this time also name the district around Chha-mo-lung-ma as Lho Chamo-long (Southern Bird Land). Today one recognizes the whole Everest massif, or the whole Everest-Makalu Group in the Khumbu Himal under the title 'Chomolungma'.

1921 Colonel C. K. Howard Bury, leader of the first Mount Everest expedition that year, was given the name Chomo Uri (Turquoise Goddess) for Mount Everest; he also heard Chomo Lungma applied to both Everest and Makalu. After several weeks of reconnaissance, Mallory and Bullock found the approach over the East Rongbuk Glacier to the North Col.

1922 The second British Expedition. Leader: General C. G. Bruce. The 8,000m. mark was passed for the first time. This was the first expedition when oxygen apparatus was tested on the mountain. An avalanche killed seven Sherpa porters.

1924 Third British Expedition. Leader: Lt. Col. E. F. Norton. On June 4 he reached a height of 8,572m. G. L. Mallory and A. C.

Irvine were lost attempting the summit; they were last seen by Odell climbing above 8,530 metres.

1933   Fourth British Expedition. Leader: Hugh Ruttledge. Camp VI was established at 8,350m. P. Wyn Harris and L. R. Wager reached a height of over 8,500m., as did F. S. Smythe a day later.

1934   Solo attempt by Englishman, M. Wilson, who died below the North Col.

1935   A strong British reconnaissance team (fifth official British Everest Expedition) arrived late in the season and only reached the North Col. The leader was E. E. Shipton. The expedition made several ascents of summits in the Everest region. The first photographs were taken looking down into the Western Cwm.

1936   Sixth British Expedition. Leader: Hugh Ruttledge. Expedition was hampered by bad weather and didn't climb far above the North Col.

1938   Seventh British Expedition. Leader: H. W. Tilman. A height of about 8,300 metres was reached.

1947   Solo attempt by Canadian E. Denman, who climbed within a short distance of the North Col. Nepal opens its borders to outsiders.

1950   First British preliminary reconnaissance of the Nepalese side of Everest by H. W. Tilman and C. S. Houston (U.S.). They came to the foot of the Khumbu Icefall.

1951   Second British reconnaissance under E. E. Shipton. First ascent of the Khumbu Icefall into the entrance of the Western Cwm (the Valley of Silence).

1951   Solo attempt by a Dane, K. B. Larsen on the North side. He reached the North Col. He forbade his Sherpas to follow him.

1952   In a scholarly article in the Himalayan Journal, B. L. Gulatee, the Director, Geodetic and Training Circle, Survey of India, wrote that the earlier figure of 8,840 metres (29,002 ft) ought to be adhered to until further observations were taken.

1952–   New measurements from the Nepalese side allowed a more
1955   precise figure to be computed. Since 1955 the official height of Everest has been 29,028 ft or 8,847.734 metres. (According to

Dir. Gulatee one should allow a plus/minus variation of 10 ft, or about 3 metres). Incidentally the Chinese observations of 1975–77 have produced almost exactly the same figure.

1952 First and second Swiss Expeditions. Leaders: E. Wyss-Dunant and G. Chevalley. The first team pioneered the route through the Western Cwm, over the Geneva Spur to the South Col and the South-east Ridge. R. Lambert and Sherpa Tenzing reached a height of 8,595m. The autumn expedition took a route over the Lhotse Face to the South Col and this has since become the classic route. (Their highest point: 8,100 m.).

1953 First ascent of Mount Everest on May 29 by E. P. Hillary and Sherpa Tenzing in the course of the British Expedition, led by Colonel J. Hunt. The first ascent of the South Summit was made two days earlier by R. C. Evans and T. Bourdillon.

1956 Third Swiss Expedition. Leader: A. Eggler. The summit of Everest was reached twice by this expedition, on May 21 by E. Schmied and J. Marmet and on the following day by A. Reist and H. von Gunten. (The first ascent of Lhoste was made on May 18 by two members of the same expedition.)

1958 Chinese-Russian Reconnaissance as preparation for a big expedition to take place in 1959 or 1960. Towards the end of 1958 a political rift between the Russian and Chinese cancelled these plans and the Chinese went to Everest alone in 1960. The leader of the Chinese Reconnaissance party was Chuj Din; of the three Russian climbers, J. Beletzki. They reached a height of 6,400 metres, below the North Col.

1960 Chinese claim an ascent of Everest via the North Ridge. Western experts have doubted whether the summit was in fact reached because of various equivocal factors and the lack of photographic documentation. Comparing such photographs as did exist with earlier material, a height of 8,500 metres (plus or minus 50 metres) was certainly reached. A Chinese film of the expedition was shown in London on 8th October 1962.

1960 First Indian Expedition under G. Singh.
1962 Second Indian Expedition under J. Dias.

1962   A group of three Americans and one Swiss make an un-authorized attempt from the North, reaching a height of 7,600m.

1963   American Expedition. Leader: N. Dyhrenfurth. On May 22 W. Unsoeld and T. Hornbein made the first traverse of Everest, climbing the West Ridge and descending the South-east Ridge. There were also two other successful ascents of the classic South-east Ridge route by J. Whittaker and Sherpa Gombu on May 1 and B. Bishop and L. Jerstad on May 22 (meeting with Unsoeld/Hornbein just under the South Col and a free bivouac at about 8,600m.)

1965   Third Indian Everest Expedition. Leader: M. S. Kohli. In four separate assaults, nine men reached the summit.

1966   Everest was closed to climbers until the summer of 1969.

1966   Second Chinese Everest Expedition – leader unknown. Route North Col. This expedition in the spirit of the Cultural Revolution proved disastrous. Of the 25 or 26 men who went to the North Col, it seems that only two came back; the thoughts of Chairman Mao did not make up for insufficient equipment.

1967   Chinese scientific expedition in the region north of Everest. Leader unknown. Probably a scientific survey party to the North Col.

1968   Third Chinese Everest Expedition – leader unknown. Followed the North Col Route without success. The attempt began in April and on May 9 everyone retreated from Base Camp.

1969   In the autumn (post-monsoon) Japanese climbers reconnoitred the possibilities of Everest South-west Face from the Western Cwm. They reached a height of 8,050m. in the Great Central Gully.

1970   A big Japanese expedition were unable to advance on 8,050m. on the South-west Face. Two members reached the summit by the South-east Ridge route. Japanese Ski Everest Expedition accomplished first ski descent (with parachute) from the South Col to the Western Cwm. Six Sherpas were lost in the Icefall.

1971   International Everest Expedition. Leader: N. Dyhrenfurth (participants from 13 nations). Reached 8,350m. on the South-west

Face; an attempt on the direct West Ridge failed.

1971   Argentine expedition under H. C. Tolosa met with no success.

1972   A European expedition under K. M. Herrligkoffer failed on the South-west Face (8,300m.).

1972   First British Expedition to the South-west Face, led by C. Bonington made no further progress.

1973   64-member Italian expedition led by Count Guido Monzino put eight men on the summit via the normal (South-east Ridge) route.

1973   48-member Japanese expedition, led by Michio Yuasa, to the South-west Face, made no significant advance beyond the great diagonal barrier (the Rock Band) (8,380m.).

1974   Unsuccessful Spanish Expedition (serious frostbite suffered).

1974   French Expedition attempted the West Ridge without oxygen. Expedition leader G. Devouassoux and five Sherpas were killed in an avalanche.

1975   Japanese Ladies' Expedition led by E. Hisano. On May 16 Junko Tabei became the first woman to stand on the summit of Everest; she was accompanied by Sherpa Sirdar Ang Tsering. A new absolute women's altitude record.

1975   Large Chinese Expedition climbed the North Ridge. The deputy leader, a Tibetan lady named Phantog, was amongst the eight Tibetans and one Chinese to reach the summit on May 27. She thus became the second woman to do so.

1975   Second British South-west Face Expedition under C. Bonington met with success. D. Haston and D. Scott (May 24, bivouac on the South Summit, 8,760m.) and P. Boardman with Sherpa Pertemba (May 26) were the summit pairs. M. Burke was lost in the vicinity of the summit on May 26; after making what was probably the first solo ascent of the mountain.

1976   Joint British and Royal Nepalese Army Expedition to Everest. Leader: T. Streather. J. Stokes and M. Lane reached the summit via the South-east Ridge. One expedition member was killed in a crevasse near camp II.

1976   American Bicentennial Expedition. Leader: P. Trimble. The summit was reached by two members, Bob Cormack and Chris

Chandler, following the South-east Ridge route.

1977   New Zealand climbers undertook the first expedition to Everest in alpine-style (without Sherpas). They reached the South Col.

1977   A South Korean expedition climbed the classic South-east Ridge route (Sang-Don-Ko and Sherpa Pemba Norbu reached the summit).

1978   First ascent of Mount Everest completely without any artificial oxygen on May 8 by R. Messner and P. Habeler. They were attached to the first Austrian Everest Expedition, led by W. Nairz. Besides these, five other expedition members (including the first German to do so, R. Karl) and a Sherpa reached the summit (May 3, 10 and 13). Second solo ascent by F. Oppurg.

1978   Autumn Expedition. A German (Leader K. Herrligkoffer) and French (Leader P. Mazeaud) Expedition during the period 14–17 October put on the summit: seven German climbers, three French, a Pole, a Swiss and an Austrian as well as three Sherpas, following the normal South Col Route. Second Everest ascent without oxygen was made by Hans Engl on 10 October. Third by the Sherpas Ang Dorje and Mingma on 17 October. The Third Female ascent was made by the Polish climber Wanda Rutkiewicz. (Hans Engl as well as Ang Dorje and Mingma made their oxygenless climb in the company of climbers who were using breathing apparatus. Hans Engl has said that he would have been unable to make the summit without the trail having been broken by Sepp Mack).

1979   Yugoslav expedition reached summit 'straightened out' the West Ridge route by not deviating onto the North Face, thus completing the hardest and longest rock climb on Everest to date. The summit team of A. Stremfelj and N. Zaplotnik (13 May), who were followed two days later by three further team members, descended via the Hornbein Couloir. Ang Phu fell to his death.

During the 1980s it became fashionable to climb Everest. No longer did the authorities stipulate only one expedition per route; instead, several teams attempting the same line became the norm. Today, most 'successes' are claimed by commercial expeditions, through whom the tourist can book guides, organisation, logistics and insurance.

1980   First complete North Face climb by Japanese T. Shigehiro and T. Ozaki on 10 May. Setting off from the Main Rongbuk Glacier they climbed in a direct line up the gully now known as the Japanese Couloir, which leads into the Hornbein Couloir.

1980   Following on from their first winter ascent of Everest three months before, Polish mountaineers achieved a notable success by following the South Pillar at the right-hand edge of the South-west Face. The rock band alone took 16 days to climb. J. Kukuczka and A. Czok reached the summit in a storm on 19 May. The route had been climbed five times by the end of 1992, while twenty more climbers followed the pillar to mid-height before traversing to the South Col.

1980   The most spectacular climb of all: R. Messner's solo ascent without supplementary oxygen, from the north. He had hoped to be able to follow the Chinese route on to the North-east Ridge, but soft snow forced him out on to the face. Upon reaching the Norton (or Great) Couloir, he climbed it almost directly to the summit, which he reached on 20 August.

1982   On the first Everest attempt by Soviet mountaineers, Russians succeeded in climbing the South-west Pillar, to the left of the great central gully on the South-west Face. The summit was reached by the leading pair of E. Myslovski and V. Balyberdin and nine others on 4 May—the highest number ever to complete a new route.

1983   After a reconnaissance in 1980 and an attempt the following year (to a height of 7600m.), American climbers completed a bold new route on the East (or Kangshung) Face. After ascending an initial 1000m. buttress, the line follows snow slopes to just below the South Summit. The summit party of L. Reichardt, K. Momb and C. Buhler (8 October) were followed the next day by a further trio.

1984   A small Australian team made an audacious ascent of the North

Face via the Norton (or Great) Couloir. The summit pair of T. Macartney-Snape and G. Mortimer were the second climbers (after R. Messner) to open a new route without the aid of supplementary oxygen. A. Henderson turned back shortly below the summit.

1986   Canadian woman, S. Wood, was not only the first female North American climber to top out on Everest, but she did so by a new route. The expedition climbed the West Shoulder from the Rongbuk Glacier. Although two previous expeditions had done the same, neither had continued to the summit. Wood and her partner D. Congden followed the 1983 American route, traversing into the Hornbein Couloir, summiting on 20 May. They remain the only climbers to have climbed this line, although in 1989 Polish climbers opened a variation by approaching it from the Khumbu Glacier and the Lho La Pass.

1988   The second ascent of the Kangshung Face was made on 12 May by an American team plus the British climber S. Venables. Having taken a line to the left of the 1983 route, three members set off from the South Col for the summit. Venables alone made it to the top becoming only the second to complete a new route solo; also this was only the third new route to have been completed without supplemental oxygen.

1993   A large-scale Japanese expedition completed the first winter ascent of the South-west Face (Bonington Route). Three ropes reached the summit.

1995   Following several unsuccessful attempts (the first in 1982 under Chris Bonington) a Japanese team was finally able to reach the summit by climbing Everest's extremely long North-east Ridge.

1996   Three-hundred-ninety-eight climbers from thirty nations, members of thirty different expeditions, congregated on Everest in the pre-monsoon season. One team from Siberia attempted a variant on the steep flank between the NNE Ridge and the North Ridge. Of the eighty-six men and women who reached the top of the world in May 1996, eleven failed to return. Among those lost were climbing guides Rob Hall and Scott Fischer.

THE EXPEDITIONS 1921-1978

	Year	Leader	Nationality	Route
1.	1921	C. K. Howard-Bury	British	North Ridge
2.	1922	C. G. Bruce	British	North Ridge
3.	1924	E. F. Norton	British	North Ridge
4.	1933	H. Ruttledge	British	North Ridge
5.	1934	M. Wilson (solo)★	British	North Ridge
6.	1935	E. E. Shipton	British	North Ridge
7.	1936	H. Ruttledge	British	North Ridge
8.	1938	H. W. Tilman	British	North Ridge
9.	1947	E. L. Denman★	Canadian	North Ridge
10.	1950	C. S. Houston/ H. W. Tilman	USA/British	Southern approach
11.	1951	K. Becker-Larsen★	Danish	North Ridge
12.	1951	E. E. Shipton	British	Southern approach
13.	1952	E. E. Shipton★	British	Northern approaches
14.	1952	E. Wyss-Dunant	Swiss	South-east Ridge
15.	1952	G. Chevalley	Swiss	South-east Ridge
16.	1952	P. Datschnolian	USSR	From the North
17.	1953	J. Hunt	British	South-east Ridge
18.	1956	A. Eggler	Swiss	South-east Ridge
19.	1960	G. Singh	Indian	South-east Ridge
20.	1960	(disputed)	Chinese	North Ridge
21.	1962	J. Dias	Indian	South-east Ridge
22.	1962	W. W. Sayre★	USA	North Ridge

★ Unsanctioned expeditions.

	Year	Leader	Nationality	Route
23.	1963	N. Dyhrenfurth	USA	South-east and West Ridges
24.	1965	M. S. Kohli	Indian	South-east Ridge
25.	1966	unknown	Chinese	North side
26.	1967	unknown	Chinese	North side
27.	1968	unknown	Chinese	North side
28.	1969		Japanese	South-west Face
29.	1970	S. Matsukuta	Japanese	South-east Ridge and South-west Face
30.	1970	A. Takahashi	Japanese	South-east Ridge
31.	1971	N. Dyhrenfurth	International Expedition	South-west Face
32.	1971	H. C. Tolosa, C. Comesana	Argentinian	South-east Ridge
33.	1972	K. M. Herrligkoffer	European Expedition	South-west Face
34.	1972	C. Bonington	British	South-west Face
35.	1973	G. Monzino	Italian	South-east Ridge
36.	1973	M. Yuasa	Japanese	South-west Face
37.	1974	J. I. Lorente	Spanish	West Ridge
38.	1974	G. Devouassoux	French	West Ridge
39.	1975	Mrs E. Hisano	Japanese	South-east Ridge
40.	1975	Shi Chan-chun	Chinese	North Ridge
41.	1975	C. Bonington	British	South-west Face
42.	1976	H. R. A. Streather	British/ Nepalese	South-east Ridge
43.	1976	P. Trimble	USA	South-east Ridge
44.	1977	K. Wood Ford	New Zealand	South-east Ridge
45.	1977	Y. Do Kim	South Korean	South-east Ridge
46.	1978	W. Nairz	Austrian	South-east Ridge
47.	1978	P. Mazeaud	French	South-east Ridge
48.	1978	K. Herrligkoffer	W. German	South-east Ridge

SUCCESSFUL ASCENTS 1953–1997

Known fatalities are marked •; ascents (including descents) without bottled oxygen are marked ★.

Date	Climber	Route	Nationality/Leader
1. 29.May.1953	E. Hillary Tenzing Norgay, Sherpa	South-east Ridge	British Expedition (J. Hunt)
2. 23.May.1956	Ernst Schmied Jörg Marmet	South-east Ridge	Swiss Expedition (A. Eggler)
3. 24.May.1956	Dölf Reist Hans-Rudolf von Günten	South-east Ridge	Swiss Expedition (A. Eggler)

25.May.1960: Chinese expedition (Shih Chan-Chan) claimed ascent from the north, by Wang Fu-Chou, Kombu and Chu Yin-Hua. Western experts doubt, due to lack of a plausible account.

Date	Climber	Route	Nationality/Leader
4. 1.May.1963	Jim Whittaker Nawang Gombu, Sherpa	South-east Ridge	American Expedition (N. Dyhrenfurth)
5. 22.May.1963	Barry Bishop Luther Jerstad	South-east Ridge	
6. 22.May.1963	Willi Unsoeld Tom Hornbein	Traverse from N.W. and down S.E. Ridge	
7. 20.May.1965	A. S. Cheema Nawang Gombu, Sherpa	South-east Ridge	Indian Expedition under (M. S. Kohli)
8. 22.May.1965	Sonam Gyatso Sonam Wangyal	South-east Ridge	
9. 24.May.1965	C. P. Vohra Ang Kami, Sherpa	South-east Ridge	
10. 29.May.1965	H. P. S. Ahluwalia H. C. S. Rawat Phu Dorje, Sherpa	South-east Ridge	
11. 11.May.1970	Naomi Uemura Teruo Matsuura	South-east Ridge	Japanese Expedition (S. Matsukuta)
12. 12.May.1970	Katsutoshi Hirabayashi Chotare, Sherpa	South-east Ridge	
13. 5.May.1973	Rinaldo Carrel Mirko Minuzzo Lhakpa Tensing, Sherpa Sambu Tamang, Sherpa	South-east Ridge	Italian Expedition (G. Monzino)
14. 7.May.1973	Fabrizio Innamorati Virginio Epis Claudio Benedetti Sonam Gyalzen, Sherpa	South-east Ridge	

Date	Climber	Route	Nationality/Leader
15. 26.May.1973	Hisashi Ishiguro Yasuo Kato	South-east Ridge	Japanese Expedition (M. Yuasa)
16. 16.May.1975	Mrs Junko Tabei Ang Tsering (First female ascent)	South-east Ridge	Japanese Ladies Expedition (Mrs E. Hisano)
17. 27.May.1975	Mrs Phantog Sodnam Norbu Lotse Samdrup Dharphuntso Kunga Pasang Tsering Tobygal Hgapo Khyen Hon Sheng-fu (the only Chinese member to reach the summit)	North Ridge (Tibetan side)	Expedition of the People's Republic of China (Shi Chan-Chun) First proven North Ridge ascent (Second female ascent)
18. 24.Sept.1975	Doug Scott Dougal Haston	South-west Face	British Expedition (C. Bonington)
19. 26.Sept.1975	Peter Boardman Pertemba, Sherpa	South-west Face	
20. 26.Sept.1975	• Mick Burke (Probable first solo summit push)	South-west Face	
21. 16.May.1976	J. H. (Brummy) Stokes M. P. (Bronco) Lane	South-east Ridge	Joint British/Royal Nepalese Army Expedition (H. Streather)
22. 8.Oct.1976	Bob Cormack Chris Chandler	South-east Ridge	American Bicentennial Expedition (P. Trimble)
23. 15.Sept.1977	Sang-Don-Ko Pemba Norbu, Sherpa	South-east Ridge	South Korean Expedition (Kim Young-Do)
24. 3.May.1978	Robert Schauer Ang Phu, Sherpa Wolfgang Nairz Horst Bergmann	South-east Ridge	Austrian Expedition (W. Nairz)
25. 8.May.1978	Reinhold Messner ★ Peter Habeler ★	South-east Ridge	
26. 10.May.1978	Oswald Ölz Reinhard Karl	South-east Ridge	
27. 13.May.1978	Franz Oppurg (Second solo ascent)	South-east Ridge	

233

Date	Climber	Route	Nationality/Leader
28. 14.Oct.1978	Sepp Mack Hubert Hillmaier Hans Engl ★	South-east Ridge	German Expedition (K. Herrligkoffer)
29. 15.Oct.1978	Jean Afanassief Nicolas Jaeger	South-east Ridge	French Expedition (P. Mazeaud)
30. 15.Oct.1978	Pierre Mazeaud Kurt Diemberger (Austrian)	South-east Ridge	
31. 16.Oct1978	Wanda Rutkiewicz (Polish) Robert Allenbach (Swiss) Siegfried Hupfauer Wilhelm Klimek Mingma, Sherpa ★ Ang Dorje, Sherpa ★	South-east Ridge	German Expedition (K. Herrligkoffer)
32. 17.Oct.1978	Georg Ritter Berndt Kullmann	South-east Ridge	Ritter went to 8500 m. without oxygen
33. 13.May.1979	Jernej Zaplotnik Andrej Stremfelj	West Ridge, Direct	Yugoslav Expedition (Tone Skarja)
34. 15.May.1979	Stane Belak Stipe Bozic • Ang Phu, Sherpa	West Ridge, Direct	
35. 1.Oct.1979	Gerhard Schmatz Hermann Wrath Hans v. Känel Pertemba, Sherpa Lhakpa Gyalzo, Sherpa	South-east Ridge	German Expedition (Gerhard Schmatz)
36. 2.Oct.1979	• Ray Genet • Hannelore Schmatz Sungdare, Sherpa Tilman Fischbach Günter Kämpfe Nick Banks Ang Phurba, Sherpa Ang Jangbo, Sherpa	South-east Ridge	
37. 17.Feb.1980	Leszek Cichy Krzysztof Wielicki	South-east Ridge	Polish Expedition (Andrzej Zawada)
38. 3.May.1980	Yasuo Kato	North Col/ North-east Ridge	Japanese Expedition (Hyoriko Watanabe)

EVEREST CHRONICLE

Date	Climber	Route	Nationality/Leader
39. 10.May.1980	Tsuneoh Shigehiro Takashi Ozaki	North Face/ Hornbein-Couloir	
40. 14.May.1980	Martin Zabaleta Pasang Temba, Sherpa	South-east Ridge	Spanish Expedition (Juan-Ignacio Lorente)
41. 19.May.1980	Andrzej Czok Jerzy Kukuczka	South Pillar	Polish Expedition (Andrzej Zawada)
42. 20.Aug.1980	Reinhold Messner ★	North Col/ North Face	Solo
43. 21.Oct.1981	Chris Kopczynski Sungdare, Sherpa	South Pillar/ South-east Ridge	American Expedition (John West)
44. 4.Oct.1981	Chris Pizzo Yong Tenzing, Sherpa Peter Hackett	South Pillar/ South-east Ridge	
45. 4.May.1982	Volodya Balyberdin Eduard Myslovski Sergei Bershov Mikhail Turkevich	South-west Pillar	Russian Expedition (Yevgeni Tamm)
46. 5.May.1982	Valentin Ivanov Sergei Yefimov	South-west Pillar	
47. 8.May.1982	Valeri Khrishchaty Kazbek Valiev	South-west Pillar	
48. 9.May.1982	Valeri Khomutov Vladimir Puchkov Yuri Golodov	South-west Pillar	
49. 5.Oct.1982	Laurie Skreslet Sungdare, Sherpa Lhakpa Dorje, Sherpa	South-east Ridge	Canadian Expedition (William March)
50. 7.Oct.1982	Pat Morrow Pemba Dorje, Sherpa Lhakpa Tshering, Sherpa	South-east Ridge	
51. 27.Dec.1982	• Yasuo Kato	South-east Ridge	Japanese Expedition (Yasuo Kato)
52. 7.May.1983	Peter Jamieson Gerald Roach David Breashears Ang Rita, Sherpa ★ Larry Nielson ★	South-east Ridge	American Expedition (Gerhard Lenser)
53. 14.May.1983	Gary Neptune Jim States Lhakpa Dorje II, Sherpa	South-east Ridge	

Date	Climber	Route	Nationality/Leader
54. 8.Oct.1983	Kim Momb Louis Reichardt Carlos Buhler	East Face/ South-east Ridge	American Expedition (James Morrissey)
55. 8.Oct.1983	Haruichi Kawamura ★ Shomi Suzuki ★	South Pillar to South-east Ridge	Japanese Expedition (Haruichi Kawamura)
56. 8.Oct.1983	Haruyuki Endo ★ • Hiroshi Yoshino ★ • Hironobu Kamuro ★	South-east Ridge	Japanese Expedition (Hiroshi Yoshino)
57. 9.Oct.1983	George Lowe Dan Reid Jay Cassell	East Face to South-east Ridge	American Expedition (James Morrissey)
58. 16.Dec.1983	Takashi Ozaki Nobru Yamada Kazunari Murakami Nawang Yonden, Sherpa	South-east Ridge	Japanese Expedition (Kazuyuki Takahashi)
59. 20.April.1984	• Hristo Ivanov Prodanov ★	West Ridge	Bulgarian Expedition (Avram Iliev Avramov)
60. 8.May.1984	Ivan G. Vulchev Metodi Stefanov Savov	West Ridge descent via South-east Ridge	
61. 9.May.1984	Nikolay Petkov Kiril Doskov	West Ridge descent via South-east Ridge	
62. 9.May.1984	Phu Dorjee, Sherpa	South-east Ridge	Indian Expedition
63. 23.May.1984	Bachendri Pal Dorjee Lhatoo, Sherpa Ang Dorje, Sherpa ★ Sonam Palzor	South-east Ridge	(Darshan Kumar Khullar)
64. 3.Oct.1984	Tim Macartney-Snape ★ Greg Mortimer ★	North Face/ Norton- Couloir	Australian Expedition (Geoffrey Bartram)
65. 8.Oct.1984	Bart Vos	South-east Ridge	Dutch Expedition (Herman Plugge)
66. 15.Oct.1984	• Jozef Psotka ★ Zoltan Demjan ★ Ang Rita, Sherpa ★	South Pillar, descent via South-east Ridge	Czechoslovakian Expedition (Frantisek Kele)
67. 20.Oct.1984	Philip Ershler	North Col/ North Face	American Expedition (Louis W. Whittaker)
68. 21.April.1985	Bjorn Myrer-Lund Odd Eliassen	South-east Ridge	Norwegian Expedition (Arne Naess)

Date	Climber	Route	Nationality/Leader
	Pertemba, Sherpa		
	Ang Lhakpa Dorje, Sherpa		
	Chris Bonington		
	Dawa Norbu, Sherpa		
69. 29.April.1985	Arne Naess	South-east Ridge	
	Stein Aasheim		
	Haavard Nesheim		
	Ralph Höibakk		
	Sungdare, Sherpa		
	Ang Rita, Sherpa ★		
	Pema Dorje, Sherpa		
	Chowang Rinzing, Sherpa		
70. 30.April.1985	Richard Bass	South-east Ridge	
	David Breashears		
	Ang Phurba II, Sherpa		
71. 28.Aug.1985	Oscar Cadiach	North Col/	Catalan Expedition
	Toni Sors	North-east	(Conrad Blanch)
	Charles Valles	Ridge	
	Ang Karma, Sherpa		
	Shambu Tamang		
	Narayan Shrestha		
72. 30.Oct.1985	Etsuo Akutsu	South-east	Japanese Expedition
	Satoshi Kimoto	Ridge	(Kuniaki Yagihara)
	Hideji Nazuka		
	Teruo Saegusa		
	Mitsuyoshi Sato		
	Kuniaki Yagihara		
	Noboru Yamada ★		
73. 20.May.1986	Sharon Wood	West Ridge	Canadian Expedition
	Dwayne Congdon	from Tibet	(Jim Elzinga)
74. 30.Aug.1986	Erhard Loretan ★	North Face/	French-
	Jean Troillet ★	Hornbein-	Swiss Expedition
		Couloir	(Pierre Béghin)
75. 22.Dec.1987	Huh Young-Ho	South-east	South Korean Expedition
	Ang Rita, Sherpa ★	Ridge	(Hahm Tak-Young)
76. 5.May.1988	Noboru Yamada	North Col/	Asian Expedition
	Ang Lhakpa Nuru, Sherpa	South Col	(Tsuneoh Shigehiro)
	Cerin Doji	Traverse	
77. 5.May.1988	Ang Phurba II, Sherpa	South Col/	Asian Expedition
	Ringen Puncog	North Col	(Kunga Sherpa)
	Da Cering	Traverse	

Date	Climber	Route	Nationality/Leader
78. 5.May.1988	Susuma Nakamura Shoji Nakamura Teruo Saegusa Munehiko Yamamoto Li Zhixin Lhakpa Sona, Sherpa	North Col/ North-east Ridge	Asian Expedition (Tsuneoh Shigehiro)
79. 10.May.1988	Sungdare, Sherpa Padma Bahadur	South-east Ridge	Asian Expedition (Kunga Sherpa)
80. 12.May.1988	Stephen Venables ★	East Face/ South Col	American Expedition (Robert Anderson)
81. 25.May.1988 82. 28.May.1988	Paul Bayne Patrick Cullinan John Muir	South-east Ridge South-east Ridge	Australian Expedition (Austin Brookes)
83. 26.Sept.1988	Jean-Marc Boivin Michel Metzger ★ Jean-Pierre Frachon Gérard Vionnet-Fuasset André Georges Pasang Tshering, Sherpa Sonam Tshering, Sherpa Ajiwa, Sherpa	South-east Ridge	French Expedition (François Poissonnier)
84. 26.Sept.1988	Kim Chang-Sun Pemba Dorje, Sherpa Uhm Hong-Gil	South Pillar/ South-east Ridge	South Korean Expedition (Choi Chang-Min)
85. 26.Sept.1988	Marc Batard ★	South-east Pillar	Solo
86. 26.Sept.1988	Jang Bong-Wan Chang Byong-Ho Chung Seung-Kwon	South Pillar/ South-east Ridge	South Korean Expedition (Choi Chang-Min)
87. 29.Sept.1988 88. 2.Oct.1988	Stacy Allison Pasang Gyalzen, Sherpa Peggy Luce Geoffrey Tabin Nima Tashi, Sherpa Phu Dorje, Sherpa Dawa Tshering, Sherpa	South-east Ridge South-east Ridge	American Expedition (James Frush)
89. 2.Oct.1988	Nam Sun-Woo	South Pillar/ South-east Ridge	South Korean Expedition (Choi Chang-Min)
90. 13.Oct.1988	Serge Koenig • Lhakpa Sonam, Sherpa Pasang Temba, Sherpa	South-east Ridge	French Expedition (Serge Koenig)

Date	Climber	Route	Nationality/Leader
91. 14.Oct.1988	Jerónimo López Nil Bohigas Lluis Giner Ang Rita, Sherpa ★ Nima Rita, Sherpa	South-east Ridge	Catalan Expedition (Lluis Belvis)
92. 14.Oct.1988	Lydia Bradey ★	South-east Ridge	New Zealand Expedition (Rob Hall)
93. 17.Oct.1988	• Jozef Just ★	South-west Face	Czechoslovakian Expedition (Ivan Fiala)
94. 10.May.1989	Stipe Bozic • Dimitar Ilijevski Ajiwa, Sherpa Sonam Tshering, Sherpa ★ Viktor Groselj	South-east Ridge	Yugoslavian OR Macedonian Expedition (Jovan Poposki)
95. 16.May.1989	Ricardo Torres • Phu Dorje, Sherpa Ang Dannu, Sherpa	South-east Ridge	American Expedition (Walt McConnell)
96. 24.May.1989	Adrian Burgess Ang Lhakpa Nuru, Sherpa Sonam Dendu, Sherpa Roddy Mackenzie	South-east Ridge	American Expedition (Karen Fellerhoff)
97. 24.May.1989	• Eugeniusz Chrobak Andrzej Marciniak	West Ridge/ Hornbein- Couloir	Polish Expedition (Eugeniusz Chrobak)
98. 13.Oct.1989	Toichiro Mitani Hiroshi Ohnishi Atsushi Yamamoto Tchiring Thebe Lama Chuldin Dorje, Sherpa	South-east Ridge	Japanese Expedition (Ken Kanazawa)
99. 13.Oct.1989	Cho Kwang-Je	South Pillar/ South-east Ridge	South Korean Expedition (Kim In-Tae)
100. 13.Oct.1989	Carlos Carsolio ★	South-east Ridge	Mexican Expedition (Carlos Carsolio)
101. 23.Oct.1989	Chung Sang-Yong Nima Rita, Sherpa Nuru Jangbu, Sherpa	West Ridge from Nepal	South Korean Expedition (Lee Suk-Woo)
102. 23.April.1990	Ang Rita, Sherpa ★ Ang Kami, Sherpa	South-east Ridge	Nepalese Expedition (Chitra Bahadur Gurung)

Date	Climber	Route	Nationality/Leader
	Pasang Norbu, Sherpa Top Bahadur Khatri		
103. 7.May.1990	Robert Link Steve Gall Sergei Arsentiev ★ Grigori Lunyakov ★ Da Cheme Gyal Bu	North Col/ North-east Ridge	International Expedition (Jim Whittaker)
104. 8.May.1990	Ed Viesturs ★ Mistislav Gorbenko Andrej Tselishchev ★	North Col/ North-east Ridge	
105. 9.May.1990	Ian Wade Da Qiong Luo Tse Ren Na Gui Sang	North Col/ North-east Ridge	
106. 10.May.1990	Yekaterina Ivanova Anatoli Moshnikov ★ Yervand Ilyinski Aleksandr Tokarev ★ Mark Tucker Wang Ja	North Col/ North-east Ridge	
107. 10.May.1990	Peter Athans Glenn Porzak Ang Jangbu, Sherpa Nima Tashi, Sherpa Dana Coffield Brent Manning Michael Browning Dawa Nuru, Sherpa	South-east Ridge	American Expedition (Glenn Porzak)
108. 10.May.1990	Peter Hillary Robert Hall Gary Ball Rudy Van Snick Apa, Sherpa	South-east Ridge	New Zealand Expedition (Robert Hall)
109. 11.May.1990	Andrew Lapkass	South-east Ridge	American Expedition (Glenn Porzak)
110. 11.May.1990	Tim Macartney-Snape ★	South-east Ridge	Australian Expedition (Tim Macartney-Snape)
111. 11.May.1990	Mikael Reuterswäld Öskar Kihlbörg	South-east Ridge	New Zealand Expedition (Rob Hall)

Date	Climber	Route	Nationality/Leader
112. 4.Oct.1990	Alex Lowe Dan Culver	South-east Ridge	American Expedition (Hooman Aprin)
113. 4.Oct.1990	Yves Salino	South-east Ridge	French Expedition (Laurence de la Ferrierè)
114. 5.Oct.1990	Hooman Aprin Ang Temba, Sherpa	South-east Ridge	American Expedition (Hooman Aprin)
115. 5.Oct.1990	Erik Decamp Nawang Thile, Sherpa Sonam Dendu, Sherpa Marc Batard ★ Christine Janin Pascal Tournaire	South-east Ridge	French Expedition (Marc Batard)
116. 6.Oct.1990	Bok Jin-Young Kim Jae-Soo Park Chang-Woo Dawa Sange, Sherpa Pemba Dorje, Sherpa	South-east Ridge	Japanese/ South Korean Expedition (Nobuo Kuwahara)
117. 6.Oct.1990	Babu Tshering, Sherpa	South-east Ridge	French Expedition (Marc Batard)
118. 7.Oct.1990	Andrej Stremfelj Mrs. Marija Stremfelj Janez Jeglic Lhakpa Rita, Sherpa	South-east Ridge	Slovenian Expedition (Tomaz Jamnik)
119. 7.Oct.1990	Cathy Gibson Aleksei Krasnokutsky Phinzo, Sherpa	South-east Ridge	American Expedition (Hooman Aprin)
120. 7.Oct.1990	Jean-Nöel Roche Bertrand "Zébulon" Roche Denis Pivot Alain Desez René De Bos Ang Phurba III, Sherpa Nima Dorje, Sherpa	South-east Ridge	French Expedition (Laurence de la Ferriere)
121. 8.May.1991	Ang Temba II, Sherpa Sonam Dendu, Sherpa Apa, Sherpa	South-east Ridge	Nepalese Expedition (Lobsang, Sherpa)
122. 8.May.1991	Peter Athans	South-east Ridge	American Expedition (Peter Athans)

Date	Climber	Route	Nationality/Leader
123. 15.May.1991	Mark Richey Yves La Forest Rick Wilcox Barry Rugo	South-east Ridge	American Expedition (Rick Wilcox)
124. 15.May.1991	Eric Simonson Bob Sloezen George Dunn Andy Politz Lhakpa Dorje, Sherpa Ang Dawa, Sherpa	North Col/ North Face	American Expedition (Eric Simonson)
125. 15.May.1991	Ed Viesturs	South-east Ridge	American Expedition (Ed Viesturs/R. Link)
126. 15.May.1991	Mingma Norbu, Sherpa Gyalbu, Sherpa	North Face/ Hornbein- Couloir	Swedish Expedition (Jack Berg)
127. 17.May.1991	Mike Perry	North Col/ North Face	American Expedition (Eric Simonson)
128. 17.May.1991	Battista Bonali ★ Leopold Sulovsky ★	North Face/ Norton- Couloir	Italian Expedition (Oreste Forno)
129. 20.May.1991	Lars Cronlund	North Face/ Hornbein- Couloir	Swedish Expedition (Jack Berg)
130. 21.May.1991	Mark Whetu Brent Okida	North Col/ North Face	American Expedition (Eric Simonson)
131. 22.May.1991	Babu Tshering, Sherpa Chuldin, Sherpa	North Col/ North Face	British Expedition (Harry Taylor)
132. 24.May.1991	Greg Wilson	North Col/ North Face	American Expedition (Eric Simonson)
133. 27.May.1991	Muneo Nukita • Junichi Futagami Nima Dorja, Sherpa Phinzo Norbu, Sherpa	North Col/ North Face	Japanese Expedition (Muneo Nukita)
134. 6.Oct.1991	Frco. José "Coque" Pérez Rafael Vidaurre José-Antonio Garcés Antonio Ubieto	South-east Ridge	Spanish Expedition (Juan-Carlos Gómez)
135. 7.Oct.1991	Volodya Balyberdin ★ Anatoli Boukreev ★	South-east Ridge	Russian Expedition (Volodya Balyberdin)

	Date	Climber	Route	Nationality/Leader
136.	10.Oct.1991	Roman Giutashvili Dan Mazur	South-east Ridge	
137.	10.May.1992	Prem Singh Sunil Dutt Sharma Kanhaiya Lal (Pokhriyal)	South-east Ridge	Indian Expedition (Hukam Singh)
138.	12.May.1992	Ned Gillette Doron Erel Cham Yick-Kai Gary Ball Douglas Mantle Rob Hall Randall Danta Guy Cotter Sonam Tshering, Sherpa Ang Dorje II, Sherpa Tashi Tshering, Sherpa Apa, Sherpa Ang Dawa, Sherpa Miss Ingrid Baeyens	South-east Ridge	New Zealand Expedition (Rob Hall)
139.	12.May.1992	Ronald Naar Edmond Oefner Dawa Tashi, Sherpa Nima Temba, Sherpa	South-east Ridge	Dutch Expedition (Ronald Naar)
140.	12.May.1992	Aleksandr Gerasimov Andrei Volkov Ilia Sabelnikov Ivan Dusharin	South-east Ridge	Russian Expedition (Vyacheslav Volkov)
141.	12.May.1992	Skip Horner Louis Bowen Vernon Tejas Dawa Temba, Sherpa Ang Gyalzen, Sherpa	South-east Ridge	American Expedition (Todd Burleson)
142.	12.May.1992	Lobsang, Sherpa Santosh Yadav Mohan Singh (Gunjyal) Sange Mudok Wangchuk, Sherpa	South-east Ridge	Indian Expedition (Hukam Singh)
143.	14.May.1992	Sergei Penzov Vladimir Zakharov Yevgeni Vinogradsky Fedor Konyukhov	South-east Ridge	Russian Expedition (Vyacheslav Volkov)

Date	Climber	Route	Nationality/Leader
144. 15.May.1992	Cristián García-Huidobro Rodrigo Jordán Juan-Sebastián Montes	East Face/ South Col	Chilean Expedition (Rodrigo Jordán)
145. 15.May.1992	Peter Athans Keith Kerr Todd Burleson Hugh Morton Lhakpa Rita, Sherpa Man Bahadur Tamang Dorje, Sherpa	South-east Ridge	American Expedition (Todd Burleson)
146. 15.May.1992	Francisco Gan Alfonso Juez Ramón Portilla Lhakpa Nuru, Sherpa Pemba Norbu II, Sherpa	South Pillar/ South-east Ridge	Spanish Expedition (Francisco Soria)
147. 15.May.1992	Mauricio Purto Ang Rita, Sherpa ★ Ang Phuri, Sherpa	South-east Ridge	Chilean Expedition (Mauricio Purto)
148. 15.May.1992	Jonathan Pratt	South-east Ridge	Czechoslovakian Expedition (Miroslav Smid)
149. 25.Sept.1992	Juan-Mari Eguillor Patxi Fernández Alberto Iñurrategi ★ Félix Iñurrategi ★	South-east Ridge	Basque Expedition (Pedro Tous)
150. 28.Sept.1992	Giuseppe Petigax Lorenzo Mazzoleni Mario Panzeri ★ Pierre Royer Lhakpa Nuru, Sherpa	South-east Ridge	Italian Expedition (Agostina Da Polenza)
151. 29.Sept.1992	Benoît Chamoux Oswald Santin	South-east Ridge	
152. 30.Sept.1992	Abele Blanc Giampietro Verza	South-east Ridge	
153. 1.Oct.1992	Josu Bereziartua	South-east Ridge	Basque Expedition (Pedro Tous)
154. 1.Oct.1992	Eugène Berger	South-east Ridge	French Expedition (Bernard Muller)
155. 3.Oct.1992	Mikel Repáraz Pedro Tous Juan Tomás	South-east Ridge	Basque Expedition (Pedro Tous)

EVEREST CHRONICLE

Date	Climber	Route	Nationality/Leader
156. 4.Oct.1992	Ralf Dujmovits Sonam Tshering, Sherpa	South-east Ridge	German Expedition (Ralf Dujmovits)
157. 7.Oct.1992	Michel Vincent	South-east Ridge	French Expedition (Michel Vincent)
158. 9.Oct.1992	Wally Berg Augusto Ortega Alfonso de la Parrá Apa, Sherpa Pasang Kami, Sherpa	South-east Ridge	American Expedition (Wally Berg)
159. 9.Oct.1992	Philippe Grenier Michel Pellé Thierry Defrance Alain Roussey Pierre Aubertin Scott Darsney	South-east Ridge	French Expedition (Michel Pellé)
160. 13.April.1993	Heo Young-Ho Ngati, Sherpa	North Ridge, descent via South-east Ridge, South Col	South Korean Expedition (Oh-In-Hwan)
161. 22.April.1993	Dawa Tashi, Sherpa • Mrs. Pasang Lhamu, Sherpa Pemba Nuru, Sherpa • Sonam Tshering, Sherpa Lhapa Nuru Nawang Thile, Sherpa	South Col/ South-east Ridge	Nepalese Expedition (Mrs. Pasang Lhamu, Sherpa)
162. 5.May.1993	Ji Mi Jia Chuo Kai Zhong Pu Bu Wang Yong Feng Wu Chin Hsiung	North Col/ North Ridge	Chinese- Taiwanese Expedition (Zeng Shu-Sheng)
163. 10.May.1993	Alex Lowe John Helenek John Dufficy Wally Berg Michael Sutton Apa, Sherpa Dawa Nuru, Sherpa Chuldin Temba, Sherpa	South Col/ South-east Ridge	American/Canadian/ South African Expedition (Todd Berleson)

245

EVEREST

Date	Climber	Route	Nationality/Leader
164. 10.May.1993	Miss Kim Soon-Joo Miss Ju Hyun-Ok Miss Choi Oh-Soon Ang Dawa, Sherpa Ang Tsering, Sherpa Sona Dendu, Sherpa Rinzin, Sherpa	South Col/ South-east Ridge	South Korean Expedition (Miss Ji Hyun-Ok)
165. 10.May.1993	Michael Groom ★ • Lobsang Tshering Bhutia	South Col/ South-east Ridge	Australian/Indian/ Macedonian Expedition (Tashi Wangchuk Tenzing)
166. 10.May.1993	Harry Taylor	South Col/ South-east Ridge	British/Canadian/American/ Australian Expedition (John Barry)
167. 17.May.1993	Miss Rebecca Stephens Ang Pasang, Sherpa Kami Tshering, Sherpa	South Col/ South-east Ridge	
168. 10.May.1993	Miss Dicky Dolma Miss Santosh Yadav Miss Kunga Bhutia Baldev Kunwer Ongda Chhiring, Sherpa Na Temba, Sherpa Kosang Dorje, Sherpa Dorje, Sherpa Miss Radha Devi Thakur Rajiv Sharma Miss Deepu Sharma Mrs. Savita Martolia Nima Norbu Dolma Miss Suman Kutiyal Nima Dorje, Sherpa Tenzing, Sherpa Lobsang Jangbu, Sherpa Nga Temba, Sherpa	South Col/ South-east Ridge	Indian/ Nepalese Expedition (Miss Bachemdri Pal)
169. 10.May.1993	Miss Mary Lefever Mark Selland Charles Armatys Pemba Temba, Sherpa Moti Lal Gurung	South Col/ South-east Ridge	American Expedition (Paul Pfau & Michael Sinclair)
170. 16.May.1993	Michael Sinclair Mark Rabold	South Col/ South-east Ridge	

Date	Climber	Route	Nationality/Leader
	Phinzo, Sherpa		
	Dorje, Sherpa		
	Durga Tamang		
171. 10.May.1993	Veikka Gustafsson	South Col/	New Zealand/Finnish
	Mrs. Jan Arnold	South-east	American/British/French
	Rob Hall	Ridge	Expedition (Rob Hall)
	Jonathan Gluckman		
	Ang Chumbi, Sherpa		
	Ang Dorje, Sherpa		
	Norbu (Nuru), Sherpa		
172. 10.May.1993	Vladas Vitkauskas	South Col/	Lithuanian Expedition
		South-east	(Vladas Vitkauskas)
		Ridge	
173. 10.May.1993	Alexei Mouravlev	South Col/	Russian Expedition
		South-east	(Alexander Volguine)
		Ridge	
174. 15.May.1993	Vladimir Janochkine	South Col/	
		South-east Ridge	
175. 16.May.1993	Vladimir Bashkirov ★	South Col/	
		South-east Ridge	
176. 17.May.1993	Vladimir Koroteev	South Col/	
		South-east Ridge	
177. 16.May.1993	Josep Pujante	South Col/	Spanish Expedition
	Ang Phurba, Sherpa	South-east	(Lluis Belvis)
		Ridge	
178. 17.May.1993	Oscar Cadiach ★	South Col/	
		South-east Ridge	
179. 16.May.1993	José Maria Onate	South Col/	Spanish Expedition
	Alberto Cerain	South-east	(Josu Feijoo)
	José Ramon Aguirre	Ridge	
	Jangbu, Sherpa		
	Ang Rita, Sherpa ★		
180. 16.May.1993	Jan Harris	South Col/	American/
	Keith Brown	South-east	Australian Expedition
		Ridge	(Keith Brown)
181. 16.May.1993	Park Young-Seok	South Col/	South Korean Expedition
	• An Jin-Seob	South-east	(Lee Jong-Ryang)
	Kim Tae-Kon	Ridge	
	Kazi, Sherpa		

247

EVEREST

Date	Climber	Route	Nationality/Leader
182. 27.May.1993	Dawson Stelfox	North Col/ North Ridge	British/Irish Expedition (Dawson Stelfox)
183. 6.Oct.1993	Park Hyun-Jae Panuru, Sherpa	North Col/ North Ridge	South Korean Expedition (Lim Hyung-Chil)
184. 6.Oct.1993	François Bernard Antoine Cayrol Eric Gramond ★ Gyalbu, Sherpa Dawa Tashi, Sherpa	South Col/ South-east Ridge	French Expedition (Alain Esteve)
185. 9.Oct.1993	Alain Esteve Hubert Giot ★ Norbu (Nuru), Sherpa Nima Gombu, Sherpa	South Col/ South-east Ridge	
186. 7.Oct.1993	Juanito Oiarzabal Ongda Chhiring, Sherpa	South Pillar	Spanish Expedition (Juanito Oiarzabal)
187. 7.Oct.1993	Miss Ginette Harrison Gary Pfisterer Ramon Blanco Graham Hoyland Stephen Bell Scott McIvor Na Temba, Sherpa Pasang Kami, Sherpa Dorje, Sherpa	South Col/ South-east Ridge	British/American/ Spanish Expedition (Stephen Bell)
188. 9.Oct.1993	Martin Barnicott David Hempleman-Adams Lee Nobmann Tenzing, Sherpa Nga Temba, Sherpa Lhakpa Gelu, Sherpa Ang Pasang, Sherpa	South Col/ South-east Ridge	
189. 9.Oct.1993	Maciej Berbeka Lhapka Nuru, Sherpa	North Col/ North Face	British/Australian/ Finnish Expedition (Jonathan Tinker)
190. 10.Oct.1993	Jonathan Tinker Babu Tshering, Sherpa	North Col/ North Face	
191. 18.Dec.1993	Hideji Nazuka Fumiaki Goto	South-west Face	JapaneseExpedition (1st Winter ascent) (Kuniaki Yagihara)
192. 20.Dec.1993	Osamu Tanabe Sinsuke Ezuka	South-west Face	
193. 22.Dec.1993	Yoshio Ogata Ryushi Hoshino	South-west Face	

Date	Climber	Route	Nationality/Leader
194. 8.May.1994	Kiyohiko Suzuki Wataru Atsuta Nima Dorje, Sherpa Dawa Tshering, Sherpa Na Temba, Sherpa Lhakpa Nuru, Sherpa	South Pillar	Japanese Expedition (Mitsuyoshi Hongo)
195. 13.May.1994	Tomiyasu Ishikawa Nima Temba, Sherpa Dawa Tahsi, Sherpa Pasang Tshering, Sherpa	South Pillar	
196. 8.May.1994	• Shih Fang-Fang	North Col/ North Face	Taiwanese Expedition (Chang Jui-Kong)
197. 9.May.1994	Lobsang Jangbu, Sherpa ★ Rob Hess ★ Scott Fischer ★ Brent Bishop Sona Dendu, Sherpa	South Col/ South-east Ridge	American Expedition (Steven Goryl)
198. 13.May.1994	Steven Goryl	South Col/ South-east Ridge	
199. 9.May.1994	Ang Dorje, Sherpa Hall Wendel Helmut Seitzel David Keaton Ekke Gundelach Rob Hall Ed Viesturs Nima Gombu, Sherpa Norbu (Nuru), Sherpa David Taylor Erling Kagge	South Col/ South-east Ridge	New Zealand/American/ German/Norwegian Expedition (Rob Hall)
200. 13.May.1994	Lhakpa Rita, Sherpa Chuwang Nima, Sherpa Man Bahadur Tamang Kami Rita, Sherpa Dorje, Sherpa Ryszard Pawlowski Robert Cedergreen Paul Morrow Peter Athans Todd Burleson	South Col/ South-east Ridge	American/British/ Polish/Canadian/ South African Expedition (Todd Burleson)

EVEREST

Date	Climber	Route	Nationality/Leader
201. 19.May.1994	David Hahn	North Col to North Face	American/ New Zealand/Australian
202. 25.May.1994	Steve Swenson ★	North Col/ North Face	Expedition (Eric Simonson)
203. 26.May.1994	Mark Whetu • Michael Rheinberger	North Col/ North Face	
204. 31.May.1994	Bob Sloezen	North Col/North Face	
205. 10.Oct.1994	Muneo Nukita Apa, Sherpa Chumang Nima, Sherpa Dawa Tshering, Sherpa	South Col/ South-east Ridge	Japanese Expedition (Takashi Miyahara)
206. 11.Oct.1994	Charlie Hornsby Roddy Kirkwood Dorje, Sherpa Dawa Temba, Sherpa	South Col/ South-east Ridge	British/American Expedition (Simon Currin)
207. 7.May.1995	Lobsang Jangbu, Sherpa ★	South Col/ South-east Ridge	New Zealand/American/ French/Polish Expedition (Rob Hall)
208. 11.May.1995	Kiyoshi Furuno Shigeki Imoto Dawa Tshering, Sherpa Pasang Kami, Sherpa Lhakpa Nuru, Sherpa Nima Dorje, Sherpa	North-east Ridge	Japanese Expedition (Tadao Kanzaki)
209. 11.May.1995	Vladimir Shataev Iria Projaev Fedor Shuljev	North Col/ North Ridge	Russian Expedition (Kazbek Khamitsayev)
210. 13.May.1995	Kazbek Khamitsayev Eugeni Vinogradski Sergei Bogomolov Vladimir Korenkov Ang Rita, Sherpa ★		
211. 12.May.1995	Piotr Pustelnik	North Col/ North Ridge	Polish/Italian Expedition (Marco Bianchi)
212. 13.May.1995	Marco Bianchi ★ Christian Kuntner ★		
213. 12.May.1995	Ryszard Pawlowski	North Col/ North Ridge	American/Russian/Polish/ Danish/French/Brazilian Expedition (Henry Todd)
214. 14.May.1995	Mozart Catao Waldemar Niclevicz		
215. 17.May.1995	Graham Ratcliffe Anatoli Boukreev ★ Nikoli Sitnikov		

Date	Climber	Route	Nationality/Leader
216. 23.May.1995	Michael Jorgensen Crag Jones		
217. 12.May.1995	Cheng Kuo-Chun Miss Chiang Hsui-Chen Mingma Tshering, Sherpa Lhakpa Dorje, Sherpa ★ Tenzing, Sherpa ★	North Col/ North Ridge	Taiwanese Expedition (Liang Ming-Pen)
218. 13.May.1995 219. 17.May.1995 220. 26.May.1995	Mrs. Alison Hargreaves ★ Contantin Lacatusu Greg Child Karsang, Sherpa Lobsang Temba, Sherpa	North Col/ North Ridge	New Zealand/ British/American/ Romanian/Australian/ Canadian/French/Finnish Expedition (Russell Brice)
221. 14.May.1995	Reinhard Patscheider ★ Teodors Kirsis Imants Zauls	North Col/ North Ridge	Latvian/Italian Expedition (Reinhard Patscheider/Teodors Kirsis)
222. 14.May.1995 223. 16.May.1995	George Mallory Jeffrey Hall Jim Litch Dan Aguillar Kaji, Sherpa Ongda Chhiring, Sherpa Wongchu, Sherpa Colin Lynch Jay Budnik Steve Reneker Kurt Wedberg Phinzo, Sherpa Jangbu, Sherpa	North Col/ North Ridge	American/Australian Expedition (Paul Pfau)
224. 14.May.1995 225. 17.May.1995 226. 24.May.1995 227. 26.May.1995 228. 27.May.1995	Luc Jourjon Babu Tshering, Sherpa George Kotov Ali Nasuh Mahruki Jeff Shea Lhakpa Gelu, Sherpa Tshering, Sherpa Patrick Hache Robert Hempstead Lama Jangbu, Sherpa Babu Tshering, Sherpa Michael Smith Patrick Falvey James Allen	North Col/ North Ridge	British/Russian/French/ American/Australian/ Turkish/Irish Expedition (Jon Tinker)

Date	Climber	Route	Nationality/Leader
229. 14.May.1995	Josef Hinding ★	North Col/ North Ridge	Austrian Expedition (Willi Bauer)
230. 15.May.1995	Brad Bull Tommy Heinrich Apa, Sherpa Arita, Sherpa Nima Rita, Sherpa	South Col/ South-east Ridge	American/ Indian/Argentinean Expedition (Bob Hoffman)
231. 16.May.1995	Tony Tonsing Musal Kazi Tamang	North Col/ North Ridge	American/Peruvian Expedition (Thor Kieser)
232. 14.Oct.1995	Jo Yong-Il • Zangbu, Sherpa	North Col/ North Ridge	South Korean Expedition (Kim Jong-Ho)
233. 14.Oct.1995	Han Wuang-Yong Hong Sung-Taek Tashi Tshering, Sherpa	North Col/ North Ridge	South Korean Expedition (Lee Dong-Ho)
234. 14.Oct.1995	Park Jung-Hun Kim Young-Tae Kipa, Sherpa Dawa Tamang	South-west Face	South Korean Expedition (Cho Hyung-Gyu)
235. 10.May.1996	Anatoli Boukreev ★ Neal Beidleman Martin Adams Klev Schoening Mrs. Charlotte Fox Tim Madsen Mrs. Sandy Hill Pittman • Scott Fischer Miss Lena Nielsen-Gammelgaard Lobsang Jangbu, Sherpa ★ Nawang Dorje, Sherpa Tenzing, Sherpa Tashi Tshering, Sherpa	South Col/ South-east Ridge	American/Danish/ Kazakhstani Expedition (Scott Fischer)
236. 10.May.1996	Jon Krakauer • Andrew Harris Michael Groom • Rob Hall • Mrs. Yasuko Namba • Douglas Hansen Ang Dorje, Sherpa Norbu, Sherpa	South Col/ South-east Ridge	New Zealand/American/ Japanese/Australian/ Canadian/South African Expedition (Rob Hall)

Date	Climber	Route	Nationality/Leader
237. 10.May.1996	Gau Ming-Ho Nima Gombu, Sherpa Mingma Tshering, Sherpa	South Col/ South-east Ridge	Taiwanese Expedition (Gau Ming-Ho)
238. 10.May.1996	• Tsewang Samanla • Tsewang Paljor • Dorje Morup (Samanla, Paljor, and Morup may not have reached summit.)	North Col/ North Face	Indian Expedition (Mohinder Singh)
239. 17.May.1996	Sange, Sherpa Hira Ram Tashi Ram Nadra Ram Kusang, Sherpa		
240. 11.May.1996	Hiroshi Hanada Eisuka Shigekawa Pasang Tshering, Sherpa Pasang Kami, Sherpa Ang Gyalzen, Sherpa	North Col/ North Face	Japanese Expedition (Mitsuo Uematsu)
241. 13.May.1996	Mamoru Kikuchi Hirotaka Sugiyama Nima Dorje, Sherpa Chuwang Nima, Sherpa Dawa Tshering, Sherpa		
242. 17.May.1996	Hirotaka Takeyuchi Pemba Tshering, Sherpa Na Temba, Sherpa	North Col/ North Face	Japanese Expedition (Koji Yamazaki)
243. 21.May.1996	Koji Yamazaki		
244. 17.May.1996	Sven Gangdal Olav Ulvund Dawa Tashi, Sherpa Dawa Tshering, Sherpa	North Col/ North Face	Norwegian/Italian/ Czechoslovakian Expedition (Jon Gangdal)
245. 18.May.1996	Morten Rostrup Josef Nezerka Fausto De Stefani Gyalbu, Sherpa		
246. 19.May.1996	Alan Hinkes Matthew Dickinson Lhakpa Gelu, Sherpa Mingma Dorje, Sherpa Phur Gyalzen, Sherpa		British/American/ Norwegian/ Dutch Expedition (Simon Lowe)
247. 20.May.1996	Petr Kouznetsov Valeri Kohanov	Couloir between	Russian Expedition (Sergei Antipine)

253

Date	Climber	Route	Nationality/Leader
	Grigori Semikolenkov	North and North-east Ridge	
248. 23.May.1996	Thierry Renard Babu Tshering, Sherpa Dawa, Sherpa	South Col/ South-east Ridge	French Expedition (Thierry Renard)
249. 23.May.1996	Ed Viesturs ★ David Breashears Robert Schauer Jamling Tenzing Norgay Miss Araceli Segarra Lhakpa Dorje, Sherpa ★ Dorje, Sherpa Jangbu, Sherpa Muktu Lhakpa, Sherpa Thilen, Sherpa	South Col/ South-east Ridge	American/Spanish/ Austrian/Indian Expedition (David Breashears)
250. 23.May.1996	Goren Kropp ★ Ang Rita, Sherpa ★	South Pillar/ South Col	Swedish Expedition (Goren Kropp)
251. 23.May.1996	Jesus Martinez ★	South Pillar/ South Col	Spanish Expedition (Jose Antonio Martinez)
252. 24.May.1996	Hans Kammerlander ★ (descent on skis)	North Col/ North Face	Italian Expedition (Hans Kammerlander)
253. 24.May.1996	Yuri Contreras Hector Ponce de Leon	North Col/ North Face	Mexican/German/ Austrian Expedition (Peter Kowalzik)
254. 25.May.1996	Ian Woodall Miss Cathy O'Dowd • Bruce Herrod Pemba, Sherpa Ang Dorje, Sherpa Lama Jangbu	South Col/ South-east Ridge	South African/ British Expedition (Ian Woodall)
255. 26.Sept.1996	Miss Clara Sumarwati Kaji, Sherpa Gyalzen, Sherpa Ang Gyalzen, Sherpa Dawa Tshering Chuwang Nima, Sherpa	North Col/ North Face	Indonesian Expedition (Miss Clara Sumarwati)
256. 11.Oct.1996	Choi Jong-Tai Shin Kwang-Chal Paneru, Sherpa	South Col/ South-east Ridge	South Korean Expedition (Lim Hyung-Chil)

Date	Climber	Route	Nationality/Leader
	Kipa, Sherpa		
	Dawa Tamang		
257. 26.April.1997	Apa, Sherpa	South Col/	Indonesian/Kazakhstani/
	Anatoli Boukreev	South-east	Polish Expedition
	Dawa Nuru, Sherpa	Ridge	(Edhie Wibowo)
	Vladimir Bashkirov		
	Misirin		
	Asmujiono		
258. 2.May.1997	Vladimir Frolov	North Col/	Kazakhstani/Russian/
	Andrej Molotov	North Face	Georgian/Canadian/
	Sergei Ovsharenko		Australian Expedition
	Vladimir Souviga ★		(Ervand Ilinski)
259. 7.May.1997	• Ivan Plotnikov		
	• Nikolai Chevtchenko		
260. 20.May.1997	Konstantin Farafonov		
	Sergei Lavrov		
	Dimitri Grekov		
	Dimitri Sobolev		
	Dimitri Mouravev		
	Mrs. Lyudmila Savina		
261. 22.May.1997	Andy Evans		
262. 7.May.1997	Lee In	North Col/	South Korean Expedition
	Ang Dawa Tamang	North Face	(Lee Dong-Yeon)
263. 8.May.1997	Antoine de Choudens ★	North Col/	French/Bulgarian
	Stephane Cagnin	North Face	Expedition
264. 20.May.1997	Doytchin Vassilev		(Antoine de Choudens)
265. 21.May.1997	Nikola Kekus	South Col/	British/Icelandic/
	Bjorn Olafsson	South-east	Mexican Expedition
	Hallgrimur Magnusson	Ridge	(Jon Tinker)
	Einar Stefansson		
	Babu Tshering, Sherpa		
	Dawa, Sherpa		
266. 23.May.1997	Mark Warham		
	Eric Blakeley		
	Hugo Rodriguez		
	Lhakpa Gelu, Sherpa		
	Da Tenzi, Sherpa		
267. 21.May.1997	Danuri, Sherpa	South Col/	Nepalese Expedition
		South-east	(Bhakta Bahadur Thakuri)
		Ridge	

Date	Climber	Route	Nationality/Leader
268. 22.May.1997	Franc Pepevnik	North Col/	Croatian/Slovenian/
269. 23.May.1997	Pavle Kozjek ★	North Face	Bosnia-Herzegovinian/
			German Expedition
			(Darko Berljak)
270. 23.May.1997	David Breashears	South Col/	American Expedition
	Peter Athans	South-east	(David Breashears)
	Jangbu, Sherpa	Ridge	
	Dorje, Sherpa		
	Kami, Sherpa		
271. 23.May.1997	Jamie Clarke	South Col/	Canadian/American
	Alan Hobson	South-east	Expedition (Jason Edwards)
	Lhakpa Tshering, Sherpa	Ridge	
	Gyalbu, Sherpa		
	Tashi Tshering, Sherpa		
	Kami Tshering, Sherpa		
272. 23.May.1997	Guy Cotter	South Col/	New Zealand/
	Ed Viesturs	South-east	American/
	Tashi Tenzing	Ridge	Finnish/Australian/
	Veikka Gustafsson ★		Spanish Expedition
	David Carter		(Guy Cotter)
	Ang Dorje, Sherpa		
	Mingma Tshering, Sherpa		
273. 23.May.1997	Mohandas Nagapan	South Col/	Malaysian Expedition
	Magendran Munisamy	South-east	(Nor Ramlle Sulaiman)
	Na Temba, Sherpa	Ridge	
	Dawa Temba, Sherpa		
	Gyalzen, Sherpa		
	Ang Phuri Gyalzen, Sherpa		
	Fura Dorje, Sherpa		
274. 23.May.1997	Andres Delgado	South Col/	British/Australian/
	Tenzing, Sherpa	South-east	Mexican Expedition
		Ridge	(Mal Duff)
275. 27.May.1997	Mrs. Brigitte Muir		
	Kipa, Sherpa		
	Dorje, Sherpa		
276. 24.May.1997	Alexandre Zelinski	North Col/	Russian Expedition
	Sergei Sokolov	North Face	(Kazbek Khamitsayev)
277. 25.May.1997	Wally Berg	South Col/	American/British
	Kami Rita, Sherpa	South-east	Expedition (Todd Burleson)
	Ang Pasang, Sherpa	Ridge	

EVEREST CHRONICLE

Date	Climber	Route	Nationality/Leader
	Pemba Tenji, Sherpa Mingma Tshering, Sherpa Lhakpa Rita, Sherpa Nima Tashi, Sherpa • Tenzing Nuru, Sherpa		
278. 27.May.1997	Yuri Contreras Ilgvars Pauls Dawa Sona, Sherpa	South Col/ South-east Ridge	British/Mexican/Latvian/ Norwegian/Irish/American/ Italian/Canadian/Australian Expedition (Henry Todd)
279. 29.May.1997	Russell Brice Richard Price	North Col/ North Face	New Zealand/Japanese/ Canadian/British/French/ Belgian/American/Dutch Expedition (Russell Brice)
280. 29.May.1997	Da Chimyi Tenzing Dorje Kai Zhong	North Col/ North Face	Chinese/Tibetan Expedition (Da Chimyi)

No ascents were made in post-Monsoon season, 1997.

The list was compiled by the author with later additions concerning fatalities and oxygen free ascents added by the english language publishers drawing on sundry sources, notably: *the American Alpine Journal, High* magazine, and the research of Xavier Eguskitza. The "ascents without bottled oxygen" refer to no use of bottled oxygen at any point in the ascent or descent, including during sleep. A number of other near "ascents without bottled oxygen" have been made. These are not noted.

1953 THE TOP OF THE PYRAMID

The opening-up of Nepal in 1949 and the closure of Tibet after the Chinese occupation, are two events which belong amongst the most significant changes in the world during this century. For mountaineers they meant a shift of the struggle for Everest from the north to the hitherto-unexplored Nepalese southern side, and the end of the 30-year British monopoly on the mountain. British climbers were, however, the first to reconnoitre the 'new' side in 1950 and 1951. In October 1951, Eric Shipton, one of the greatest British explorers, was the first to tread the celebrated Khumbu Icefall and negotiate it up to where at its top, a massive crevasse system splits the valley from side to side, like a moat defending the Western Cwm (this Welsh name was given to the Everest Sanctuary in 1921 by George Leigh Mallory). Shipton was unable to enter the basin of the Western Cwm. This expedition, sponsored by the Himalayan Committee (newly formed by the Alpine Club and the Royal Geographical Society to replace the old Everest Committee), also included Edmund Hillary, Tom Bourdillon and Dr Michael Ward.*

Then in 1952, the Swiss came; the expedition leader was Dr Wyss-Dunant (who coined the conception of the Death Zone). Sirdar of the Sherpas was Tenzing Norgay. What they achieved during the period April 23 to May 28 was phenomenal and well worth remembering. On May 28 Lambert and Tenzing reached a height of 8,500 metres on the South-east Ridge (only 348 metres below the summit) but having then reached their limit, they were forced to turn back.

Above Base Camp at 5,050 metres, they had erected eight camps — the first three: at the foot of the Icefall, in the Icefall and directly above it; their Advance Base Camp, Camp V at 6,800 metres was at the end of the four and a half kilometre long Western Cwm (to which the Swiss gave the beautiful name 'Valley of Silence'). Their line of attack was to follow the massive rock ridge leading directly up to the South Col (known ever since as the Geneva Spur). Camp V had been installed on May 12, and on May 26 Camp VI was placed on the 7,986-metre-high South Col. Because of

* The party was completed by W. H. Murray and E. P. Riddiford.

the danger of falling ice, there was only an equipment dump, a staging post, between these two. Lambert and Tenzing made their bid for the summit from a tent on the South-east Ridge.

After this considerable but incomplete success, the Swiss launched a second expedition in the August of 1952, this time led by Dr Gabriel Chevalley — new to the team were Ernst Reiss and Norman Dyhrenfurth. They built their main standing camp in the middle of the Western Cwm at 6,400 metres, as a strong launching pad for their attempt. After a fatal accident on the Geneva Spur, they opened a route across the Lhotse slopes to the South Col camp, with two intermediate camps on the face, and they reached the South Col on November 19 (Reiss, Tenzing and seven Sherpas). There they faced unbelievable difficulties and were forced to retreat on November 20 in the face of hurricanes and arctic cold.

Without the benefit of this Swiss experience — general, tactical and practical — the British success in 1953, coinciding fortuitously with the coronation of their young Queen, would not have been possible. John Hunt says in his book on the expedition:

'The significance of all these other attempts is that, regardless of the height they reached, each one added to the mounting sum of experience, and this experience had to reach a certain total before the riddle could be solved. The building of this pyramid of experience was vital to the whole issue; only when it had attained a certain height was it within the power of any team of mountaineers to fashion its apex. Seen in this light, other expeditions did not fail; they made progress. They had reached this stage when we prepared to try again last winter (1952–53). By that time, *but not before*, the defences by which the mountain had so far withstood assault were well enough known; it only remained to study them and draw the right conclusions. . . . We of the 1953 Everest Expedition are proud to share the glory with our predecessors.' And of the Swiss contribution in particular, Hunt says eloquently, 'Our ascent was linked at almost every step with their attempt.'

As events proved strikingly, the strategic and tactical planning was faultless, and the preparation, the journey to, and the time spent on the mountain were equally undertaken with precision and elasticity. It is noteworthy that Eric Shipton was not in the final analysis selected by the

Himalaya Committee as leader of this expedition (he was by preference a small-expedition man, and no lover of the use of oxygen); in John Hunt, a high-ranking army officer (at that time with the Central European Command) with three Himalayan expeditions to his credit from his years serving in Bengal, they had found an enthusiastic and highly competent alpinist . . . a man, therefore, with valuable practical experience in tactics and leadership by reason of his profession, and in the alpine field by reasons of inclination.

Hunt took extensive advice, notably from the Swiss and from the French, who in 1950 with their ascent of Annapurna, became the first to conquer an eight-thousand metre peak. It was given to him freely, and two veterans of the Everest struggle also gave him especially valuable counsel. Norton, who in 1924 had reached about 8,600 metres on the North Ridge, advised: 'Put your assault camp on, or very close under the Southern Summit. . . . I shall never have any great hope of success unless a final camp is so placed.' And Longstaff (his many achievements included the first ascent of a seven-thousand metre mountain, Trisul, 7,120 metres, in 1907) recommended: 'Make it your very personal responsibility to erect this final camp.' Hunt accepted the advice of both. The ridge camp was erected at 8,504 metres and Hunt himself carried a load up to the Southeast Ridge, to a height of 8,336 metres.

The expedition resolved to use oxygen apparatus. Hunt discusses the decision in detail in his book. The following quotation is noteworthy: 'Oxygen may be looked upon as a height-reducer, producing conditions comparable with climbing on more familiar mountains.' The barrier to natural acclimatization, Hunt believed, lay at around 6,500 metres; above that, physical and mental deterioration sets in and becomes progressively more marked. Consequently, for a man to find success on an 8,000 metre peak from a height of 6,500 metres, he really needs to speed up his rate of progress and employ 'rush' tactics. But this he cannot do. To climb those 2,400 metres (from 6,500 to 8,848 metres) in the course of a day, or at most two, is clearly beyond the bounds of possibility.

How quickly and forcibly the lack of oxygen affects someone at 8,800 metres, who has been climbing with supplementary oxygen, is revealed in the following quotation from Hillary's famous account of his summit climb. He turned off his set on the summit, took off the facemask and set the apparatus down. He noticed: 'After some ten minutes of this, I realized I was becoming rather clumsy-fingered and slow-moving, so I quickly replaced my oxygen set and experienced once more the stimulating effect of even a few litres of oxygen. . . .'

The British team comprised: John Hunt as leader, Edmund Hillary, Tenzing Norgay, George Lowe, Wilfrid Noyce, Charles Evans, Alfred Gregory, Tom Bourdillon, Charles Wylie, Michael Westmacott, Michael Ward (Doctor), Griffith Pugh (Physiologist), Tom Stobart (Cameraman) and James Morris (Correspondent for *The Times*). Nine of the team reached as far as the South Col, three of them twice. Of the nine, seven went on to over 8,200 metres, four climbed the 8,760 metre South Summit, two reached the Main Summit. Three of the nine remained four days and nights above 7,900 metres, three stayed on an additional three days and nights. Even though some were very tired, there was no case of complete collapse from exhaustion.

Of the 27 Sherpas, 19 climbed to the South Col, six of those twice. The highest camp was erected at 8,504 metres and was, Hunt declared the supreme test of the support party: 'On those two days, 26th and 28th May, the tasks of Sherpas and Sahibs were no longer complementary, they were identical'.

The expedition had left Kathmandu on March 10/11. Before commencing climbing, the team had spent a week of acclimatization and training, and familiarizing themselves with the oxygen equipment. On May 1, from a fully-equipped Advanced Base Camp (Camp IV, 6,462 metres) the climb over the Lhotse Face began — Camp V (6,706 metres), Camp VI (7,010 metres), Camp VII (7,315 metres) — Camp VIII on the South Col (7,986 metres) was erected on May 22. On May 26 the first summit pair of Bourdillon and Evans reached the South Summit (8,760 metres); the first loads for the Ridge Camp (IX) were carried by Hunt and some Sherpas to 8,336 metres on the South-east Ridge. On May 28 the Ridge Camp was established at 8,504 metres for the second assault. Gregory, Lowe and Ang Nyima withdrew back to Camp VIII right away, leaving Hillary and Tenzing in the camp. They passed a relatively good night using oxygen at two-hourly intervals; there were some extremely strong gusts of wind and the temperature dropped to -27°C.

On May 29, they left the tent at 6.30 a.m., were on the South Summit at 9 and at 11.30, after five hour's climbing, were the first men on the summit of Everest. 32 years had passed since the struggle for 'The Third Pole' had begun.

Hillary confessed to a 'terrific feeling of exposure' throughout their passage along the summit ridge. Of the view down the South-west Face, he said, 'It was a great thrill to look straight down this enormous rock face and to see 8,000 feet below us, the tiny tents of Camp IV in the Western Cwm.' The other side of the ridge was equally awe-inspiring, 'great contorted cornices, overhanging masses of snow and ice, stuck out like twisted fingers over the 10,000 foot drop of the Kangshung Face.' The 15 metre-high rock barrier which since then has been known as 'The Hillary Step', 'the rock itself smooth and almost holdless', he tackled by jamming himself into a narrow crack between the cornice and the rock, and straddling his way upwards with 'a fervent prayer that the cornice would remain attached to the rock'.

After 15 minutes on the summit they turned to go. It only took an hour to get back to the South Summit, and at 14.00 hours they were back in the Ridge Camp. Tenzing got the stove going and made hot lemonade. They felt weak and exhausted. They had to cut steps down to the South Col — Hillary for 60 metres, Tenzing a further 30 metres. Just short of the tents their oxygen ran out.

The next day they all climbed down to Camp IV. Lowe gave the thumbs-up signal to the tiny figures coming to meet them, and waved his ice axe in the direction of the summit. John Hunt described the scene graphically: 'Everyone was pouring out of the tents; there were shouts of acclamation and joy. The next moment I was with them: handshakes — even, I blush to say hugs — for the triumphant pair.'

In the closing passages of his fine book, Sir John also ponders over the future: 'Some day Everest will be climbed again. It may well be attempted without oxygen, although I do not rate the chances of success very high at present. Let us hope for the opening of the frontier dividing Nepal and Tibet to climbers from both sides of that political barrier, for the route to the top of the mountain by the North Face remains to be completed. The time may come when the prospect of traversing across the summit, climbing up by one ridge and descending by another, may no longer be fantasy'. That climbers would also seek to climb the formidable South-west Face, and would succeed, Sir John didn't at that time, 1953, foresee. But it has happened during the intervening years, as have his other prophesies, all been fulfilled.

Sources: John Hunt, *The Ascent of Everest*, Hodder and Stoughton, 1953; G. O. Dyhrenfurth, *To the Third Pole*, English-language edition — Werner Laurie 1955.

1963 THE FIRST TRAVERSE

In May 1963, exactly ten years after the first ascent, the first American Expedition, led by Norman G. Dyhrenfurth, succeeded in making the first traverse of Everest. The big expedition — 19 Americans, one Briton, a Nepalese Liaison Officer and 32 Sherpas — built up two chains of camps on the mountain. Base Camp was situated just before the Khumbu Icefall at 5,425 metres; Camp I above the Icefall at 6,160 metres; Advance Base Camp II at 6,500 metres in the middle of the Western Cwm; Camp III-S (South) on the Lhotse Face at 6,980 metres; IV-S at 7,950 metres; V-S on the South Col at 7,986 metres; and Camp VI-S at 8,370 metres on the South-east Ridge just below the South Summit, at an altitude therefore 478 metres less than the Main Summit. From the Advance Base, a Camp III-W (West) was erected close under the West Shoulder at 7,250 metres; between these two there was only a Dump Camp, for the monstrous snow slope up to the West Shoulder presented a constant avalanche threat. In fact four Sherpas cooking tea at the Dump Camp were swept down the mountain with their two tents in the powder-snow avalanche. It was an astonishing incident — with no injuries, luckily, but the loss of a fair amount of equipment. Camp IV-W stood at 7,650 metres on a ledge where the snow met the steep rock of the summit ridge; and finally, a storm camp was established (Camp V-W) at 8,300 metres, in other words 548 metres height-difference from the summit.

263

The expedition went to great pains not to let news of their ambitious intention leak to the press beforehand. Indeed, the decision to definitely attempt the West Ridge was only made on the march-in, after discussions amongst the team, and the work of preparing the route to the West Shoulder was initially considered merely as 'Reconnaissance'. The summit via the South Col route had priority.

On March 29 (having left Kathmandu on February 20) the Advance Base Camp was established; on April 16 the South Col Camp V-S was set up and it was fully equipped in ten days of load carrying. The first assault on the summit began on April 27 from Camp II. Oxygen was used above Camp III-S. When the expedition's cameraman, Dr Doody, was forced to withdraw (thrombosis), Norman Dyhrenfurth took over the film work and, with his Sherpa Ang Dawa IV, made up the support party for the summit partnership of James W. Whittaker (known as 'Big Jim' as he is 6 feet 5 inches tall) and the Sherpa, Nawang Gombu. Eight Sherpas carried loads from the South Col camp to the site of the ridge camp on April 30, and they helped to chisel out a platform for two small, linking tents.

On May 1, after quite a comfortable night sleeping on oxygen, the summit pair Whittaker/Gombu set off around 6.30. The weather was windy and the visibility limited (they only occasionally glimpsed nearby Lhotse, phantomlike in the drifting mists). At 8,660 metres they each dumped a partly-filled oxygen cylinder for the journey down. At 11.30 on the South Summit (8,760 metres) the storm eased slightly. The Hillary Step presented no special difficulties. At 13.00 hours, after six and a half hours climbing, they stood on the summit. The last few steps they had taken together, side by side. They plunged an aluminium stake bearing the American flag into the summit snows, but of the bust of Mao, claimed to have been left there by the controversial Chinese Expedition of 1960, they saw no sign. This was the fourth definite ascent of Everest and they were the seventh and eighth visitors to the Third Pole.

As they began their descent, they noticed that their oxygen cylinders had run out. The 188 metres with the Hillary Step and the (short) uphill stretch to the South Summit, they had therefore to do without oxygen, gasping for breath. Finally, when they did reach the oxygen bottles they

264

had left on the way up, with what relief they gulped in the reviving gas. The descent was very slow; it took them four hours altogether before, staggering with fatigue, they regained Camp VI-S. It was 17.30; they had spent ten and a half hours on the climb.

Dyhrenfurth with his Sherpa had that same day reached 8,600 metres — clearly higher than the summit of Lhotse — filming, and had turned back only when more than half of their oxygen was exhausted, arriving back in Camp VI-S at 13.30. Both parties spent two nights in Camp VI and at least 40 hours around the 8,000 metre level (with more or less extensive intervals without artificial oxygen).

Resting and recuperating afterwards in Base Camp with the entire team, the decision was finally taken to venture an attempt on the traverse. It was obvious that far more oxygen would be needed, and they would have therefore to reckon on reduced rations. Timetables were worked out for the West and South teams, with the object of a meeting on the summit. What did turn out to be difficult, was to persuade the Sherpas to support this (double) attempt.

In the night of May 16/17, the West Ridge team met with a catastrophe in Camp IV-W (7,650 metres). It was during one of the wildest storms they had ever encountered. Two tents, linked together and housing the Americans, Auten and Corbet, and four Sherpas, ripped free from their sustaining guylines and began to slide down over the West Flank towards the drop on the Tibetan side (down to the Rongbuk Glacier). A snow drift halted their progress close to the cliff edge. Auten struggled back up to fetch Tom Hornbein and Willi Unsoeld, whose tent had remained intact. Everyone had come out of the ordeal alive, but Camp IV was nothing but a ruin, and the attempt had been dealt a crushing blow. But there was no talk of surrender, and after two days' rest, they pushed on again to re-establish Camp IV and then to place one high camp, instead of the two originally planned, as high as possible. This they did on May 21 at a height of 8,300 metres, only 548 metres lower in altitude than the summit, and 100 metres higher than the Ridge Camp under the South Summit. The camp site was a tiny ledge 50 centimetres x 2.5 metres. Willi Unsoeld and Tom Hornbein stayed there alone whilst their support team retired down the mountain. They had kept to their timetable, and on the other side of the mountain, up in Camp VI-S, Barry Bishop and Luther Jerstad were also ready.

The West Ridge pair left at 7 a.m. on May 22. Their route was more difficult than they had expected. The 'Hornbein Couloir' (not very far to the right of the classical Great Couloir on the North Face) narrowed to a crack, the climbing was difficult, and the wind's full strength caught the steep knife-edged ridge. They had to remove their crampons and over-boots while they climbed their cautious way along the smooth flank of the ridge for a distance of four rope-lengths, creeping one at a time along a series of tiny cracks and holds, which brought them 'truly high'. They were now, in fact, higher than Everest's South Summit. Then, coming over the last snow slope, they saw the American flag in the last rays of the evening sun, 'the flag stiff and streaming in the winds of space'. At 18.15 they approached the summit together. After 11 hours and 15 minutes. It was the sixth ascent, the first (and so far the only) by this new West Ridge Route.

Jerstad and Bishop, meanwhile, had left their camp at 8 o'clock that morning and reached the summit at 15.30, the fifth ascent of the South-east route, and the second summit success of this expedition. Looking down the West Ridge, they could see nothing of their expected friends, they called but received no answer. After a long rest, they slowly climbed down. It was 20.00 when from a height of 8,625 metres, they looked back up and saw the light of a torch. They waited two full hours until Unsoeld and Hornbein joined them there and their lamps had all burnt out. Before they reached the South Summit none of the tracks were visible. In complete darkness, without torches and without oxygen (it had long since been exhausted by both parties), they kept going till midnight, step by step, trying to find the way down. Slipping, staggering, un-sure. Just after midnight, they huddled down together on a rock below the line of the ridge, for the highest of all free bivouacs. They survived. Chomolungma, the Goddess Mother, had smiled graciously, the wind dropped.

On the evening of May 24, they were all back in Base Camp. Unsoeld, Bishop and Jerstad had to be carried out to Namche Bazar with severely frostbitten feet, and from there, flown on to Kathmandu. Unsoeld and

Bishop lost all their toes. Hornbein and Jerstad suffered no permanent damage. The total cost of the expedition was 405,263 dollars.

Sources: Norman Dyhrenfurth's description in *Die Alpen IV/1964* and *Alpinismus 2/1965,* as well as an article by James Ramsey Ullman, who had accompanied the expedition, in *Life* Magazine 20.9.63. (See also: James Ramsey Ullman, *Americans on Everest,* Lippincott, USA 1964, and Michael Joseph, London 1965, and T. F. Hornbein, *The West Ridge,* Sierra Club 1964.)

1969-1975 TO THE SOUTH-WEST FACE

The problem on Everest which in 1953 Sir John Hunt in his look into the future had not predicted — the 2,200 metre-high South-west Face of Everest — first began to capture climbers' interest sixteen years later in the autumn of 1969. After five attempts, it was finally climbed in 1975 in exemplary style, another success for British mountaineers.

The huge forbidding face rises from the upper basin of the Western Cwm, from a height of 6,600 metres. It has a wide, steep flank, of ice and rock fore-wall, which at 7,000 metres narrows into an increasingly steepening couloir, the Great Central Gully. Above 8,000 metres this gully ends abruptly at the foot of a 400 metre-high Rock Band, hundreds of metres wide. Above that are snow slopes, broken by relatively short, but difficult rock steps. The average angle of the slope is 49 degrees, and for 1,100 metres of the climb it is estimated to be 58 degrees. The bulwark of the Rock Band, which is tilted gently from left to right, is almost vertical, and its climbing difficulties are graded as V and VI. The Rock Band stopped all the earlier attempts at heights between 8,050 and, at most, 8,370 metres. The 8,050 metres was reached by the first Japanese reconnaissance party in 1969; the Spring of 1970 brought a veritable Japanese invasion to the Western Cwm (the South-west Face, the South-east Ordinary Route were attempted, as well as a Ski Expedition to the South Col) — 59 participants in all. Then there was an International South-west Face Expedition with members from 13 nations; a European Expedition, and another big

Japanese Expedition with 48 members (Everest was climbed by them, but by a repeat of the South Col Route — see table).

In Autumn 1972, in other words after the monsoon, British climbers under their leader, Chris Bonington, made their first attempt to force the formidable cliff face at 8,300 metres. The nucleus of the team was the climbers who in 1970 had made the first ascent of Annapurna South Face, the first of the really big Himalayan faces to be climbed (exactly one month before the ascent of the Rupal Face on Nanga Parbat, which at 4,500 metres of actual face height, is the biggest face of all). Bonington's team were the first to consider tackling the steep rock barrier by a gully on its left (west) side, seeing a possibility of reaching the upper snowfields this way, and in 1975 to take full advantage of the fine weather period, they began their climb during the last weeks of, and immediately after the end of, the monsoon (August/September). They had found the key to the problem; they had the required skills; the results of their 1975 expedition was the proof.

From the end of August to the middle of September, they built up their chain of camps to Camp V in the upper part of the Great Central Gully at 7,800 metres. From here on September 9, Tut Braithwaite and Nick Estcourt breached the Rock Band. The route across to the narrow left-hand gully led them over some steep, friable ribs of rock, sheathed in a layer of unstable powder snow. This was clearly one of the hardest sections of the whole climb. Then they climbed into the unknown gully, which was both steep and dark. After climbing a small chockstone pitch, almost covered with snow, they found — as they had hoped — a 'tongue of hard, avalanche-pressed snow' which brought them up through the gully for 200 metres to an ampitheatre at the top. Instinct led them to try a narrow 65 degree ramp under overhanging rock, and this brought them out of the gully to the upper snowfields and a possible site for Camp VI at 8,300 metres. The way to the summit lay open. On fixed ropes they returned to Camp V.

As first assault team, Chris Bonington selected Dougal Haston and Doug Scott; as a second group, Martin Boysen, Peter Boardman, Mick Burke and Sherpa-Sirdar Pertemba; after that, Nick Estcourt and Tut Braithwaite with Ronnie Richards and Ang Phurba would make up a third group; and finally, if all else failed, Chris Bonington, Mike Thompson, Allen Fyfe and Lapka Dorje as a fourth team could make an attempt.

On September 22, Scott and Haston followed the ropes put up by Estcourt and Braithwaite, and they reached a steep snow arête, the starting point for a long traverse across the upper snowfields, the site for Camp VI. Ang Phurba, Pertemba, Thompson, Bonington and Burke followed them up with all the necessary equipment for the camp. 'Theirs was an impressive carry,' said Scott afterwards.

The next day, Scott and Haston covered the next part of the route, a snow couloir, rock sections ('rotten rock and soft powdery snow') and fixed ropes for a distance of 500 metres. Back in Camp VI, breathing oxygen, they passed a fairly comfortable night. For the summit climb (September 24) Scott decided against wearing his heavy down suit; he did however pack a stove and billycan; Haston took down boots and a bivouac sheet with him; each had two 'dead men' (snow anchors), four pegs, one hammer and his oxygen equipment. They had two cylinders apiece which they hoped, by using them sparingly, would suffice to bring them to the summit and back. It was 15.30 hours before they reached the South Summit. Haston had been experiencing difficulties with his oxygen apparatus. In the couloir, leading to the South Summit, the rock was inclined at 65 degrees and covered in show — in one 60-metre section, the snow was literally chest-deep. Climbing this was a strength-consuming, ticklish business.

Dougal Haston wanted to bivouac on the South Summit before going on, but Doug Scott persuaded him — while they made themselves a drink of warm water — that they should go on and start the summit ridge right away. They found the Hillary Step to be simply a '40-foot bank of snow' which they climbed in 30 minutes. There was no talk now of turning back. Not long afterwards, Scott noticed a smudge of red along the ridge ahead. When they reached it, they found that the red object was 'a tripod festooned with red ribbons and crowned with a rosette, like a May Pole'. Doug Scott described the event, 'We took off our masks and I could see Dougal's face lit up in the setting sun and filled with happiness . . . we thumped each other's backs and congratulated each other. The wind had dropped to nothing as we stood up there in wonder at the scene before us. It was everything and more than we had dared to hope for. Beyond the Rongbuk Glacier silver threads meandered out north and west across the brown land of Tibet. Peak after peak in all directions. We tried to name them, and also spent time looking down the north side, picking out features from the history books. The sun filtered down behind layers of cloud, occasionally breaking through in an explosion of light. We watched this happen several times — one sunset after another — until we had only about half-an-hour left before it got dark. . . . We left nothing on top, because we had nothing to leave. . . .'

When they got back to the South Summit, it was already pitch dark. They bivouaced there at 8,760 in a snow-hole. (the 11 year American record for the highest bivouac had been broken.). Their oxygen ran out at 8.30 p.m. and the stove was finished by midnight. They drank hot water. Concentrating their minds on survival, the nine hours of the Everest night seemed like an eternity. At 5.30 in the morning they crawled out of their hole, and by 9 o'clock were back in their tent at Camp VI. 'We reached the tent and safety . . . got into our sleeping bags, put a brew on, and lay back breathing oxygen; then we radioed Chris with the news. . . .'

On the 26th, the second group set off for the summit — Peter Boardman, Pertemba, Martin Boysen and Mick Burke. Having lost a crampon and experiencing difficulty with his oxygen set, Boysen decided to return to Camp VI. Burke went on alone in the tracks of Boardman and Pertemba. In constantly poor visibility and worsening weather, the first pair reached the summit, but they only stayed there for a couple of minutes. Fifteen minutes after beginning their descent, they could make out Mick Burke looming through the mist towards them 'cine camera in his hand and eager for the summit'. He tried to persuade them to go back up with him, but they were reluctant to do so, and Burke carried on alone. They last saw him disappearing into the mist towards the summit. They waited for him in vain on the South Summit for an hour or more, by which time visibility was down to a few feet. 'They then had to battle for their own survival, in the face of a fierce wind . . . they made the decision to go down. It was well after dark when they finally stumbled in to Camp VI. . . .' Fateful Himalaya.

Doug Scott completed his expedition report with a few reflections on the future of big mountaineering. Amongst other things, he said: 'Only time will tell whether or not our ascent has any major historical significance. It certainly does not mark an end to this facet of mountaineering. Why should it, when there are still two major face routes on Everest waiting to be climbed — the North-west face direct from the Rongbuk Glacier and the East Face from the Kangshung Glacier? Then there is the huge South Wall of Dhaulagiri, and the South Face buttresses of K2. . . . On all but the world's three highest peaks, where the logistics will remain complex, and where oxygen will no doubt continue to aid hard climbing, the scene is set for near-alpine ascents of the major problems. . . . Already scores of Himalayan peaks have been climbed in alpine style. . . . Once climbers begin to combine the tactics and lessons learnt from these mountains, with some of the equipment and survival techniques that have resulted from the recent Everest, Makalu and Annapurna ascents, the future will offer unlimited scope for fantastic adventures.'

Sources: Doug Scott's report 'Everest South-west Face Climbed' in *Mountain* No. 47, Jan/Feb 1976 and personal notes of Dougal Haston's lecture in Munich in October 1977. (See also: Chris Bonington, *Everest, The Hard Way*, Hodder and Stoughton, 1976.)

1975 TWO WOMEN ON THE ROOF OF THE WORLD

In the Spring of 1975 Everest was again in the headlines, twice. Women reached the Roof of the World for the first time: On May 16 a Japanese woman, Junko Tabei, became the very first woman to stand on Everest, and then on May 27, a Tibetan woman, Phantog, Deputy Leader of a big Chinese Expedition, was one of nine people to reach the summit.

The People's Republic of China had reported in the year 1960 that three Chinese climbers — Wang Fu-chou, Chan Ying-hua, Lui Lien-man — and a Tibetan, Konbu, had climbed Everest by the North Col-North Ridge route. The summit was said to have been reached on May 25 at 4.20 Peking Time (2.20 Local Time), in other words, in the middle of the night.

271

A bust of Mao Tse-tung was left behind on the summit. There were no summit photographs and the published account was very vague in its descriptions. No subsequent climbers ever found the bust of Mao, and by and large, this reputed ascent was seriously doubted in the West. (This expedition is mentioned in the *Table of Expeditions*, elsewhere in this book; in the chronological list of 'Summiters', the four climbers have not been given serial numbers.)

As China becomes relatively more open, and Western correspondents are given more freedom, a final clarification of this point should eventually become possible. At any event, there can be no doubt at all about the successful ascent on May 27, 1975. The author of the official expedition report is apparently the same Wang Fu-chou who was in the 1960 summit party, and was a leading member of the 'Party Committee' for the organization of this 1975 climb. The report also, for the first time, gives Everest the name 'Qomolangma Feng'. The Tibetan climber of that 1960 expedition, Gonpo (formerly given as Konbu) was again a member of this expedition. As well as the published report and many photographs, a very impressive documentary film of the expedition was made, with footage right up to the summit. It was shown at the Trento Mountaineering Film Festival of 1976 and on British television.

The expedition set off amidst carnival celebrations in Lhasa on the great square under the Potala — with Tibetan dancing in traditional dress, banner-waving children and the letting off of countless colourful balloons. A long convoy of lorries brought the expedition through the wide, tarred streets to the Himalayan chain. Base Camp was established at 3,000 metres near the Rongbuk Monastery (which wasn't however shown in the film). In layout this camp, with its dozen or so large tents on either side of a wide camp street and its parade ground, resembled a military camp for a battalion or more. Military — indeed paramilitary — leadership and order were evident with roll-calls, flag parades, issuing of orders, staff conferences and speeches.

Wang Fu-chou records how troops were used as a transport column and it was obvious they were employed in fact to above the North Col. Special 'scouts' (a dozen trainers with young climbers) also prepared the climbing route as far as the North Col, 7,007 metres. Criss-crossed with crevasses

Members of the 1975 Chinese Expedition just below Everest summit.
(Oxygen cylinders clearly visible in their loads.)

and under threat of avalanches, it was reconnoitred and established with ropes and ladders. A group of soldiers and Tibetans, led by trainers, according to Wang 'climbed the North Col five times in six days'. They carried up all the equipment, including hundreds of cylinders of oxygen, to Camp IV, the Advance Base. The first assault attempt, which was divided into two parties, were active on the mountain between April 24 and May 8, but their bid finally had to be called off as a result of continuous storms. 33 men and seven women had by this time reached Camp VI at a height of 8,200 metres. After 13 days on the mountain the climbers 'were nearing the end of their physical resources' and were ordered back to Base Camp.

Few actual details are given of the second attempt, except that Camp VI was moved higher by 100 metres, to 8,300 metres, and the final assault camp was raised to 8,680 metres.

On May 17 and 18 two groups comprising three women and 15 men set out from Base Camp under the leadership of the 29-year old Tibetan climber, Sodnam Norbu, and 37-year old Phantog, the Deputy Leader of the Expedition, and who during the course of the expedition was made a member of the Communist Party.

Strong troops of supporters accompanied the team. Reaching Camp VI on May 25, two women and seven men had to drop out because of extreme fatigue. May 26 was a day of storms and gales, but by midday it had cleared a little and the Party Committee commanded that some of the team should 'probe and prepare' the route ahead, which consisted of ice sections and vertical rock steps; they would fix ropes and instal metal ladders whilst the second half of the nine-strong summit team, make a forced climb to the assault camp, some 380 metres higher. In the words of Wang Fu-chou, 'The ridge runs from the assault camp to the Second Step'. Both groups fulfilled their tasks and joined forces in the assault camp that evening. At 11 o'clock that night a Party branch meeting was called in the camp and it was decided that all nine should attempt the summit.

On May 27 they set off in two ropes while it was still dark, and after one and a half hours of uninterrupted climbing, they reached the top of the Second Step at 9.30 a.m.

There are anomolies here. The Second Step we know should lie between 8,570 and 8,600 metres and be 30 metres high, a completely smooth rock wall with an inclination of 60 to 70 degrees, above which rises a further three metres of completely vertical rock. This must then have had to be prepared the afternoon before. But the height of the upper camp has been given as 8,680 metres — if correct, this would mean the camp was above the level of the top of the Second Step.

During a ten-minute rest stop on top of the Second Step, all climbers 'inhaled oxygen for two or three minutes at a flow of two to five litres per minute'. The climbers were in high spirits, but the conditions remained difficult. While they were still 60 metres from the summit, an 'almost perpendicular ice slope blocked their advance', and they had to make a detour to the north till they could find a way up the rocks. One of the climbers became very faint at this stage, but was revived with oxygen. At 14.30 hours the summit was reached.

They planted a three-metre high tripod on the summit, unfurled the five-star flag, photographed, filmed, collected rock samples, and made ice and snow observations. Phantog underwent an ECG test by telemetry, which required her to lie down flat on the summit for seven minutes. The climbers remained on top for 70 minutes in all, and obviously there must have been hardly any wind. During this time, none of them used any supplementary oxygen at all. Each member carried an oxygen cylinder and special mention is made of the fact that Phantog carried her own, just like the others. The assault camp was regained without incident during the evening and on May 29 they were all back in Base Camp. It had been a great success.

The climbers were: Tibetans — Phantog (37, mother of three), Sodnam Norbu (29), Lotse (37), Samdrup (23), Dharphuntso(30), Kunga Pasang (29), Tsering Tobygal (29), Hgapo Khyen (21), and the single Chinese: Hon Sheng-fu (36). Five belong to the Army in one capacity or another. Lotse and Hon Sheng-fu were members of the successful Shisha Pangma Expedition in 1964 (8,015 metres) and the 1960 Everest Expedition. Phantog had previously climbed Mustagh Ata and Kong Tiubie Tagh, two seven-thousanders. The Chinese, as mentioned earlier, gave Everest the name of 'Qomolangma Feng', although both Chomolungma and Jolmo Lungma were also quoted.

When Phantog stood on the top of Everest on May 27, she did not know she was not the first woman to do so, and the Japanese lady, Junko Tabei, similarly, when she stood there on May 16, did not know that within only 11 days, she would have to share the women's world altitude record with another. In 1978 a third woman reached the summit of Everest. She was Wanda Rutkiewicz, a Polish climber, member of Dr Herrligkoffer's post-monsoon expedition. Junko Tabei is 37 and although she is strongly built, has all the elegance one associates with oriental women, but above all she is a very warm, sympathetic person, married and the mother of a daughter who was aged three at the time of Everest. Mrs Tabei climbed her first mountain as a schoolgirl in the fourth grade. After finishing her studies she made the first women's winter ascent of Tanigawa-dake, the most popular and at the same time, the most dangerous (over 600 dead) mountain for Japanese climbers. The climb took three days and the route (Ojo-Gampeki Route) is Grade VI. She met her husband through climbing. In 1970 she visited the Himalayas for the first time and climbed Annapurna III (7,577 metres) as a member of another all-women's expedition. Her historical achievement on Everest she sees as the natural further development of her own climbing career, but equally, 'as the success of the whole team'.

This team comprised 15 women, led by 42-year old Eiko Hisano. Junko Tabei was the climbing leader. The expedition was organized by the newly-formed Japanese Ladies Himalayan Club, or more exactly 'Ladies Club for the Preparation and Execution of Himalayan Expeditions'. A strong team of Sherpas assisted the hopeful women to accomplish their ambition.

It demanded strong nerves and steadfastness for during the night of May 4, an avalanche poured down from the slopes of Nuptse, completely engulfing their Camp II, which was situated not far from the upper limit of the Khumbu Icefall, on a little raised area. Seven women and six Sherpas received minor injuries and valuable equipment was lost. They had to be dug out, but nevertheless were lucky to still be alive. Courageously, they overcame the shock. On May 15, the decisive Camp VII was placed at a height of 8,500 metres on the South-east Ridge by Mrs Yurioko Watanabe (she has two children, aged five and six) and Ang Tsering. Watanabe had herself carried a ten kilo load as high as Camp IV (7,600 metres) and was considered for a further summit assault which didn't, in the event, materialize.

After the night in the Ridge Camp, Junko Tabei together with Sherpa-Sirdar Ang Tsering reached the summit at midday on May 16 in fine weather. Nowhere is it reported that she saw any signs of movement as she looked down the North Ridge and onto the North Col below, from which one concludes that she knew nothing of the Chinese expedition at that time.

Sources: Various references in *Mountain* and *Alpinismus* during 1975, as well as personal notes on the official Chinese film.